Oscar Israelowitz's

Guide to Jewish U.S.A.

Volume I — The Northeast

Library of Congress Catalogue Card Number: 87-080153
International Standard Book Number: 0-9611036-5-5
Printed in the United States

Cover Photos

Temple Emanu-El of Borough Park - Stained Glass Window

Touro Synagogue in Newport, Rhode Island

Contents

FORWARD

The Guide to Jewish U.S.A. is designed for the world traveller, student, and historian who has visited many ports-of-call in search of Jewish communities and yet has not had the time nor the opportunity to discover the myriads of Jewish communities and historic sites right here in their own backyard—in the U.S.A.

The guide contains brief histories of the first Jewish settlements in each state. There are listings and background stories of Jewish historic landmarks, Jewish museums, synagogues, kosher restaurants and hotels, and mikvehs.

This guide has a special feature called "The Old Neighborhoods." As the original Jewish settlers of a town or city moved away from the "Jewish" section, the old synagogues were often "left behind." The guide contains listings of hundreds of these former synagogue buildings. Some of the buildings have been demolished as the slum areas were cleared and replaced with Urban Renewal projects. Many of the former synagogues, however, are still extant, but have undergone a metamorphosis. They are now churches, day-care centers, playhouses, office complexes, or warehouses. Although the buildings have undergone a change of ownership, it is still possible to find the original Judaic symbols such as the Star of David or a cornerstone bearing the Hebrew inscriptions or the date of construction in Hebrew characters.

This guide is designed for the explorer who wishes to discover the great Jewish "treasures" that have been abandoned and forgotten by the Jewish communities. This book is also a tribute to all of the Jewish pioneers who helped establish Jewish communities throughout the United States.

A special note of thanks is due to all of the people who assisted in providing information, historical data, and photographs for this guide. There's so much to see and do in Jewish U.S.A., so let's begin.

IMPORTANT NOTE: Although every effort has been made to ensure accuracy, changes will occur after the "guide" has gone to press. Particular attention must be drawn to the fact that kosher food establishments change hands often and suddenly, in some cases going over to a non-kosher ownership. No responsiblity, therefore, can be taken for the absolute accuracy of the information, and visitors are advised to obtain confirmation of kashruth claims.

INTRODUCTION

The first Jewish settlers in America were largely Sephardic. They were descendants of those Jews who had lived in Spain and Portugal for over one thousand years but were forced, in the year 1492, either to accept Christianity or leave the country. This Spanish Inquisition was just one event in their Diaspora and their search for freedom and a peaceful existence.

In 1654, Portugal conquered Brazil and expelled the Jews living in the city of Recife. The Jews set sail in the Caribbean Sea but were captured by Spanish pirates. They were subsequently rescued and brought to New Amsterdam. Their troubles were not over yet. The governor of New Amsterdam, Peter Stuyvesant was a notorious anti-Semite. He refused to let Jews into his colony. It was not until pressure was applied by his commanding officers in Amsterdam that the first twenty three Jews were permitted to live freely in America. This was the first official Jewish settlement in North America.

For the first two centuries after their settlement in New Amsterdam, the Jewish community in America increased very slowly. By the time of the American Revolution in 1776, of a total population of three million, only some two thousand were Jews. From the Colonial period through the early 1800s, a sizable percentage of America's Jewish community assimilated into Christian society through marriage and by lapse.

Between 1820 and 1850, about 200,000 Jews arrived from the Ashkenazic countries of Germany and Bohemia. They were fleeing from political oppression and grinding poverty. It was during this period that the Reform movement developed in Europe and in the United States.

Most of these German Jews started their business careers as peddlers. They would journey out into the country, knocking on doors of isolated farmhouses and tried to sell to the farmwives a few stockings, spools of cotton thread, needles or cheap household crockery. They worked long hours and saved every penny until they could purchase a horse and wagon, or set up a small dry goods shop. This was the beginning of such great department stores as B. Altman's, Macy's, Bamberger's, Filene's, and Bloomingdale's.

The third and largest wave of immigration came between 1881 and 1925. The new arrivals were Yiddish-speaking Jews from Russia, Poland, Galicia, Roumania, and Hungary. The Russian Jews fled from their country in the wake of the bloody pogroms instigated by the Czar's government. Oppressive laws combined with the constant threat of massacre to drive the Jews of Eastern Europe from their homes in tremendous numbers. When this wave of immigration was stopped by U.S. law in 1924, the Jewish population in the United States had grown to nearly 4½ million.

Most of the Eastern European Jews settled in the large cities such as New York City, Philadelphia, Baltimore, Newark, Boston, and Pittsburgh. In the 1880s, attempts were made by the Baron de Hirsch Fund to shift poor Jewish families from the teaming tenements of the city slums to farm villages. Rural settlements were established in New Jersey, Connecticut, New York, the Dakotas, Kansas, and other states. Most of these Jewish Agricultural settlements failed and were abandoned, because the Jews lacked both experience and guidance in farming. Those in New Jersey, however, did prosper. There are still many Jewish egg and poultry farmers in Southern New Jersey.

During the turbulent 1960s, many Jews moved from their established Jewish communities in the major cities and settled in the suburbs. During this mass exodus to suburbia, hundreds of synagogues were literally "left behind."

The Jewish population in the United States is approximately 6,000,000.

Connecticut

There were Jewish traders living in Connecticut as early as the 1650s. The Jewish communities from New York and Rhode Island fled to Connecticut from the invading British forces during the Revolutionary War. A permanent Jewish community did not take root in Connecticut, however, until the early 1840s, with the arrival of German Jews in New Haven, Waterbury, and Hartford. The first congregation was organized in New Haven in 1840, when a number of families from Bavaria formed what is today Congregation Mishkan Israel. Other early congregations in the state included Hartford's Temple Beth Israel, established in 1843, and Bridgeport's Congregation B'nai Israel (Park Avenue Temple), organized in 1859.

Among the early German Jewish settlers was Gershon Fox who established a one-room "fancy goods" store in Hartford in 1847. This little store eventually became Hartford's leading department store, as well as a New England landmark—G. Fox Department Store.

In the 1880s, the pogroms of Russia brought thousands of Eastern European Jews to Connecticut. Most of these immigrants settled into the established Jewish neighborhoods throughout the state. Many, however, with the help of the Baron de Hirsch Fund, were settled on farms in the vicinity of Colchester. Not all of these farmers were successful as farmers. Some could not survive from their crop produce alone so they took in boarders into their farmhouses. Eventually, they converted their farmhouses into small hotels. Colchester was once known as the "Catskills of Connecticut," since it attracted thousands of Jewish visitors for their summer vacations.

There are still several Jewish farmers in Connecticut but they have shifted their farm productions to dairy farming, tobacco growing, and egg farming. As you drive along the back roads near Colchester, you will still discover quaint little synagogues in such towns as Hebron or Columbia.

In the 1960s and 1970s, the mass movement of the Jewish communities in the major cities was to the suburbs. In the wake of this movement, the scores of magnificent synagogues and temples were literally "left behind." If you drive through these "old neighborhoods" you will discover isolated remnants of these once-vibrant Jewish communities. Some have been purchased by local churches, day-care centers, athletic clubs, or even playhouses.

The Jewish population of Connecticut is approximately 95,000.

HARTFORD

CONGREGATION BETH ISRAEL
701 Farmington Avenue

The first recorded mention of Jews in Hartford occurs in 1659, when court records show that "David the Jew" received a 20 shilling fine for selling wares in homes when heads of families were absent. In 1843, a special enactment of the Connecticut Legislature provided that Jews wishing to form religious societies had the same rights, powers, and privileges as Christians. Hartford's first synagogue, Congregation Beth Israel, was founded that year. The first location of the congregation was at 942 Main

Street. It was known as Touro Hall, but was originally the North Baptist Church. The congregation remained at that location from 1856 to 1876. In 1876, Congregation Beth Israel constructed its own synagogue at 21 Charter Oak Avenue. It remained in that location until 1936 when it moved to its present site at 701 Farmington Avenue, in West Hartford.

The present site of Congregation Beth Israel was constructed in 1936 and consists of a 12-sided building of Byzantine design and has a dome which is said to be a replica of the Santa Sophia dome in Constantinople. The twelve sides represent the twelve tribes of Israel and the totality of united Israel.

The Charter Oak Avenue Temple, 1876 - 1935.

The foyer has a vaulted ceiling of a warm amber color, 18 feet in height. The foyer is lined entirely in genuine Italian travertine marble (which is volcanic lava from the region of Tivoli) with a floor of Tennessee marble laid in ornamental design. On January 3, 1942, the Meeting House of the First Church of Christ (Congregational) in West Hartford was destroyed by fire. On the same day, Temple Beth Israel offered to that congregation the use of its ornate foyer for its Sunday services. In 1947, the First Church of Christ presented a bronze plaque to the temple thanking it for its neighborly kindness.

There are also a library of Judaica and an exquisite Jewish museum housed in Temple Beth Israel. For information about library and museum hours, please call 233-8215.

The Charter Oak Temple Restoration Association is in the process of saving Connecticut's oldest synagogue structure. It is planning to convert the building, built for Congregation Beth Israel in 1876, but abandoned in 1972, into a cultural center and a museum of Connecticut's Jewish history. For further information about this project, contact the Association at 115 North Beacon Street, Hartford, Connecticut 06105.

Congregation Beth Israel of West Hartford.

NEW HAVEN

CONGREGATION MISHKAN ISRAEL
Orange Avenue and Audobon Street

The first documented Jewish family in New Haven were the Pinto brothers who arrived in 1758. Ezra Stiles, the president of Yale University in 1772, reported on how one Jewish family observed the traditional Sabbath. In 1840, the first congregation in Connecticut, Mishkan Israel, was established by Bavarian Jews. It became Reform as early as 1856 and its 1897 temple was located at the corner of Orange and Audobon Streets. In the 1960s, the majority of New Haven's Jewish community moved to the suburbs. Congregation Mishkan Israel is now located in Hamden. The original Orange Street synagogue building is now the New Haven Arts Center.

Mishkan Israel, Connecticut's oldest congregation, now houses the New Haven Performing Arts Center.

CONGREGATION BETH ISRAEL
232 Orchard Street

The last surviving congregation in the "old section" of New Haven, Congregation Beth Israel, is located at 232 Orchard Street. It was organized in 1913 and built in 1926. Its exquisite bleached mahogany Holy Ark was designed in New York City and displays reliefs of two bold lions flanking the Ten Commandment Tablets and a noble eagle perched above. There are still several elderly Jewish families living in the area. The congregation's rabbi, Rabbi Hecht, lives several miles from the synagogue, but "walks in" on the Sabbath to conduct the services. The congregation follows the Orthodox tradition.

The Jewish community of Greater New Haven numbers about 23,000 out of a total population of approximately 250,000. Most of the Orthodox community is concentrated in Westville. The oldest Jewish cemetery in Connecticut (established in 1843) is located in Westville.

HOLOCAUST MEMORIAL
Whaley Avenue (Westville)

A most haunting Holocaust Memorial, designed by architect Augustus Franzoni in 1977, is located in a park just across the street from Congregation Beth El Kesser Israel (85 Harrison Street). This was the first Holocaust Memorial in the United States to be constructed on city parkland and was built under the joint auspices of the New Haven Jewish Federation and the City of New Haven.

Holocaust Memorial in New Haven was designed by Augustus Franzoni in 1977.

NEW LONDON

CONGREGATION BETH EL
660 Ocean Avenue

Paul Rudolph, known in American architecture for his mega-structure projects (Boston Government Service Center, Yale University - School of Art & Architecture), and direct structural expression associated with Brutalism, engaged in synagogue architecture as well. Congregation Beth El of New London wished to expand its existing synagogue, which was designed by Percival Goodman (ca. 1950). Paul Rudolph was commissioned for the extension. Based

Interior view of New London's Congregation Beth El.

on a retaining wall of brick, the sanctuary, clad in steel sheathing, is a collection of sculptural forms each housing skylights, and is quite removed in appearance from the flexible plan attached in the complex. The design is close to monumental.

The main sanctuary contains sculptural manifestations. There are exquisite tapestries along the walls, an elegant menorah, but no ark! Rather, there are six independently-supported clear lucite cylinders, each containing one Torah. The space evokes the feeling of a modern museum, where the Torahs appear in showcases.

Congregation Beth El, New London.

THE OLD NEIGHBORHOODS

The following list contains information about synagogues which are no longer functioning as Jewish houses of worship. These addresses are located in the old sections of the city or town. It is advisable to take extra precautions while driving through these neighborhoods.

Ansonia Beth El Congregation *95 Factory Street*

Bridgeport Congregation Agudas Achim *Madison Avenue & Grand Street*

Congregation Ahavath Achim *41 Cherry Street 725 Hancock Avenue*

Congregation Anshe Lubavitch Nusach Ho'ari *43 High Street*

Congregation Bikur Cholim *69 Green Street*

Congregation B'nai Israel *1100 Park Avenue*

Congregation Ein Jacob *746 Connecticut Avenue*

Congregation Rodeph Sholom *36 Court Street Park and Capital Avenues*

United Hebrew Orthodox Congregation *1159 Park Avenue*

Jewish Community Center *360 State Street*

Congregation Sephardic Bikur Cholim *725 Hancock Avenue*

Congregation Shaare Torah *3050 Main Street*

Danbury Congregation B'nai Israel *Liberty Street*

Danielson Temple Beth Israel *11 l'Homme Street*

Derby Congregation Sons of Israel *Main Street*

Greenwich Hebrew Institute *23 East Elm Street*

Hartford Congregation Adas Israel *250 Market Street*

Congregation Agudath Achim *298 Market Street 221 Greenfield Street*

Congregation Beth Israel *Charter Oak Avenue*

Congregation B'nai Israel *47 Pleasant Street*

Congregation Ohave Zedek *37 Wooster Street 370 Garden Street*

Congregation Shaare Torah *8 Winthrop Street*
Congregation Tifereth Israel *74 Pleasant Street*
Congregation Ateres Israel *92 Barbour Street*
Blue Hills Synagogue *300 Cornwall Street*
Congregation Chevre Lamdei Mishnayoth *150 Bedford Street*
Congregation Emanu-El *500 Woodland Street*
Jewish Community Center *1015 Asylum Street*
Congregation Kneset Israel *265 Enfield Street*
Congregation Ohav Zedek *370 Garden Street*
Hebrew Congregation *339 Cornwall Street*

Colchester Beth Jacob Synagogue *49 Church Street*
Jewish Aid Congregation *Mill Street*

Manchester Temple Beth Sholom *Myrtle & Linden Streets*

Meriden Congregation B'nai Abraham *38 Cedar Street*

Middletown Congregation Adath Israel *Union Street*

Moodus Congregation Rodfe Zedek *North Moodus Road*

New Britain Congregation Brethren of Israel *Elm Street*

New Haven Congregation Beth Hamedrash Hagadol
10 Rose Street
George & Dwight Streets
Congregation Bikur Cholim B'nai Abraham *19 Factory Street*
Congregation B'nai Jacob *345 George Street*
Congregation B'nai Sholom *96 Olive Street*
Congregation Kesser Israel *132 Foote Street*
165 Sherman Avenue
Congregation Magen David *16 Bradley Street*
Congregation Mishkan Israel *Orange & Audobon Streets*
Congregation Shaare Torah *67 York Street*
Congregation Sheves Achim *Factory Street*
White Street Synagogue

New London Congregation Ahavath Chesed
8 Shapely Street

Norwalk Congregation Zera Kodesh *13 North Avenue*

Norwich Brothers of Joseph *230 West Main Street*
Congregation Beth Jacob *63 Church Street*

Congregation Sons of Israel *Forest Street*
Congregation Agudath Achim *34 High Street*

South Norwalk Congregation Beth Israel
Concord & South Main Street
17 West Avenue

Stamford Congregation Agudas Sholom *16 Greyrock Place*
29 Grove Street
Jewish Center *132 Prospect Street*
Congregation Temple Beth El *144 Prospect Street*
Temple Sinai *54 Grove Street*

Torrington Congregation Sons of Jacob *Spear & Park Avenues*

Waterbury Congregation Beth Israel *24 Kingsbury Street*
Congregation Shearith Israel *33 Kingsbury Street*
15 Woodlawn Terrace
Congregation Temple Israel *100 Willow Street*

Willimantic Congregation Sons of Israel *41 Temple Way*
469 Pleasant Way

KOSHER RESTAURANTS

Fairfield Moishe's Deli & Bakery *2081 Blackrock Turnpike (203) 333-3059*

Hamden Able's Restaurant *2100 Dixwell Avenue 281-3434*

New Haven Gutkin's Food Shop *363 Whalley Avenue 562-6184*

Norwich Bagel Coffee Shop *327 Central Avenue 889-0423*

Stamford Deli-Land *850 Highbridge Road 322-3649*
Nosherye *1035 Newfield Avenue 329-7862*

West Hartford Crown's Supermarket *2471 Albany Avenue 236-1965*

SYNAGOGUES

[Note: All area codes are 203]

Bloomfield 06002 Congregation Beth Hillel (C) *160 Wintonbury Avenue 242-5561*
Congregation Tiferes Israel (O) *27 Brown Street 243-1719*
Congregation Tikvoh Chadashah (C) *180 Still Road 243-3576*

Bridgeport 06604 Congregation Adath Israel (O) *540 East Washington Avenue 336-3929*
Congregation Agudas Achim (O) *85 Arlington Street 335-6353*
Congregation B'nai Israel (R) *2710 Park Avenue 336-1858*
Congregation Rodeph Sholom (C) *2385 Park Avenue 334-0159*
Congregation Shaare Torah (O) *3050 Main Street 372-6513*

Congregation Bikur Cholim *1541 Iranistan Avenue 336-2272*

Bristol 06010 Congregation Beth Israel (C) *339 West Street 583-6293*

Cheshire Temple Beth David (R) *3 Main Street 272-0037*

Columbia 06237 Congregation Agudath Achim (O)

Colchester 06415 Congregation B'nai Israel (C) *193 Clapboard Ridge Road 792-6161*
United Jewish Center (R) *141 Deer Hill Avenue 748-3355*

Danielson 06239 Temple Beth Israel (C) *Killingly Drive 774-9874*

Derby 06418 Beth Israel Synagogue (C) *300 Elizabeth Street 777-1264*
Congregation Sons of Israel (C) *6 Anson Street*

Deep River Congregation Beth Shalom (C) *93 Union Street 526-5649*

East Hartford 06118 Temple Beth Tefiulah (C) *465 Oak Street 569-0670*

Ellington 06029 Congregation Knesseth Israel (O) *Pinney Street 875-3623*

Fairfield 06432 Congregation Ahavath Achim (O) *1571 Stratfield Road 372-6529*
Congregation Beth El (C) *1200 Fairfield Woods Road 374-5544*

Greenwich 06830 Temple Sholom (C) *300 East Putnam Avenue 869-7191*

Hamden 06517 Temple Beth Sholom (C) *1809 Whitney Avenue 288-7748*
Congregation Mishkan Israel (R) *785 Ridge Road 288-3877*

Hartford 06117 Congregation Adas Israel *215 Pearl Street 525-3590*
United Synagogue of Greater Hartford (O) *840 North Main Street 236-3576*

Hebron 06248 Congregation Agudas Achim (O)

Madison Temple Beth Tikva (R) *Durham Road 245-7028*

Manchester 06040 Temple B'nai Abraham (C) *400 East Middle Turnpike 643-9563*

Meriden 06450 Temple B'nai Abraham (C) *127 East Main Street 235-2581*

Middletown 06457 Congregation Adath Israel (C) *Broad & Old Church Streets 346-4709*

Milford 06460 Temple B'nai Sholom (C) *88 Noble Avenue 874-1010*

New Britain 06052 Temple B'nai Israel (C) *265 West Main Street 224-0479*
Congregation Tifereth Israel (O) *76 Winter Street 229-1485*

New Haven 06515 Congregation Beth El–Kesser Israel (C) *85 Harrison Street 389-2108*
Congregation Beth Israel (O) *232 Orchard Street 776-1468*
Congregation Bikur Cholim Shevet Achim (O) *278 Winthrop Avenue 776-4997*
Congregation B'nai Jacob (C) *75 Rimmon Road 389-2111*
Westville Synagogue (O) *74 West Prospect Street 389-9513*
Young Israel (O) *292 Norton Street 776-4212*

New London 06320 Congregation Ahavath Chesed (O) *590 Montauk Avenue 442-3234*
Congregation Beth El (C) *660 Ocean Avenue 442-0418*
Temple Israel *Park Street (summer only)*

New Milford 06776 Temple Sholom (R) *122 Kent Road North 354-0273*

Newington 06470 Congregation B'nai Sholom (C) *26 Church Street 667-0826*
Temple Sinai (R) *41 West Hartford Road 561-1055*

Newtown 06470 Congregation Adath Israel (C) *Huntington Road 426-6761*

Norwalk 06851 Congregation Beth El (C) *109 East Avenue 838-2710*
Beth Israel Synagogue (O) *40 King Street 866-0534*
Temple Sholom (R) *259 Richards Avenue 866-0148*

Norwich 06360 Beth Jacob Synagogue (C) *400 New London Turnpike 886-2459*

Congregation Brothers of Joseph (O) *2 Broad Street 887-3777*

Orange 06477 Temple Emanu-El (R) *150 Derby Avenue 397-3000*

Orange Synagogue Center (C) *205 Old Grassy Hill Road 795-0386*

Putnam 06260 Congregation Sons of Zion (C) *Church Street 928-4496*

Ridgefield Temple Shearith Israel (R) *46 Peaceable Street 438-6589*

Riverside Greenwich Reform Synagogue (R) *200 Riverside Avenue 637-4463*

Rockville 06066 Congregation B'nai Israel (C) *54 Talcott Avenue 871-1818*

Simsbury Farmington Valley Jewish Congregation (R) *55 Bushy Hill Road 658-1075*

South Windsor 06074 Temple Beth Hillel (R) *1001 Foster Street 644-8466*

Stamford 06902 Congregation Agudath Sholom *301 Strawberry Hill Avenue 325-3501*

Temple Beth El (C) *350 Roxbury Road 332-6901*

Temple Sinai (R) *Lakeside Drive 322-1649*

Young Israel(O) *69 Oakland Avenue 323-3390*

Stratford 06497 Temple Beth Sholom (C) *275 Huntington Road 378-6175*

Torrington 06790 Beth El Synagogue (C) *124 Litchfield Street 482-8263*

Trumbull 06611 Congregation B'nai Torah (C) *5700 Main Street 268-6940*

Wallingford Beth Israel Synagogue (C) *22 North Orchard Street 269-5983*

Waterbury 06710 Congregation Beth El (C)359 Cooke Street 756-4659

Congregation B'nai Sholom (O) *135 Roseland Avenue 754-4159*

Temple Israel (R) *100 Williamson Drive 574-1916*
Congregation Shares Israel *94 Randolph Avenue*

Waterford Temple Emanu-El (R) *29 Dayton Road 443-3005*

West Hartford 06117 Congregation Agudas Achim (O) *1244 North Main Street 233-6241*
Beth David Synagogue (O) *20 Dover Road 236-1241*
Temple Beth El (C) *2626 Albany Avenue 232-9696*
Congregation Beth Israel (R) *701 Farmington Avenue 233-8215*
Chabad House (Lubavitch) (O) *798 Farmington Avenue 523-5860*
Emanu-El Synagogue (C) *160 Mohegan Drive 236-1275*
Congregation Sinai(C) *426 Washington Avenue 934-7946*
Congregation Kehilath Chaverim *141 Ballard Drive*
Young Israel of West Hartford (O) *2240 Albany Avenue 233-0103*
Young Israel of Hartford (O) *1137 Trout Brook Drive 523-7804*

Westport 06880 Temple Israel (R) *14 Coleytown Road 227-1293*

West Haven Congregation Sinai (C) *426 Washington Avenue 934-7946*

Wethersfield 06109 Temple Beth Torah (C) *130 Main Street 529-2410*

Willimantic 06226 Temple B'nai Israel (C) *345 Jackson Street 423-3743*

Winsted 06098 Temple Beth Israel (C) *74 Park Place*

Woodbridge 06525 Congregation B'nai Jacob (C) *75 Rimmon Road 389-2111*

MIKVEHS

Fairfield 1326 Stratfield Road *(203) 374-2191*
New Haven 86 Hubinger Street *387-2184*
Norwich 2 Broad Street *889-7982 or 887-1412*
Stamford 301 Strawberry Hill Avenue *325-3501*
Waterbury 135 Roseland Avenue *754-4159*
West Hartford 61 North Main Street *521-9446*

Delaware

Following the Dutch annexation of Delaware from the Swedish in 1655, Jewish traders from New Netherland (namely, New Amsterdam) arrived. This was just one year after the arrival of the first Jews in North America. There was not, however, a permanent Jewish community in Delaware until 1872. This was due primarily because of the remoteness of the greater part of the state from the main northern and southern travel routes. Another reason was because of the proximity of Wilmington, the only large city, to Philadelphia. Since Delaware and Pennsylvania were considered as virtually a single state until after the Revolution, there were undoubtedly Jews from Pennsylvania who had commercial interests in Delaware, but few of them lived there.

The first synagogue services in Delaware were conducted for the High Holy Days of 1873. The first congregation, Ohabe Sholom, was dedicated on March 19, 1880 and conducted services in Wilmington's Lieberman Building. The first enduring congregation, Adas Kodesh, was founded in 1885. It acquired the old Zion Lutheran Church and converted it into the first synagogue building in the state. Wilmington's first Reform congregation, Beth Emeth, was organized in 1906.

Between 1910 and 1920, many East European Jews received grants from the Baron de Hirsch Fund and were settled on farms near Dover by the Jewish Agricultural Society. Congregation Beth Sholom was organized in 1946 by these Jewish farmers.

The Jewish population of Delaware is approximately 9,500.

WILMINGTON

ADAS KODESCH SHEL EMETH CONGREGATION
Washington Boulevard and Torah Drive

In 1885, the Orthodox Adas Kodesch Congregation was founded. Its first locations were rented spaces in Downtown Wilmington. In 1898, the congregation purchased the Zion Evangelical Lutheran Church, located at the southwest corner of 6th and French Streets. This was the site of the first public school in Wilmington. The price of the building was $5,625.

In 1900, a group of Jews who preferred the Sephardic ritual established the Chesed Shel Emeth Congregation. In 1916, they erected a synagogue on Shipley, below Third Street, which it occupied until its merger in 1957 with Adas Kodesch.

The present synagogue, located in the Brandywine Hills section, was designed by Percival Goodman. The building was to cost $650,000, without any furnishings. The synagogue is located on 3½ acres and is designed in a modern, rustic style.

Adas Kodesch Shel Emeth's original French Street building.

THE OLD NEIGHBORHOODS

The following list contains information about synagogues which are no longer functioning as Jewish houses of worship. These addresses are located in the old sections of the city or town. It is advisable to take extra precautions while driving through these neighborhoods.

Dover Congregation Beth Sholom *Hartley Road*
Wilimington Congregation Adas Kodesh *6th & French Streets*
Congregation Beth Emeth *10th & Washington Streets*
Congregation Chesed Shel Emeth *229 Shipley Avenue*

KOSHER RESTAURANTS

Wilmington Modern Kosher Meats *1708 Naamana Road (302) 475-9300*
Baker's Rack *1705 Concord Pike* 654-3165
Brandywine Pastry Bakery *4117 Silverside Road* 475-1180

SYNAGOGUES

[Note: All area codes 302]

Dover 19901 Congregation Beth Sholom (C) *Queen & Clara Streets 734-5578*

Newark 19711 Temple Beth El (R) *301 Possum Park Road 366-8330*

70 Amstel Avenue

Wilmington 19802 Congregation Adas Kodesh Shel Emeth (O) *Washington Boulevard & Torah Drive 762-2705*

Congregation Beth Emeth (R) *300 Leo Boulevard 764-2393*

Congregation Beth Sholom (C) *18th Street & Baynard Boulevard*

District of Columbia (Washington, D.C.)

WASHINGTON HEBREW CONGREGATION
Massachusetts Avenue and Macomb Street, N.W.

In 1795, Isaac Polock, a merchant and resident of Savannah, Georgia, took up residence in Washington. He was the earliest known Jewish resident in the nation's capital. He was well-known in the city's business and social life. As an important builder, Polock built six large brick houses in 1796, of which one became the residence of James and Dolly Madison, while Madison was Secretary of State. The "Polock House" was located at 2109 Pennsylvania Avenue, N.W.

In 1857, the 34th Congress enacted the legislation which gave the city's first Jewish congregation full equality with the Christian churches. Organized in 1852, the Washington Hebrew Congregation first met in private homes then moved into a room in the Concordia Lutheran Church, located at 20th and G Streets. In1863, the congregation purchased the South Methodist Church, on 8th Street, between H and I Streets. In 1897, the Washington Hebrew Congregation built an impressive Moorish-style synagogue. President William McKinley and his cabinet participated in the cornerstone-laying.

In 1952, President Harry S. Truman was the speaker at the Washington Hebrew Congregation's centennial anniversary and the laying of the cornerstone of its new building. The present building of the congregation, located at Massachusetts Avenue and Macomb Street, N.W., was dedicated on May 6, 1955 at ceremonies addressed by President Dwight D. Eisenhower.

ADAS ISRAEL CONGREGATION
Third and G Streets, N.W.

The city's second congregation, Adas Israel Synagogue, dedicated its first house of worship at 6th and G Streets in 1878, in the presence of President Ulysses Grant and members of his cabinet. The congregation was organized in 1869 by some 35 members who left the Washington Hebrew Congregation, then newly-Reform, but previously ultra-Orthodox. By 1907, the congregation had outgrown this structure and moved to a new building at 6th and Eye Streets, N.W. where it remained until moving to its present location at Connecticut Avenue and Porter Street, N.W.

The original building was sold to St. Sophia's Greek Orthodox Church, and some years later became the home of the Evangelical Church. For two decades beginning in 1946, the building—altered for commercial use—became a grocery and carry-out shop.

In 1968, the entire block was selected for the headquarters site of the Washington Area Metropolitan Transit System—Metro. This meant demolition of the remaining buildings, including the abandoned grocery, former church, and former synagogue.

A Washingtonian who knew the history of the old synagogue building, felt its demolition would be a tragedy, and suggested to some Jewish friends that they attempt to save it. But this meant finding a new site and raising the necessary funds to move the building, all this before the wrecker's ball was to strike.

Like a modern miracle it was accomplished, but only through the untiring efforts of a great many dedicated people. Responding

Moving the original Adas Israel Synagogue to its new site.

to a strong appeal from the Jewish Historical Society, Adas Israel Congregation, and a host of concerned individuals, the Mayor and the City Government ordered a halt to demolition, and the City agreed to lease a new site for the building at 3rd and G Streets, N.W. A vigorous volunteer effort brought in the necessary funds.

On December 18, 1969, the 270 tons of decaying brickwork and lumber, strapped with steel bands, were delicately lifted onto huge dollies. The historic three-block move down city streets to the present site took two and a half hours, all with traffic stopped and the news cameras grinding.

The crisis had been averted, but that was just the beginning. The almost-hollow shell had to be placed on a new foundation, then restored and refurnished. It took five years of delicate handwork to remove the first floor store windows and to restore the exterior and interior based on old photographs and descriptions furnished to architects by congregants who had been there as children.

The first floor, where classrooms and the ritual bath were originally located, was completely altered when the building was converted for the grocery business. Refurbished, that floor now houses the museum and its archives, and the offices of the Historical Society.

The second floor sanctuary still had the original Ark for the Torahs and part of the women's gallery. One of the original pews was traced to a country church in Southern Maryland and trucked back. Craftsmen were hired to make faithful reproductions so that the present pews are a blend of the original and the restored. The same is true of the bimah, the floors, the gallery and its railings.

Architecturally, the building was of plain, late Colonial design, with a simplicity reminiscent of a 19th Century Quaker meeting house. Outside the original cupola and the wood sunburst design over the main entrance and over many of the windows remain. The simple Federal design is a marked contrast to the Byzantine architecture in vogue in the late 19th Century.

A beautifully landscaped garden and walk surround the old synagogue. The unusual wrought iron fence with its Magen David and menorah motif was inspired by a similar design seen in a

400-year-old synagogue on the Island of Rhodes visited by a long-time member of Congregation Adas Israel. He designed and contributed the fence as a memorial to his father, a master designer and ironwork artisan.

After 99 years, the original Adas Israel was rededicated on June 22, 1975. Adas Israel Congregation was the first Jewish house of worship erected in the nation's capital. It now stands as an official landmark—the second synagogue ever to be listed in the National Register of Historic Places. The museum is named for Albert Small and his wife, whose substantial gift made possible the completion of the restoration work. For further information about the museum, please call (202) 789-0900 or (301) 881-0100.

EMBASSY OF ISRAEL
3514 International Drive, N.W.

The Embassy of Israel, located at 3514 International Drive, N.W. houses the official mission to the United States of America. In the Embassy are the offices of Israel representatives who deal with diplomatic, military, economic, information, cultural, scientific, agricultural, labor, and other affairs. The Embassy is headed by the Ambassador to the United States.

The structure was designed by Israeli architects and resembles typical Jerusalem architecture, with its domes, arches, windows, and characteristic desert color. A representative collection of contemporary Israeli art is featured in the interior.

Israel has maintained an Embassy in Washington since 1948. The present building was opened in December, 1980. It is not open to the general public. For further information about the Embassy of Israel, please call (202) 364-5500.

The Israeli Embassy

B'NAI BRITH BUILDING
1640 Rhode Island Avenue, N.W.

The international headquarters of the B'nai Brith, the oldest and largest Jewish service organization in the world, is located at 1640 Rhode Island Avenue, N.W. In addition to the offices, the building also houses the Klutznick Exhibit Hall and the B'nai Brith Library. The research library contains material relating to human rights and Jewish history. The Klutznick Exhibit Hall is Washington's first Jewish museum. The exhibit hall seeks to tell the story of Jewish contributions to American life and to portray the development of the American Jewish community since 1654. Among the notable items on permanent exhibit is the famous letter George Washington wrote to the Hebrew congregation at Newport, Rhode Island, a collection of letters from American presidents to B'nai Brith, and the Horowitz and Kanof collections of Jewish ceremonial objects, both modern and traditional 17th to 19th century pieces. For further information, please call (202) 857-6600.

THE OLD NEIGHBORHOODS

The following list contains information about synagogues which are no longer functioning as Jewish houses of worship. These addresses are located in the old sections of the city or town. It is advisable to take extra precautions while driving through these neighborhoods.

Congregation Adath Israel *6th & I Streets*
Congregation Ohave Sholom *5th & I Streets*
Congregation B'nai Israel *16th & Crittenden Streets, N.W.*
Talmud Torah Congregation *467 East Street, S.W.*
Valiener Anshe Sfard Congregation *607 S Street, S.W.*
Washington Hebrew Congregation *8th Street (between H & I Streets)*

SYNAGOGUES

[Note: All area codes 202]

Adath Israel Congregation 20003 (C) *2850 Quebec Street N.W. 362-4433*
Congregation Agudath Achim *6343 13th Street, N.W.*
Congregation Beth Sholom (O) *13th Street & Eastern Avenue, N.W. 726-3869*
Congregation Ezras Israel *7101 7th Street, N.W.*
Congregation Kesher Israel (O) *2801 N Street, N.W., 1134 25th Street, N.W.*
Temple Michah (R) *600 M Street, S.W. 544-3099*
Congregation Ohav Sholom (O) *1600 Jonquil Street, N.W. 882-7225*
Temple Sinai (R) *3100 Military Road, N.W. 363-6394*
Congregation Tifereth Israel (C) *7701 16th Street, N.W. 882-1605*
Washington Hebrew Congregation (R) *3935 Macomb Street, N.W. 362-7100*

Maine

There was a Jewish community in the city of Bangor as early as the 1840s. These German Jewish settlers were engaged in various retail businesses catering to the workers in the lumber industry centered around Bangor. When the prime timbering areas had been cut and the industry moved west, most of the Jews moved away. Significant Jewish settlement in Maine began only after the Civil War.

Immigrants from Eastern Europe who settled in Portland and in the factory towns of Lewiston, Auburn, Bangor, and Waterville founded the present Jewish community in the early 1880s. The Jewish population in Maine was considerable in 1884, since in that year the State Legislature repealed the Sunday "Blue Laws," permitting Jews who kept their places of business closed on Saturdays to work at their regular trades and vocations on Sundays.

Although there was a small Jewish enclave established in the city during the 1860s, Portland's Jewish community arrived with the 20th century. In 1900 there were only 80 Jewish families in Portland, but in the early years of this century, as the events of the Russian Revolution unleashed the floodgates of Eastern Europe, Jewish immigrants streamed into the city from Russia, Poland, Latvia, and Lithuania. By 1907, there were 1,500 Jews in Portland; by 1912, 2,000; and by 1920, 3,000.

A great many of the pioneer Jewish families in Portland before the turn of the century were merchant tailors and clothiers. Others became junk dealers, working out of pushcarts. The children of these junk dealers very often became college graduates. From peddlers to professionals in one generation.

The original Jewish neighborhood in Portland settled at the foot of Munjoy Hill, in a few blocks around Hampshire and Newberry Streets. They worked in shops along Fore Street, in the Old Port section. Portland's first synagogue, Shaarey Tphiloh, was established in 1904 and was located on Newberry Street. In 1921, Congregation Etz Chaim was established and is still located on Congress Street. In 1927, the Jewish Home for the Aged was opened atop Munjoy Hill.

Portland's Jews became part of the general population drift to the suburbs in the 1940s. By the mid-1940s, half of Portland's Jewish population was living off the urban peninsula in the Wood-

Bangor's Temple Beth Israel.

fords Corner area. By 1956, enough of the Orthodox community had moved from the East End to the Woodfords section that Shaarey Tphiloh moved to new quarters on Noyes Street.

Bangor boasts Maine's oldest and most traditional Jewish community. There are today three congregations in Bangor; the Orthodox Beth Abraham Congregation, the Conservative Beth Israel, and the Reform Beth El Congregation which conducts services in the Unitarian Church.

There is presently a new trend of returning to one's Jewish roots throughout rural Maine. They are young Jewish people who moved out to the small rural communities. Many were part of the counterculture in the '60s and '70s. Now, in the 1980s, they are approaching middle age, have children, and may have become business and professional people. They have sought out the Jewish community again. The Reconstructionist Temple Shalom in the Lewiston-Auburn area attracts many of these "born-again" Jews.

The Jews in the Lewiston-Auburn area have been left in peace by the larger community. Anti-Semitism, say local Jews, has never been a great problem in the mill town. The apparent tolerance can be explained in terms of the local history. Lewiston has no middle class. There never was a Yankee population of landed gentry. Lewiston is an artifically conceived city like Lowell, Massachusetts, or Manchester, New Hampshire. The population is all [French-Canadian, Irish, and predominantly Lithuanian Jews] immigrants. They all came to work in the mills. They have the same historic experience in common.

There are about 10,000 Jews throughout Maine of which about 5,000 live in the greater Portland area.

THE OLD NEIGHBORHOODS

The following list contains information about synagogues which are no longer functioning as Jewish houses of worship. These addresses are located in the old sections of the city or town. It is advisable to take extra precautions while driving through these neighborhoods.

Auburn Congregation Beth Abraham *68 2nd Street*
Congregation Tiferes Anshe Sfard *4 Mill Street*
Bangor Congregation Toldos Itzchok *37 Essex Street*
142 York Street
Lewiston Congregation Bais Jacob *169 Lisbon Street*
Old Town Congregation Sons of Israel *Stillwater Avenue*
Portland Congregation Adath Israel *79 Middle Street*
Congregation Anshe Sfard *Cumberland Avenue & Wilmot Street*
Congregation Shaaray Tphiloh *147 Newberry Street*
Temple Israel *204 Federal Street*
Rockland Congregation Adas Jeshurun *Willow Street*

KOSHER RESTAURANTS

Bangor The Bagel Shop *1 Main Street (207) 947-1654*
Portland Penny-Wise Market *182 Ocean Avenue 772-8808*
Dunkin' Donuts *546 Deering Avenue 772-1536*

SYNAGOGUES

[Note: All area codes 207]

Auburn 04210 Congregation Beth Abraham (C) *Main Street & Laurel Avenue* 783-7450
Temple Sholom Synagogue (Rec.) *Bradman Road* 786-4201

Augusta Temple Beth El *Woodlawn Street* 622-7450

Bangor 04401 Congregation Beth Abraham (O) *145 York Street* 945-5940
Congregation Beth El (R) *275 Union Street* 945-9442
Congregation Beth Israel (C) *144 York Street* 945-3433

Bath 04530 Beth Israel Congregation (C) *862 Washington Street* 443-5181

Biddeford 04005 Congregation Etz Chaim (C) *34 Bacon Street* 284-5771

Caribou Aroostock Hebrew Congregation *1 Sumner Street*

Lewiston 04240 Congregation Beth Jacob (O) *Shawmut & Sabbatus Streets*
Jewish Community Center *134 College Street*

Old Orchard 04064 Congregation Beth Israel (O) *49 East Grand Avenue* 934-2973

Old Town Temple Israel *Center Street* (summer only)

Portland 04103 Temple Beth El (C) *400 Deering Avenue* 774-2649
Congregation Etz Chaim (O) *267 Congress Street* 773-2339
Congregation Shaaray Tphilo (O) *76 Noyes Street* 773-0693
Young Israel (O) *96 Morning Street*
Jewish Community Center *57 Ashmont Street* 772-1959

Rockland Hebrew Congregation *34 Fulton Street*

Waterville 04901 Congregation Beth Israel (C) *291 Main Street* 872-7551

MIKVEHS

Bangor 133 Pine Street *(207) 947-0876 or 945-5940*
Portland 76 Noyes Street *773-0693 or 774-0693*

Maryland

Baltimore's Jewish history dates back to pre-Revolutionary days. There were eight Jews who helped defend Fort McHenry during the War of 1812. Among those eight was a member of the Cohen family, whose brothers were founders of the Baltimore and Ohio Railroad and the Baltimore Stock Exchange.

Jews were denied the right to hold any local or state public office until a "Jew Bill" was passed in the Maryland State Legislature in 1826. Within a few months after this Jew Bill became law, Solomon Etting and Jacob Cohen, two of Maryland's most prominent Jews at the time, were elected to the Baltimore City Council. The first Jewish organization in Maryland, Congregation Nidche Israel, was organized in 1830. This congregation was known as the Baltimore Hebrew Congregation.

The majority of the membership of the Baltimore Hebrew Congregation were immmigrants from Germany who arrived in the 1830s and 1840s. Most started as peddlers but, within two generations, became part of the city's leading mercantile and industrial enterprises. The early immigrants lived primarily in East Baltimore, around Lloyd and Lombard Streets. It was on Lloyd Street that the Baltimore Hebrew Congregation built Maryland's first synagogue in 1845.

Splinter groups that broke away from the Baltimore Hebrew Congregation created Baltimore's other early synagogues such as Congregation Har Sinai, organized in 1842, Congregation Shearith Israel, organized in 1851, and Congregation Oheb Shalom, organized in 1853. The city's first rabbi was Abraham Rice. He was the first rabbi to be ordained in the United States and occupied the pulpit of the Baltimore Hebrew Congregation from 1840-1849. Har Sinai was Baltimore's first Reform congregation. Benjamin Szold, father of Henrietta Szold, was Congregation Oheb Shalom's rabbi for about 40 years.

At the outbreak of the Civil War, Baltimore's Jewish population was about 7,000. There were many secessionist sympathizers, including Rabbi Bernard Illoway of the Baltimore Hebrew Congregation, who defended and justified slavery and endorsed secession from the Union. Many Jews joined the Confederate Army.

In the 1880s, the Eastern European Jews settled in East Baltimore. By that time, the original (German) Jewish settlers, had become wealthy and had moved to the uptown section of town. The old synagogues were "recycled" and were now used by the newly-arrived Orthodox and Yiddish-speaking Jews of Eastern Europe. There were attempts by the uptown Jews to settle some of the new immigrants on agricultural settlements such as the one at Halofield, just outside Ellicott City, Maryland, in 1902. These attempts were short-lived.

The Baltimore Evening Night School, the first of its kind in the United States, was organized by Henrietta Szold in 1889 for the benefit of the East European Jews. It was a way of "Americanizing" these immigrants, by teaching them the English language and a trade. Henrietta Szold is best known, however, as the founder of Hadassah in 1912.

The center of Jewish life in Baltimore moved successively from Lloyd Street to Eutaw Place to Park Circle and Garrison Boulevard to upper Park Heights Avenue and Liberty Road and then to the suburbs of Pikesville, Reisterstown, and Randallstown. There are large Jewish communities in Silver Spring, College Park, and Rockville. The Jewish population of Maryland is approximately 120,000.

BALTIMORE

THE LLOYD STREET SYNAGOGUE
15 Lloyd Street

The Lloyd Street Synagogue, the first synagogue to be erected in Maryland, was built in 1845 by the Baltimore Hebrew Congregation. There are only two existing synagogue buildings in the United States that are older than the Lloyd Street Synagogue. They are the Touro Synagogue in Newport, Rhode Island, which was built in 1763, and Congregation Beth Elohim in Charleston, South Carolina, which dates from 1841 and replaces an even older building which had been destroyed by fire in 1840.

The Baltimore Hebrew Congregation, which was founded in 1830, conducted services in various rental halls prior to the building of the Lloyd Street Synagogue. The building was designed in Greek Revival style by Robert Carey Long, Jr. who was the most important Baltimore architect of the period.

Both the exterior and interior of the building today are very much as they were in 1845, except for a 30 foot extension of the eastern end of the building added when it was enlarged in 1860. The architect for the extension was William H. Reasin of Baltimore. Several changes were made at the time of the 1860 improvements. Originally, there was only one large entrance doorway; the two smaller doorways, now flanking the large one, were added at that time. The reading desk, in the open space in the front center, was originally directly in front of the Ark. When the east wall was moved back 30 feet, the reading desk remained in its present position.

In 1845, candle power was the lighting used in the synagogue. In 1860 the chandeliers were converted to gas and, subsequently, remodeled for electricity. The present chandeliers can be lowered to the floor for cleaning and servicing by means of pulleys in the ceiling chamber. These chandeliers are of an age antedating the synagogue building itself.

When the new east wall was built, the present handsome, sweeping curve was designed to embrace a new Ark, resembling in shape the Corinthian portico of a large mansion. This Ark was subsequently removed when the Baltimore Hebrew Congregation moved into a new synagogue building on Madison Avenue and Robert Street, and has since disappeared. An exact replica of the 1860 Ark has been constructed, following the details of a photograph of the original, supplemented by newspaper accounts of 1860.

In Baltimore, as in most large cities, there are constant shifts of population, and when most of the membership of a congregation move to another part of the city, their church or synagogue usually seeks a new location. This was the case in 1888, when the Baltimore Hebrew Congregation started to build a new synagogue "uptown," and sold this building to a Lithuanian Roman Catholic congregation known as the Church of St. John the Baptist. In 1905, the Lithuanian group, in turn, migrated to the western portion of the city, and sold the building to the Jewish congregation of Shomrei Mishmereth.

The Lloyd Street Synagogue, built in 1845, is an official Historic Landmark.

Several years ago, the synagogue was about to be abandoned because its congregation had dwindled to a few elderly men, and plans were under consideration to sell it to be converted into a garage and parking lot. Mr. Wilbur H. Hunter, Jr., Director of the Peale Museum, who, in 1959, had prepared a paper describing the synagogue for the "Historic American Buildings Survey," alerted some members of the Jewish community, and in 1963, it was purchased by the Jewish Historical Society of Maryland, to be restored as a historic monument.

The Greek Revival building has a Doric portico with a flight of steps on each side leading up to the gallery which ran on three sides. The portico, with trilyph frieze on four fluted, Greek Doric columns, extends over the whole height of the front. There are two small circular windows on the façade in the stair wells flanking the portico. In addition to these, there is a large, round, stained glass window over the Ark. This seems to be the first recorded use of the Star of David as exterior decoration in any American synagogue. The window was relocated in the new east wall when the synagogue was enlarged in 1860, and remained intact until only a few years ago. Fortunately, the lead molding and some of the original glass remained and was skillfully matched and pieced together, showing no discernible difference between the original and the restored portions of the present window.

The Beit Hamedrash, on the ground floor, is typical of such rooms in all Orthodox synagogues of the period. The brick floor dates from 1845. However, the furnishings of the room belonged to the Shomrei Mishmereth Congregation and were in active use until the congregation ceased to function in the early 1960s.

At the east end of the ground floor are two mikvehs, or ritual baths, one dating from 1845, and the other from the period of the Shomrei Mishmereth occupancy.

Several of Baltimore's leading congregations today trace their beginnings to the Baltimore Hebrew Congregation: Har Sinai (1842), Oheb Shalom (1853), Chizuk Amuno (1870), Shearith Israel (1879), Fells Point Synagogue (1838).

The Lloyd Street Synagogue is owned and maintained by the Jewish Historical Society of Maryland and is on the City of Baltimore's list of historic buildings and the United States Register of Historic Places.

A few meters away from the Lloyd Street Synagogue, the original Baltimore Hebrew Congregation, stands another historic synagogue. In 1875, Congregation Chizuk Amuno built its Moorish-Gothic synagogue at 27 Lloyd Street. In 1895, Chizuk Amuno moved to another location, McCulloh and Mosher Streets, and sold its first building to Congregation B'nai Israel. This is the only operating synagogue in downtown Baltimore. The original handcarved wooden Ark is still extant.

Adjoining the B'nai Israel Synagogue is the new home of the Jewish Historical Society of Maryland (15 Lloyd Street). The building contains a museum, gallery, and library. There are changing displays of cultural and historical material from the Society's collections, travelling exhibits and articles on loan, books and periodicals, audio-visual equipment, and a community resource for study and research. For further information, please call (301) 732-6400.

BALTIMORE HEBREW CONGREGATION
7401 Park Heights Avenue

The second home of the congregation was located at Madison Avenue and Robert Street. It was designed in 1890 by Charles L. Carson in Byzantine Revival style. The massive proportions suggest grandeur in simplicity in every outline of round arch, pointed gable and octagonal towers. The reds and browns of the Spanish tiles on the dome-shaped roof contrast effectively with the light color of the Port Deposit granite and Ohio sandstone carvings which form decorations.

In the broad recess at the back of the Temple stands the Shrine, supported on fluted columns with handsomely carved capitals and cornices. The Ark, of Moorish style modeled after the one in the ancient synagogue in Toledo, Spain, is of carved oak decorated with ivory, enamel and gold tracings. The cost of construction was $150,000.

Baltimore Hebrew Congregation's former Madison Avenue Temple.

HAR SINAI CONGREGATION
6300 Park Heights Avenue

This is the second oldest congregation in Baltimore. It was organized in 1842 and is said to be America's oldest continuous Reform congregation. Its previous locations include High Street, near Fayette Street (1849-1873), Lexington Street, near Pearl and Pine Streets (1873-1893), Bolton and Wilson Streets (1893-1959).

TEMPLE OHEB SHALOM
7310 Park Heights Avenue

Organized in 1853 by German Jews, the first home of the congregation was on Hanover Street. In 1892, the congregation built its lavish Eutaw Place Temple. That Moorish Revival structure was designed by J. Evans Sperry. The old Eutaw Place Temple now houses a Masonic Temple. The present temple building was designed in 1960 by architect Walter Gropius. Although Gropius' fame is world wide and he has designed a diversity of structures, Oheb Shalom was the first synagogue to which he brought his skill and talents. Although not a Jew, he fled Hitler's Germany in order to find freedom of expression and belief in America.

On entering the Sanctuary, it will be noticed that the floor grades upward in a gradual sweep toward the Ark. Dr. Gropius wished to convey the feeling of ascent, possibly inspired by the 24th Psalm. This upward sweep insures unhindered vision from any part of the Sanctuary or the auditorium in the rear when it is in use during High Holy Day services.

The grid-system along the Ark wall has been used as a motif in Gropius' high-rise office and residential structures. The Shabbat Menorah is made of bronze with colorful cloisonné enamel. The congregation follows the Reform ritual.

Temple Ohab Shalom's former Eutaw Place Temple.

Holy Ark design by Walter Gropius.

BALTIMORE HEBREW COLLEGE
5800 Park Heights Avenue

This institution houses a Hebrew College which trains teachers for Jewish religious schools, a women's institute of Jewish education, a high school department, the Board of Jewish Education, and the Jewish Historical Society of Maryland. For further information, please call (301) 588-2808.

NER ISRAEL RABBINICAL COLLEGE
400 Mt. Wilson Lane

The first American institution of Jewish higher education to be accorded the right to grant graduate degrees in Talmudic Law by the Maryland State Board of Education. It is run under Orthodox auspices.

ELLICOTT CITY

The Jewish agricultural colony, called Yaazor, was organized by the German (uptown) Jews of Baltimore for the newly-arrived East European Jews in 1902. It was located on the 351 acres on Johnnycake Road, between Rolling Road and the Patapsco River, northeast of Ellicott. The colony did not prosper and the residents returned to Baltimore.

ROCKVILLE

JEWISH COMMUNITY CENTER (JCC) OF GREATER WASHINGTON
6125 Montrose Road

The Jewish Community Center houses the first Jewish museum in this Washington suburban area. There is a permanent collection of Judaica and archeological artifacts. The Hebrew Home of Greater Washington is located within the JCC complex. For further information about museum exhibits and adult and youth programs at the JCC, please call (301) 881-0100.

THE OLD NEIGHBORHOODS

The following list contains information about synagogues which are no longer functioning as Jewish houses of worship. These addresses are located in the old sections of the city or town. It is advisable to take extra precautions while driving through these neighborhoods.

Annapolis Congregation Knesseth Israel *Prince George & E Streets*

Baltimore Congregation Adath Yeshurun *127 South Exeter Street*
Congregation Agudas Achim *132 South Eden Street*
High & Stiles Streets
132 South Caroline Street
Congregation Ahavas Scholom *122 South Popleton Street*
Congregation Aitz Chaim *Eden & Baltimore Streets*
Congregation Anshe Amunoh *511 Hanover Street*
Congregation Anshe Kolk *106 Albermarle Street*
Anshe Sfard *148 North High Street*
Baltimore Hebrew Congregation *Madison & Robert Streets*
Congregation Berocho Zedek *8 West Hill Street*
Congregation Beth Israel *247 South Eden Street*
Beth Hamedrash *13 Lloyd Street*
Beth Haknesseth *1601 East Baltimore Street*
Congregation Beth Jacob *144 North High Street*
Congregation Beth Jacob Anshe Kurland *114 North Exeter Street*
Congregation Bikur Cholim *High Street near Lexington Street*
Congregation B'nai Israel *27 Lloyd Street*
Congregation B'nai Jacob *2006 Christian Street*
Bobrusker Congregation *211 Aisquith Street*
Congregation Chizuk Amuno *McCulloh & Mosher Streets*

Congregation Emanu-El *1725 East Baltimore Street*
Congregation Har Sinai *Bolton & Wilson Streets*
Chaye Adom *112 Aisquith Street*
Knesseth Israel Anshi Sfard *27 Sough High Street*
Machzikei Hadas *1737 East Baltimore Street*
Mikro Kodesh *21 South High Street*
Mishkan Israel *2410 Madison Street*
Mogen Abraham *402 South Bond Street*
Moses Montefiore Amunas Israel *535 Smallwood Street*
Oheb Sholom *Eutaw Place & Lanvale Street*
Ohel Yacob *611 Aiquith Street*
Or Chodosh *1005 Pennysylvania Avenue*
Rodfei Zedek *8 West Hill Street*
Shearith Israel *2103 McCulloh Street*
Shomrei Hadass *1010 East Pratt Street*
Tiferes Israel *220 Harrison Street*
West End Hebrew Congregation Kneses Israel *743 West Lexington Street*
Western Ahavas Achim *2006 Christian Street*
Congregation Zichron Jacob *1531 East Baltimore Street*

Brunswick Beth Israel Synagogue *A Street*
Frederick Hebrew Congregation *East Church Street*
Frostburg Congregation B'nai Israel *East Church Street*
Salisbury Congregation Beth Israel *302 Main Street*

KOSHER RESTAURANTS

Baltimore The Knish Shop *508 Reisterstown Road (301) 484-5850*
O-Fishel's Kosher Restaurant *5700 Park Heights Avenue 466-3474*
O-Fishel's Kosher Restaurant *3506 Gwynbrook Avenue 356-5200*
Royal Restaurant *1630 Reisterstown Road 484-3544*
Tov Pizza *6313 Reisterstown Road 358-5238*
Danielle's Cuisine *401 Reisterstown Road 486-1487*
Jack's Deli *6311 Reisterstown Road 764-1616*
Liebe's Kosher Deli *607 Reisterstown Road 653-1977*
Shapiro's *Reisterstown & Old Court Roads 484-2400*
8515 Liberty Road 922-1600
Goldman's Kosher Deli *6848 Reisterstown Road 358-9625*
Silver Spring Shalom Kosher *2307 University Boulevard West 946-6500*
Shaul's Deli *11238 Georgia Avenue 949-8477*
Bagel Master *2646 University Avenue West 903-0200*
Wheaton World's Greatest Pizza *11419 Georgia Avenue 942-5900*
The Wooden Shoe Pastry Shop *11301 Georgia Avenue 942-9330*
The Jaffa Gate *2420 Blue Ridge Avenue 933-9331*

SYNAGOGUES

[Note: All area codes 301]

Annapolis 21403 Congregation Kneseth Israel (O) *Hilltop Lane & Spa Road 269-0740*

Arnold 21012 Temple Beth Sholom (R) *1461 Old Annapolis Road 974-0900*

Baltimore 21208 Adath Yeshurun - Magen Abraham Congregation (O) *Old Court & Rolling Roads 655-7818*
Congregation Agudath Israel (O) *6202 Park Heights Avenue 764-7778*
Baltimore Hebrew Congregation (R) *7401 Park Heights Avenue 764-1587*
Beth Abraham Congregation (O) *6208 Wallis Avenue (301) 358-7456*
Congregation Beth Am *Eutaw Place & Chauncey Street*
Congregation Beth El (C) *8101 Park Heights Avenue 484-0411*
Congregation Beth Isaac Adath Israel (O) *4398 Crest Heights Road 486-8338*
Beth Jacob Congregation (O) *5713 Park Heights Avenue 466-1266*
Congregation Beth Jacob Wisheer (O) *1016 Hillen Street*
Beth Tefilo Congregation (O) *3300 Old Court Road 486-1900*
B'nai Israel Synagogue (O) *15 Lloyd Street 358-9417*
Congregation B'nai Jacob *6605 Liberty Road*
Congregation B'nai Jacob (O) *3615 Seven Mile Lane 358-8969*
Congregation B'nai Reuben (O) *3725 Milford Mill Road 922-7990*
Chabad House (O) *5721 Park Heights Avenue*
Congregation Chizuk Amuno (O) *Eutaw Place & Chauncey Street*

Congregation Chofetz Chaim–Adath B'nei Israel (O)
3702 West Rogers Avenue 578-0774
Congregation Darchei Torah (O) *7124 Park Heights Avenue 764-0262*
Garrison Forest Beth Knesseth (O) *2 Hiawatha Circle*
Har Brook Hebrew Congregation (Temple B'nai Sholom)
4303 Govenor Richie Highway.
Har Sinai Congregation (R) *6300 Park Heights Avenue 764-2882*
Congregation Kahal Arugas Hobosem (O) *6615 Park Heights Avenue 358-9722*
Liberty Jewish Center (O) *8615 Church Lane 922-1333*
Lloyd Street Synagogue *Lloyd & Watson Streets*
Congregation Machzikei Torah (O) *6216 Baltimore Avenue 358-0885*
Congregation Magen Abraham (O) *3114-C Parkington Avenue*
Ner Israel Rabbinical College (O) *400 Mount Wilson Lane*
Ner Tamid Congregation (O) *6214 Pimlico Road 358-6500*
Temple Oheb Sholom (R) *7310 Park Heights Avenue 358-0105*
Congregation Ohel Yaakov (O) *3200 Glen Avenue 578-9336*
Pickwick Jewish Center (O) *6221 Greenspring Avenue 358-9660*
Congregation Shaari Tfiloh (O) *2001 Liberty Heights Avenue 523-4375*
Shaar Zion Congregation 660 Park Heights Avenue
Congregation Shearith Israel (O) *Glen & Park Heights Avenues 466-3060*
Congregation Shomrei Emunah (O)
6213 Greenspring Avenue 358-8604
Congregation Toras Chaim (O) *7504 Seven Mile Lane 484-6114*
Woodmore Hebrew Congregation *3607 Milford Mill Road*
Young Israel (O) *5724 Clover Road*

Bel Air Hartford Jewish Center (R) *2405 Freshman Drive 734-6429*

Bethesda 20814 Congregation Beth El (C) *8215 Old Georgetown Road 652-2606*
Bethesda Jewish Congregation *6601 Bradley Boulevard 469-8636*

Bowie 20715 Congregation Nevey Sholom (C) *12218 Torah Lane 262-4020*
Temple Solel (R) *2901 Mitchelvale Road 249-CHAI*

Chevy Chase 20015 Congregation Ohr Kodesh (C) 8402 Freyman Drive 589-3880
Temple Sholom (R) *8401 Grubb Road 589-3889*

Columbia Temple Isaiah (R) *5885 Robert Oliver Place 730-8277*

Cumberland 21502 Congregation Beth Jacob (C) 11 Columbia Street 722-6350
Temple B'er Chayim (R) *107 Union Street 722-5688*

Easton 21601 Temple B'nai Israel (C) *Adkins Avenue*

Essex Congregation B'nai Sholom *401 Eastern Boulevard*

Frederick 21701 Congregation Beth Sholom (C) *20 West 2nd Street*

Gaithersburg 20879 Hebrew Congregation (C) 9915 Appleridge Road 869-7699

Greenbelt 20770 *Congregation Mishkan Torah (C)*

Ridge & Westway Roads 474-4223

Hagerstown 21740 *Congregation B'nai Abraham (R)* 53
East Baltimore Street 733-5039

Havre de Grace 21078 Adas Sholom Temple (R) *8 North Earlton Road 939-9763*

Hyattsville 20782 Congregation Beth Torah (C) 6700 Adelphi Road

Kensington 20795 Temple Emanu-El (R) 10101 Connecticut Avenue 942-2000

Laurel Congregation Oseh Sholom *Briarwood Drive off Route 197*

Lexington Park 20653 Beth Israel Synagogue (C) 335 Midway Drive 863-8886

Mount Rainier Northeast Hebrew Congregation 4601 Eastern Avenue

Pikesville Congregation Chizuk Amuno (C) *8100 Stevenson Road 486-6400*

Pocomoke City 21851 Congregation of Israel (C) *3rd Street*

Potomac 20854 Beth Ami Congregation *8213 Lakeheath Road*
Beth Sholom Congregation *11825 Seven Locks Road*
Congregation Har Sholom (C) *11510 Falls Road 299-7087*
Washington Hebrew Congregation *Fall & Tuckerman Roads*

Randallstown 21133 Congregation Beth Israel (C) 9411 Liberty Road 922-6565
Randallstown Synagogue Center (O) *8729 Church Lane 655-6665*

Winands Road Synagogue (O) *8701 Winands Road 655-1353*
Congregation Magen Abraham (O) *3800 Pikewood Drive*
Liberty Jewish Center (O) 8615 Church Lane

Reisterstown Jewish Center *109 Cherry Valley Road 833-5307*

Rockville 20853 Temple Beth Ami (R) *800 Hurley Avenue 340-6818*
Congregation Beth Tikvah (C) *2200 Baltimore Road 762-7338*
Congregation B'nai Israel (C) *6301 Montrose Road 881-6550*

Salisbury 21801 Congregation Beth Israel (C) *600 Camden Avenue 742-2564*

Silver Spring 20910 Congregation Agudas Achim 2107 Briggs Road
Congregation Har Tzeon–Agudath Achim (C) *1840 University Boulevard West 649-3800*

Congregation Ezras Israel *8055 13th Street*
Temple Israel (C) *420 University Boulevard East 439-3600*
Congregation Shaare Tefila (C) *11120 Lockwood Drive 593-3410*
Silver Spring Jewish Center *1401 Arcola Avenue*
Southeast Hebrew Congregation (O) *1090 Lockwood Drive 593-2120*
Young Israel–(O) *1132 Arcola Avenue*
Young Israel–Shomrei Emunah (O) *811 University Boulevard West 593-4465*

Stevenson Congregation Chizuk Amuno *8100 Stevenson Road*

Temple Hill 20748 Congregation Shaare Tikvah (C) 5404 Old Temple Hills Road 894-4303

MIKVEHS

Baltimore 3500 West Rogers Avenue *(301) 664-5834*

Silver Spring 8901 Georgia Avenue *587-2014 or 565-3737*
1401 Arcola Avenue 649-4425 or 649-2799

Massachusetts

Solomon Franco, a Portuguese Sephardi, arrived in Boston in 1649, making him the first Jew to land in the Colonies. Judah Monis, an Italian Jew, received his Master's degree from Harvard College in 1720. He was hired to teach Hebrew at Harvard only after renouncing his Judaism and publicly converting to Christianity. During the American Revolution, several Jews served with the Massachusetts regiments, fought in the battle of Bunker Hill, and witnessed George Washington take command of the Continental Army.

After the Revolution, when there were still only a few Jewish residents in Massachusetts, mostly in Boston, there still was no organized Jewish community in the state. One of Boston's leading citizens was Moses Michael Hayes, a Portuguese Sephardi Jew. He helped found the First National Bank of Boston, the Boston Marine Society, and the Massachusetts Mutual Fire Insurance Company. His son Judah and his nephews Abraham and Judah Touro (whose father had built the Touro Synagogue in Newport, Rhode Island) helped establish the Massachusetts General Hospital, the Athenaeum, and the Bunker Hill Monument. When Moses Michael Hayes died, in 1805, he had to be buried in Newport, Rhode Island, since Jewish cemeteries were not permitted in Boston at the time.

The first organized Jewish community began in the mid-19th century, with the arrival of Jews from Germany. Settling at first in the newly-filled land of the South End of Boston. These German immigrants organized the first synagogue in the state in 1843.

Congregation Ohabei Shalom built its first synagogue on Warren (now Warrenton) Street in 1852. In 1844, the congregation established the first Jewish cemetery in the city. Jews no longer had to be buried in Albany, Newport, or New York City.

In 1854, several Bavarian Jews broke away from Congregation Ohabei Shalom and organized Congregation Adath Israel (today's Temple Israel). Late in the 19th century Adath Israel, under the leadership of Rabbi Solomon Schindler, introduced such Reform practices as organ music, family pews, Sunday services, and vernacular prayers.

In 1858, Boston's third congregation, Mishkan Tephila, was organized by a group of Jews from Posen (in eastern Germany).

Following the Civil War, the Jewish community shifted to Boston's North End. The Civil War industrial boom in the New England cotton and woolen mills and shoe factories attracted new Jewish immigrants, a few as factory workers, but most as tradesmen and peddlers. From the factories and sweatshops, from piece-work and peddling, grew small stores and businesses—and occasionally, like that of Lynn's William Filene, very large stores and businesses.

While the German Jews had established themselves in Boston's South End, the East European Jews, who began arriving in the late 1870s and early 1880s, settled at first in the city's North End. By 1900, the North End was similar to New York City's Lower East Side. The area was filled with peddlers and pushcarts. There were many social clubs *(landsmanschaften)*, library programs, and settlement houses. The North End spawned many notable individuals such as Sophie Tucker (who lived on Salem Street), Senator Barry Goldwater's grandfather, art critic and philosopher Bernard Berenson, and Leopold Morse, Massachusetts' first Jewish congressman.

At the turn of the century, there were seven Yiddish newspapers and Yiddish theater flourished in the area around Dover and Washington Streets. As more immigrants arrived, the Jewish neighborhoods extended into the city's West End and beyond, to Chelsea and Lynn. By 1920, the Jews had largely abandoned the North End and East Boston to the massive Italian immigration.

Around the First World War, Jews began moving to Roxbury and from there eventually to Dorchester and Mattapan.

The period following World War I was Boston Jewry's "Golden Age." There were about 50,000 Jews living in Roxbury, Dorchester, and Mattapan, making it the largest Jewish community in the northeast outside New York City. During this period, many new Jewish edifices were built including Beth Israel Hospital, Temple Israel on Commonwealth Avenue (now Boston University's Morse Auditorium), Temple Mishkan Tefila on Seaver Street, the original site of Hebrew College in Roxbury, Kehilath Israel's synagogue on Harvard Street, and Temple Ohabei Shalom on Beacon Street.

After the Second World War, the movement of the Jewish community was away from the Roxbury, Dorchester, and Mattapan area and into the nearby towns of Brighton, Brookline, Newton, Randolph, Marblehead, and Swampscott. There is now a trend for young professionals to return to the "old neighborhoods" of Chelsea and downtown Boston.

The history of the Jewish communities of Worcester and Springfield begins in the late 1880s. Immigrant Jewish families came north from New York City and settled in Springfield's North End section. As in many other places, the heads of Jewish families were often peddlers.

The first synagogues were organized in the early 1890s. By 1905, the community numbered several hundred families, and there were five Orthodox congregations in the North End. By World War I, heavy Jewish settlement in Forest Park, in the southern part of the city, took place and a Conservative and an Orthodox congregation were established. By the mid-30s, as many Jews lived there as in the North End.

In the mid-30s, Jewish settlement began in Longmeadow, once an exclusive suburb. The growth of Longmeadow as a Jewish area increased after World War II. Today, the center of Jewish life is located in Forest Park and adjoining Longmeadow, a complete shift from the North End of a century ago.

There have been Jews in the Berkshires since before the Civil War. The early settlers, usually individual men rather than the families common to later years, came from Bavaria in Germany and had often been peddlars for a number of years prior to settling down and opening a store or other business. While not directly employed by the textile mills that were the area's industrial base, the Jews who came in those early years were often involved in collecting the rags the mills needed to operate.

Pittsfield today has three congregations. Temple Anshe Amunim was formed by about forty families as an Orthodox congregation in 1869. By 1879, it was following the Reform ritual. Another congregation was formed in 1893 and was known as Kneses Israel. This congregation was also Orthodox and remained so until the early 1950s, when it became Conservative. A third congregation, Ahavath Sholom, formed in 1911 and, known as the "little shul," remains an Orthodox synagogue to this day.

The Jewish population of Massachusetts is approximately 255,000.

AMHERST

NATIONAL YIDDISH BOOK CENTER
Old East School Street 253-9201

The Center provides speakers and offers classes on a variety of topics related to Yiddish language and literature and Jewish history. Each summer the Center sponsors a week-long, residential summer program at Hampshire College which attracts lovers of Yiddish of all ages. The Center has also saved more than 350,000 Yiddish books from certain oblivion, making its holdings the largest collection of Yiddish books ever. Its collection is growing at a rate of 1,000 books per week!

BOSTON

CONGREGATION ADATH ISRAEL (TEMPLE ISRAEL)
Plymouth Street and Longwood Avenue 566-3960

Temple Israel was established in 1854, making it the second oldest congregation in Boston. It is the largest congregation in New England. It follows the Reform ritual. Its first synagogue building was located at the corner of Columbus Avenue and Northampton Street. That 1885 structure is still extant and is occupied by the Zion African Methodist Episcopal Church. Temple Israel's second location was at 602 Commonwealth Avenue. That building, with its impressive dome, is now known as the Alfred L. Morse Auditorium, and is part of Boston University.

Temple Israel on Columbus Avenue in Boston's South End, 1885.

OLD VILNA SHUL
16 Phillips Street

A traditional Orthodox congregation, located in Beacon Hill's Historic District. It was founded by Lithuanian immigrants in the 1890s. There are weekly Friday evening and Sabbath morning services.

CHARLES RIVER PARK SYNAGOGUE
55 Martha Road

This synagogue is the successor to the old North Russell Street Shul, Congregation Beth Hamedrash Hagadol Beth Jacob, which was demolished along with the rest of the old West End by the urban renewal of the 1960s. Members of the original synagogue won a $313,000 payment from the city to rebuild in the Charles River Park Apartments area, near Massachusetts General Hospital.

The structure itself is noteworthy for its modern design. It is an Orthodox congregation in most ways (only men are called to the Torah and lead services), except that there is a section for mixed seating in addition to separate men's and women's sections. It is the only shul in downtown Boston and serves the existing elderly and newly-moved-in young professional membership.

BROOKLINE

HEBREW COLLEGE
43 Hawes Street

Formerly known as the Hebrew Teachers College, the Hebrew College was founded in 1921. It is New England's only accredited schoool of Judaic studies. It trains Hebrew teachers for Jewish schools and grants B.A. and M.A. degrees in Hebrew language and literature, Bible, rabbinic literature, Jewish history, Jewish thought and contemporary Jewish studies. The original site of the Hebrew College was in the Roxbury section, adjoining Temple Mishkan Tefila. Above the front façade of the 122 Elm Hill Avenue building is the half-erased Hebrew inscription, "*Talmud Torah K'neged Kulam.*" That building now houses the Afro-American Arts Center.

TEMPLE OHABEI SHALOM
1187 Beacon Street

Founded in 1842 by German and Polish immigrants, Ohabei Shalom was the first synagogue in Massachusetts. The first synagogue was located on Warren (now Warrenton) Street and was built in 1851. The second location of the congregation was at 11 Union Park Street, from 1887 to 1921. That building is presently occupied by a Greek Orthodox church. The present building of Temple Ohabei Shalom is located in Brookline. Although it was originally Orthodox, it changed to the Reform ritual in 1871, becoming the first Reform congregation in New England.

NEW ENGLAND CHASSIDIC CENTER CONGREGATION BETH PINCHAS (BOSTONER REBBE)
1710 Beacon Street (Brookline)

The Grand Rabbi Itzchak Horowitz, the Bostoner Rebbe, is the first American-born Chassidic rabbi. The New England Chassidic Center was founded in 1915 in Boston's West End. According to the Bostoner Rebbe, "Boston's Orthodox community combines the best of two worlds, those of Torah and intellect. This combi-

Ohabei Shalom, founded in 1842, is the oldest congregation in Massachusetts.

nation has been instrumental in providing a vibrant Torah community within a modern community. We are accessible to Jews from all walks of life, with or without religious background." The Center is available to host visiting groups for lectures on Jewish and Chassidic interest. An annual matzoh-baking session and a Purim se'udah (meal) are open to the public.

The Chassidic Center is housed in a fashionable townhouse on Beacon Street. The elongated space on the first level houses the synagogue. The women are separated during services (since this is an Orthodox congregation) by a very unique mechitzah (partition). In the late 1960s, the just-completed John Hancock Building in Downtown Boston, was having some problems with its newly-installed windows. Apparently, the-windows were not properly designed for this hermetically-sealed skyscraper. After several weeks, windows started "popping out" and came crashing down to the sidewalk. The missing glass windows were replaced with plywood boards. The building, designed by the architectural firm of I.M. Pei, was dubbed the "Plywood Skyscraper."

At this point, all of the windows in the building were removed and replaced with now-properly-designed windows. The surplus original windows were now on the market—up for sale. The Bostoner Rebbe purchased two of these special windows and are serving as the mechitzah (partition) between the men's and women's sections in his shul.

The mechitzah, according to Jewish law, must be a specific height and must not allow the women to be seen by the men during services. These special windows fulfilled all of these requirements. One side of the window was reflective (mirrored) and faces the men's section, while the reverse side of the window was see-through and faces the women's section. For information about services, please call 734-5100.

CAMBRIDGE

CONGREGATION BETH ISRAEL ANSHE SFARD
238 Columbia Street

This former synagogue was built in 1901 and still displays its two inscribed cornerstones on its front façade. The building was converted into artist's lofts in the early 1970s.

Rabbi Levi I. Horowitz, the Bostoner Rebbe.

DORCHESTER

CONGREGATION CHEVRE SHAS
65 Ashton Street

This congregation had great expectations when it was organized in the 1920s. They built the ground floor Beit Hamedrash (daily chapel) with the intent of later constructing a massive elegant synagogue above. Hard times hit during 1929, the Stock Market Crash and subsequent Depression. The congregation literally never got off the ground floor. It did, however, design a very impressive Art Deco main entrance, complete with limestone blocks, terra cotta trim, and the Ten Commandment Tablets. A similar situation occurred in New York City during the same period, at the Intervale Jewish Center, in the South Bronx.

ROXBURY

CONGREGATION ADATH JESHURUN
22 Blue Hill Avenue

This twin-towered former synagogue was built in 1906 for Congregation Adath Jeshurun. Although this building is used by the First Haitian Baptist Church the Stars of David are still present, atop each of the copper domes. The marble plaques with the names of the founding fathers of the congregation are still present on the front façade of the building.

The former Adath Jeshurun Synagogue in the Roxbury section.

TEMPLE MISHKAN TEFILA
200 Seaver Street

Founded in 1858, Mishkan Tefila is Boston's third oldest congregation. Its first location was on Moreland Street. Its second location was in the Roxbury section, on Seaver Street, opposite the Boston Zoo. The massive limestone structure was built atop a hill in the early 1920s. Around the corner from the temple was the first home of the Hebrew College. That structure now houses the Afro-American Arts Center and is located at 122 Elm Hill Avenue.

The magnificent Temple Mishkan Tefila structure stands abandoned. The interior is entirely gutted. The glorious marble columns which once supported the upper galleries are strewn about the front and side lawns. Temple Mishkan Tefila is still functioning. The congregation relocated to Newton and is the oldest Conservative congregation in the area. The Rubenovitz Jewish Museum, housed in the Newton building, contains a large collection of Jewish ceremonial objects and material on Boston's Jewish history. For further information about the congregation and its museum, please call (607) 332-7770.

The magnificent ruins of the old Temple Mishkan Tefila on Seaver Street.

Detail of the menorah on the old Mishkan Tefila in Roxbury.

WALTHAM

BRANDEIS UNIVERSITY

Named for Justice Louis D. Brandeis, the first Jew appointed to the Supreme Court of the United States, Brandeis University was established in 1948 and was the first nonsectarian institution of higher education in the Western Hemisphere to be founded by Jews. The University occupies a 300-acre campus overlooking the Charles River.

For the undergraduate Judaic studies major, Brandeis offers a wide range of courses within a variety of disciplines, including history, language, and biblical texts. There is a combined Master's

Doctoral program that takes five years to complete. Brandeis University sponsors many Jewish-oriented lectures, forums, films, and exhibits throughout the year.

The world-famous Three Chapels area at Brandeis consists of separate Jewish, Catholic, and Protestant houses of worship (similar, in concept, to the three chapels at Kennedy International Airport, in New York City), grouped around a heart-shaped pool. The architects, Harrison and Abramovitz (designers of the Jewish Chapel at West Point Military Academy), designed these chapels in 1954 to "reflect the similarity of all faiths, while respecting their doctrinal differences." The buildings are so placed around the pool that no one overlooks the other. There are no external religious symbols on the buildings. There are outdoor services for events of common significance, such as Thanksgiving and the like.

In the synagogue, two curved windowless walls surround the congregation and focus attention on the Ark and the view of trees and sky through the window behind it. The Jewish chapel houses the Hillel of Brandeis University. It offers an unusually wide variety of Sabbath and holiday services, as well as classes, concerts, speakers, interest groups, lectures, and kosher meals. For further information, please call 647-2178.

The Holocaust Monument, near the Jewish Chapel, is a statue of Job cast in bronze. It was designed by Nathan Rapaport, who designed the original statue for the Yad Vashem Museum in Jerusalem. Ashes from the Treblinka Concentration Camp are buried at the base of the statue.

AMERICAN JEWISH HISTORICAL SOCIETY
2 Thornton Road 891-8110

Founded in 1892, the American Jewish Historical Society collects, catalogues, displays, and publishes material relating to the Jewish experience in America. It contains the largest collection of American Hebraica in the world. It maintains a library of over 78,000 volumes and six million pages of manuscripts as well as an extensive photo collection and periodical listing. The American Jewish Historical Society is located on the Brandeis University campus and is open to visitors as well as scholars and researchers the year round.

The Jewish Chapel on the Brandeis University campus was designed by Harrison & Abramovitz.

THE OLD NEIGHBORHOODS

The following list contains information about synagogues which are no longer functioning as Jewish houses of worship. These addresses are located in the old sections of the city or town. It is advisable to take extra precautions while driving through these neighborhoods.

Acton Congregation Beth Elohim *82 High Street*
Athol Congregation Agudas Achim *Pine Street*
Attleboro Congregation Agudas Achim *Pearl Street*
North Main Street
Arlington Jewish Community Center *370 Mass. Avenue*
Congregation B'nai Jacob *16 Burton Street*
Belmont Congregation Beth El *270 Lexington Street*
Beverly Congregation Sons of Abraham *39 Bow Street*
Boston Congregation Adath Israel *94 Brighton Street*
Congregation Agudas Achim *82 Lowell Street*
Congregation Agudath Israel *222 Woodrow Avenue*
Congregation Anshe Sfard *11 Ashland Street*
16 Davis Street
Congregation Atereth Israel *107 Northampton Street (Moreland Street)*
Congregation Beth Am Hagadol *105 Crawford Street*
Congregation Beth David *2 Paris Place (East Boston)*
Beth El *94 Fowler Street*
Beth Hamedrash Hagadol *28 North Russell Street*
Congregation Beth Medrash *24 Wall Street*
Congregation Beth Israel *Baldwin Place*
Congregation B'nai Israel *Atlantic Avenue*
Chevre Chai Adom *101 Nightingale Street*
Temple Emanu-El *471 Warren Street*

Congregation Ezrat Israel *333 Bryant Street*
Congregation Eperion *575 Warren Street*
Temple Israel *Columbus Avenue & Northampton Street*
Congregation Kehilath Israel *Harvard & Thorndike Streets*
Congregation Knesseth Israel *335 Harrison Avenue*
15 Emerald Street
Linas Hazedek Anshe Sfard *62 Poplar Street*
77 Chelsea Street
Congregation Machzikei Torah *43 Auburn Street*
Congregation Mishkan Shlomo *71 Poplar Street*
Congregation Ohel Jacob *Paris & Cove Streets*
Congregation Shaare Zedek *5 Baldwin Place*
Congregation Shaare Zion *35 Barton Street*
Congregation Shaare Jerusalem *112 Salem Street*
Congregation Sons of Jacob *210 Dover Street*
338 Harrison Avenue
South Boston Hebrew Congregation *484 East 4th Street*
Temple Ohabei Sholom *11 Union Park Avenue*
Congregation Tikvas Israel *114 Southern Avenue*
Woburn Hebrew Center *10 Greene Street*
Congregation Shaare Tefila *11 Otisfield Street*

Brockton Congregation Agudas Achim *56 Old Colony Square*
251 Crescent Street
Temple Beth Emunah *34 Cottage Street*
Congregation Anshe Sfard *Bay Street*

Cambridge Congregation Beth Israel *238 Columbia Street*
Jewish Community Center *298 Harvard Street*
Yavno Congregation *222 Webster Avenue*

Canton Congregation Brith Abraham *Revere Street*

Charleston Congregation Beth Jacob *212 Main Street*

Chelsea Congregation Ahavas Achim Anshe Sfard *15 Elm Street*
Congregation Beth Hamedrash Hagadol *5th, Walnut, & Poplar Streets*

Congregation Beth Jacob Anshe Sfard *111 3rd Street*
Congregation Poale Zedek Gemilas Chesed *83 Chestnut Street*
Congregation Shearith Israel *131 Arlington Street*
Walnut Street Synagogue
Congregation Torat Chaim *23 Heard Street*

Clinton Poresky Congregation *48 High Street*

Dorchester Congregation Chevre Shas *65 Ashton Street*
Mooreland Street Temple *19 Washington Street*
Young Israel *75 Astoria Street*

Everett Congregation Tifereth Israel *172 Union Street*

East Lexington Congregation Beth Jacob *68 Sylvia Street*

East Saugus Congregation Ahavath Sholom *Briston Street*

Fall River Congregation Adas Israel *48 Washington Street*
48 Pearl Street
Congregation Agudas Machzikei Harav *231 Union Street*
Congregation Ahavas Achim *137 Flint Street*
Congregation Bais David *Vale Street*
Congregation Brothers of Israel *266 Union Street*
Congregation Sons of Jacob *183 Quarry Street*

Fitchburg Congregation Agudath Achim *158 Sumner Street*

Framingham Congregation Beth Sholom *48 Clinton Street*

Gardner Congregation Ohav Sholom *175 Nichols Street*

Haverhill Congregation Agudas Achim *Washington Street*
Congregation Beth Jacob *River Street*
334 Broadway
Congregation Knesseth Israel *14 River Street*
Temple Emanu-El *640 Main Street*

Holyoke Congregation Anshei Rodfei Sholom *300 Park Street*

Jamaica Plains Congregation Anshe Brith Sholom *65 Bickford Street*

Lawrence Congregation Tifereth Anshe Sfard *85 Concord Street*
Congregation Sons of Israel *70 Concord Street*

Leominster Congregation Agudas Achim *Mechanic Street*
71 Pleasant Street

Lowell Congregation Kehillas Jacob *8 McIntyre Street*
Congregation Sons of Montefiore *132 Howard Street*
Temple Emanu-El *1224 Middlesex Street*

Lynn Congregation Ahavath Sholom *65 Church Street*
Congregation Agudath Israel *91 Blossom Street*
Congregation Anshe Sfard *12 West Street*
Congregation B'nai Jacob *Flint Street*
Jewish Community Center *45 Market Street*
Temple Beth El *16 Breed Street*
Congregation Chevre Tehillim *58 Shepard Street*

Malden Congregation Adath Israel *356 Cross Street*
Congregation Beth Israel *Faulkner Street*
Congregation Mishkan Tefilah *48 Granville Avenue*
Tifereth Israel Temple *68 Myrtle Street*
Young Israel *342 Ferry Street*

Mattapan Congregation Hadrat Israel *235 Woodrow Avenue*
Temple Beth Hillel *800 Morton Street*
Congregation Kehilat Jacob *18 Fessenden Street*

Medford Jewish Community Center *42 Water Street*

Melrose Hebrew Association *52 Grove Street*
American Jewish Center *34 Crystal Street*

Millis Congregation Beth Jacob *Willough Street*

Natick Temple Israel *44 North Avenue*

New Bedford Congregation Ahavath Achim *Howland Street*
Congregation Tifereth Israel *6th & Madison Streets*
Temple Sinai *169 William Street*
Congregation Chesed Shel Emes *86 Kenyon Street*
Congregation Lenas Hatzekek *334 South 1st Street*

Newton Congregation Kehilat Jacob *858 Walnut Street*
Congregation Agudath Achim *114 Adams Street*
Congregation Beth Medrash *Watertown Street*
Temple Reyim *321 Chestnut Street*

North Adams Congregation Chai Adam *Ashland Street*
Congregation House of Israel *7 Francis Avenue, 45 Center Street*

Northampton Congregation B'nai Israel *14 Bridge Street*

Peabody Congregation Anshe Sfard *45 Main Street*
Congregation Sons of Israel *Elliot Place & Spring Street*
Hebrew Community Center *42 Washington Street*

Pittsfield Congregation Anshe Amonim *Mellville Street, Fenn & Willis Streets*
Congregation Kneseth Israel *165 Linden Street, 11 Wendell Avenue*
Congregation Hebrew Alliance *Robbins Avenue*

Quincy Congregation Ahavath Achim *129 School Street*
Jewish Community Center *10 Merrymont Road*
Temple Beth El *1245 Hancock Street*

Roxbury Congregation Adath Jeshurun *532 Warren Street*
Congregation Agudath Achim *37 Intervale Street*
Congregation Beth Hamedrash Hagadol *105 Crawford Street*
Congregation Linas Zedek *20 Michigan Avenue*
Congregation Shaare Tefila *11 Otisfield Street*
Temple Mishkan Tefila *200 Seaver Street*
Young Israel *161 Ruthuen Street*

Salem Congregation Sons of Jacob *4 Derby Square*

Somerville Congregation Anshe Sfard *85 Webster Avenue*

South Framingham United Hebrew Congregation *Collidge Street*

Springfield Congregation Adath Yeshurun *565 Chestnut Street*
Congregation B'nai Yakir *114 Ferry Street*
Congregation Beth El *148 Fort Pleasant Avenue*
Congregation Beth Israel *24 Gray's Avenue*
Congregation Kesser Israel *329 Chestnut Street*
Congregation Kadimah *285 Dickinson Street 17 Oakland Street*
Congregation Sons of Israel *34 Sharon Street, 1321 Dwight Street*

Congregation Tifereth Israel *Liberty Hall Ferry & North Streets*
Young Israel 40 *Scott Street*

Stoughton Congregation Ahavath Achim *Washington Street*

Waltham Temple Beth Israel 50 *Russel Street*

West Newton Temple Reyim 321 *Chestnut Street*

Whitman Hebrew Congregation 112 *Rock Street*

Worecester Congregation Anshe Sfard 66 *Harrison Street*
Congregation Beth Israel 835 *Pleasant Street*
Congregation Beth Judah 889 *Pleasant Street*
Congregation Chesed Shel Emeth *Harrison & Penn Avenues*
Congregation Good Brothers 9 *Pond Street*
Jewish Community Center 111 *Elm Street*
Congregation Shaare Torah, Sons of Abraham 12 *Waverly Street*
Congregation Sons of Abraham 25 *Coral Street*
Congregation Sons of Jacob 14 *Woodford Street*
Congregation Sons of Israel 24 *Providence Street*
Congregation Tifereth Israel 42 *Harrison Street*
6 *Sahanto Road*
Congregation Tower of Truth 16 *Gold Street*

KOSHER RESTAURANTS

Boston Milk Street Cafe *50 Milk Street (617) 542-2433*
Brighton Kosher Mart *154 Chestnut Hill Avenue 254-9529*
Brookline The Butcherie *428 Harvard Street 731-9888*
Cafe Shalom *404A Harvard Street 277-0698*
Rubin's Restaurant *500 Harvard Street 566-8761*
Eagerman's Bakery *415 Harvard Street 566-8771*
Canton The Butcherie *110 Washington Street 828-3530*
Framingham Bread Basket *151 Cochituate Road 875-9441*
Rain's Bakery *55 Nichols Road 877-3927*
Hull Weinberg's Bakery *519 Nantasket Avenue 925-9875*

Longmeadow Kimmell's Deli *800 Williams Avenue (413) 567-3304*
Westerman's Bakery *791 Maple Road 567-9122*

Lynn Lynn Kosher Deli *224 Lewis Street (617) 599-7220*

Malden Cissy's Bakery *517 Main Street 321-4717*

Medford Donuts With A Difference *33 Riverside Avenue 396-1021*

Natick Eagerman's Bakery *810 Worcester Road 235-1092*

Newton Gosman's *333 Nahanton Street 965-7410*
Traditionally Yours *709 Washington Street 769-0439*
All You Knead *316 Walnut Street 244-6252*
Diamond Bakery *1136 Beacon Street 527-3740*

Peabody Horowitz Kosher Foods *672 Lowell Street 535-9725*

Pittsfield Samuel's Deli *115 Elm Street 442-5927*

Randolph Zeppy's Bakery *937 North Main Street 963-9837*

Revere Myer's Kosher Kitchen *176 Shirley Avenue 289-2063*
The Bakery *107 Shirley Avenue*

Springfield Abe's Kosher Meats *907 Sumner Avenue (413) 733-3504*
Liberty Bakery *801 Liberty Street 734-2114*

Stoughton Ruth's Bake Shop *987 Central Street 344-8993*

Swanscott Newman's Bakery *248 Humphrey Street 592-1550*

Worcester Ruth's Kitchen (Kosher Chinese) *1098 Pleasant Street 754-2450*

SYNAGOGUES

[Note: All area codes 617, except 413, where indicated]

Acton Congregation Beth Elohim *Hennessey Drive*

(413) 263-3061

Amherst 01002 Chabad House (O) *30 North Handley Road 253-9040*

Jewish Community Center *742 Main Street 256-0160*

Andover 01810 Temple Emanu-El (R) *7 Haggett's Pond Road 470-1356*

Athol 01331 Temple Israel (C) *107 Walnut Street*

Attleboro 02703 Agudas Achim Congregation (C) *Toner & Kelley Boulevards 222-2243*

Ayer 01432 Congregation Anshe Sholom *Cambridge Street 772-0896*

Bellingham 02019 *Congregation Beth Chaverim 16 Yvonne Road*

Belmont 02178 Beth El Temple Center (R) *2 Concord Avenue 484-6668*

Beverly 01915 Temple B'nai Abraham (C) *200 East Lothrop Street 927-3211*

Congregation Ohav Sholom (O) *3 Beckford Street 922-2495*

Boston 02215 Chabad House (O) *491 Commonwealth Avenue 424-1191*

Charles River Park Synagogue (T) *55 Martha Road 523-0453*

Old Vilna Shul (O) *16 Phillips Street 227-0587*

Temple Israel (R) *Plymouth Street & Longwood Avenue 566-3960*

Braintree 02184 Temple B'nai Sholom (C) *41 Storrs Avenue 843-3687*

Brighton 02135 Temple B'nai Moshe (C) *1845 Commonwealth Avenue 254-3620*
Congregation Kadimah–Toras Moshe (O) *113 Washington Street 254-1333*
Lubavitch Shul (O) *239 Chestnut Hill Avenue 782-8340*

Brockton 02401 Congregation Agudas Achim (O) *144 Belmont Avenue 583-0717*
Temple Beth Emunah (C) *Torrey & Pearl Streets 583-5810*
Temple Israel (R) *184 West Elm Street 587-4130*

Brookline 02146 Congregation Beth David (O) *64 Corey Road 232-2349*
Congregation Beth Pinchas (Bostoner Rebbe) *1710 Beacon Street 734-5100*
Temple Beth Zion (C) *1566 Beacon Street 566-8171*
Congregation Chai Odom (O) *77 Englewood Avenue 734-5359*
Temple Emeth (C) *194 Grove Street 469-9400*
Congregation Kehilath Israel (C) *384 Harvard Street 277-9155*
Congregation Lubavitch (O) *100 Woodcliff Road 469-9007*
Maimonides School Minyan (O) *Philbrick Road & Boylston Street 232-4452*
Temple Ohabei Sholom (R) *1187 Beacon Street 277-6610*
Sephardic Congregation of New England (O) *1566 Beacon Street 734-3743*
Sephardic Congregation of Greater Boston (O) *62 Green Street 277-9429*
Temple Sinai (R) *50 Sewall Avenue 277-5888*
Young Israel of Brookline (O) *62 Green Street 734-0276*

Burlington 01803 Temple Sholom Emeth (R) *14-16 Lexington Street 272-2351*

Cambridge 02139 Temple Beth Sholom (C) *8 Tremont Street 864-6388*
Hillel House *74 Mount Auburn Street 495-4696*

Canton 02021 Temple Beth Abraham (C) *1301 Washington Street 828-5250*
Temple Beth David (R) *250 Randolph Street 828-2275*
Young Israel (O) *6 Ridgehill Road*

Chelmsford 01824 Congregation Sholom (R) *Richardson Road 251-8091*

Chelsea 02150 Congregation Agudas Sholom (O) *145 Walnut Street 884-8668*
Congregation Ahavas Achim Anshe Sfard (O) *57 County Road 889-2016*
Congregation Shaare Zion (O) *76 Orange Street 884-0498*
Congregation Shomrei Linas Hazedek *140 Shurtleff Street 884-9443*
Temple Emanu-El (C) *Cary Avenue & Tudor Street 884-9699*

Chestnut Hill 02167 Temple Emeth (C) *194 Grove Street 469-9400*
Congregation Mishkan Tefila (C) *300 Hammond Pond Parkway 332-7770*

Clinton 01510 Congregation Shaare Zedek (C) *Water Street 365-5157*

Dover 02030 (T) 7 Donnelly Drive 426-9292

Dudley 01570 Congregation Sons of Israel (O) *43 West Main Street*

Everett 02149 Congregation Tifereth Israel (T) *34 Malden Street 387-0200*

Fall River 02720 Congregation Adas Israel (O) *1647 Robeson Street 674-9761*
Temple Beth El (C) *385 High Street 674-3529*
Congregation Agudas Machzikei Horav (O) *470 Madison Street*

Falmouth 02541 Jewish Congregation (C) *37 Hatchville Road 540-0602*

Fitchburg 01420 Congregation Agudas Achim (T) *40 Boutelle Street 342-7704*

Framingham 01701 Congregation Bais Chabad (O) *74 Joseph Road 877-8888*
Temple Beth Am (R) *300 Pleasant Street 872-8300*
Temple Beth Sholom (C) *Pamela Road 877-2540*
Congregation Shaare Sholom (R) *112 Main Street 749-8103*

Gardner 01440 Congregation Ohav Sholom (C) *152 Pleasant Street 632-2779*

Gloucester 01930 Temple Ahavath Achim (C) *86 Middle Street 281-0739*

Great Barrington 01230 Chevre of Great Barrington (R) *(413) 528-0160*
Congregation Love of Peace (R) *29 North Street*

Greenfield 01301 Temple Israel (C) *27 Pierce Street (413) 773-5884*
Hebrew Congregation (C) *89 Burnham Road 774-5796*

Haverhill 01830 Congregation Anshe Sholom (O) *427 Main Street 372-2276*
Temple Emanu-El (R) *514 Main Street 373-3861*

Hingham 02043 Congregation Shaare Sholom (R) *1112 Main Street 749-8103*

Holbrook 02343 Temple Beth Sholom (C) *95 Plymouth Street 767-4922*

Holliston 01746 Temple Beth Torah (C) *2162 Washington Street 429-6268*

Holyoke 01040 Congregation Rodfey Sholom (O) *1800 Northampton Street 534-5262*
Congregation Sons of Zion (C) *378 Maple Street 534-3369*

Hull 02045 Temple Beth Sholom (C) *600 Nantasket Avenue 925-0091*
Temple Israel (T) *Samoset Avenue & Wilson Street 925-4860*

Hyannis 02601 Cape Cod Synagogue (R) *145 Winter Street 775-2988*

Hyde Park 02136 Temple Adas Hadras Israel (C) *28 Arlington Street 364-2661*

Lawrence 01841 Congregation Anshei Sholom (O) *411 Hampshire Street 683-4544*
Congregation Tifereth Anshai Sfard Sons of Israel (C) *492 Lowell Street 686-0391*
Temple Emanu-El (R) *483 Lowell Street 682-8443*

Leominster 01453 Congregation Agudath Achim (C) *268 Washington Street 534-6121*

Lexington 02173 Temple Emunah (C) *9 Piper Road 861-0300*
Temple Isaiah (R) *55 Lincoln Street 862-7160*

Longmeadow 01106 Congregation Beth Israel (O) *1280 Williams Street (413) 567-7354*
Congregation B'nai Jacob (C) *2 Eunice Drive 567-0058*

Lowell 01851 Temple Beth El (C) *105 Princeton Boulevard 453-0073*
Temple Emanu-El (R) *101 West Forest Street 454-1372*
Montefiore Synagogue (O) *460 Westford Street 454-5264*

Lynn 01905 Congregation Ahavat Sholom (O) *151 Ocean Street 593-9255*
Congregation Anshei Sfard (O) *150 South Common Street 599-7131*
Congregation Chevre Tehillim (O) *12 Breed Street 598-2964*

Malden 02148 Congregation Agudas Achim (T) *160 Harvard Street 322-9380*
Congregation Beth Israel West (O) *10 Dexter Street 322-5686*
Temple Ezrath Israel (C) *245 Bryant Street 322-7205*
Congregation Beth Israel East (O) *58 Almont Street*
Temple Tifereth Israel (R) 539 Salem Street 322-2794
Young Israel (O) *45 Holyoke Street 322-9438*

Marblehead 01945 Temple Emanu-El (R) *393 Atlantic Avenue 631-9300*
Temple Sinai (C) *1 Community Drive 631-2244*

Marlborough 01752 Temple Emanu-El (C) *130 Berlin Road 485-7565*

Mattapan 02126 Congregation Ohel Torah (O) *149 Greenfield Road 298-1366*

Medford 02155 Temple Sholom (C) *475 Winthrop Street 396-3262*

Medway 02053 Congregation Agudath Achim (C) *73 Village Street*

Melrose 02176 Temple Beth Sholom (R) *21 East Foster Street 665-4520*

Milford 01757 Congregation Beth Sholom (T) *49 Pine Street 473-1590*

Millis 02054 Congregation House of Jacob (O) *332 Village Street 376-5894*

Milton 02187 Congregation B'nai Jacob (O) *100 Blue Hills Parkway 698-0698*
Temple Sholom (C) *180 Blue Hills Parkway 698-3394*

Natick 01760 Temple Israel (C) *145 Hartford Street 653-8591*

Needham 02192 Temple Aliyah (C) *1664 Central Avenue 444-8522*
Temple Beth Sholom (R) *670 Highland Avenue 444-0077*

New Bedford 02740 Congregation Ahavath Achim (O) *385 County Street 994-1760*
Congregation Tifereth Israel (C) *145 Brownell Avenue 997-3171*

Newburyport 01950 Congregation Ahavas Achim (C) *Washington & Olive Streets 462-2461*

Newton 02168 Agudas Achim Congregation (O) *168 Adams Street*
Boston Reconstructionist Havurah *964-2791*
Temple Beth Avodah (R) *45 Puddingstone Lane 527-0045*
Congregation Beth El Atereth Israel (O) *561 Ward Street 244-7233*
Congregation Chevre Shas (O) *35 Morseland Avenue 969-0925*
Congregation Lubavitch (O) *100 Woodcliff Road 469-9007*
Congregation Mishkan Tefila (C) *300 Hammond Pond Parkway 332-7770*
Temple Emanu-El (C) *385 Ward Street 332-5770*
Temple Emeth (C) *194 Grove Street 469-9400*
Newton Congregation for Humanistic Judaism *16 Duxbury Street 964-8409*

Temple Reyim (C) *1860 Washington Street 527-2410*
Temple Sholom (R) *175 Temple Street 332-9550*

North Adams 01247 Congregation Beth Israel (C) *265 Church Street (413) 663-5830*

Northampton 01060 Congregation B'nai Israel (C) *253 Prospect Street (413) 584-3593*

North Easton Temple Chayai Sholom (C) *9 Mechanic Street 238-4896*

Norwood 02062 Temple Shaare Tefilah (C) *556 Nichols Street 762-8670*

Onset 02558 Congregation Beth Israel (O) *Locust & Main Streets 295-4226 (summer only)*

Peabody 01960 Temple Tifereth Israel *8 Pierpont Street 531-8135*
Temple Beth Sholom (R) *489 Lowell Street 535-2100*
Temple Ner Tamid (C) *368 Lowell Street 532-1293*

Pittsfield 01201 Temple Anshe Amunim (R) *26 Broad Street (413) 442-5910*
Congregation Kneset Israel (C) *16 Colt Road 445-4872*

Plymouth 02360 Congregation Beth Israel (R) *8 Pleasant Street 746-1575*

Quincy 02169 Beth Israel Synagogue (O) *33 Grafton Street 472-6796*
Congregation Adas Sholom (C) *435 Adams Street 471-1818*
Temple Beth El (C) *1001 Hancock Street 479-4309*

Randolph 02368 Congregation Beth Am (C) *871 North Main Street 963-0440*
Young Israel (O) *374 North Main Street 961-9817*

Revere 02151 Congregation Ahavas Achim (O) *89 Walnut Street 289-1026*
Congregation Tifereth Israel (O) *43 Nahant Avenue 284-9255*
Temple B'nai Israel (C) *1 Wave Avenue 284-8388*

Roxbury (West) 02132 Temple Hillel B'nai Torah (C) *120 Corey Street 323-0486*

Salem 01970 Temple Sholom (C) *287 Lafayette Street 744-9709*

Saugus 01906 Congregation Ahavas Sholom (C) *343 Central Street*

Sharon 02067 Temple Adath Sharon (C) *18 Harding Street 784-7201*
Temple Israel (C) *125 Pond Street 784-3986*
Temple Sinai (R) *100 Ames Street 829-8587*
Young Israel (O) *9 Dunbar Street 784-6112*

Somerville 02145 Temple B'nai Brith (C) *201 Central Street 625-0333*
Havurat Sholom *113 College Avenue 623-3376*

Springfield 01108 Temple Beth El (C) *979 Dickinson Street (413) 733-4149*
Congregation Kesser Israel (O) *19 Oakland Street 732-8492*
Congregation Kadimoh (O) 124 Sumner Avenue 781-0171
Temple Sinai (R) *1100 Dickinson Street 736-3619*

Stoneham 02180 Temple Judea (C) *188 Franklin Street 665-5752*

Stoughton 02072 Congregation Ahavath Torah (C) *1179 Central Street 344-8733*

Sudbury 01776 Congregation Beth El (R) *Hudson Road 443-9622*
Congregation B'nai Torah (R) *80 Woodside Road 443-2082*

Swampscott 01907 Temple Beth El (C) *55 Atlantic Avenue 599-8005*
Temple Israel (C) *837 Humphrey Street 595-6635*

Taunton 02780 Congregation Augdath Achim (C) *36 Winthrop Street 822-3230*

Vineyard Haven 02568 Martha's Vineyard Hebrew Center (R) *Center Street 693-0745*

Wakefield 01880 Temple Emanu-El (C) *120 Chestnut Street 245-1886*

Waltham 02154 Temple Beth Israel (C) *25 Harvard Street 894-5146*

Ware 01082 Hebrew Congregation (C) *89 Main Street*

Wayland 01778 Temple Shir Tikvah (R) *141 Boston Post Road 358-5312*

Webster 01570 Congregation Sons of Israel *281 Main Street*

Wellesley 02181 Temple Beth Elohim (R) *10 Bethel Road 235-8419*

Westborough 01581 Congregation B'nai Sholom (R) *9 Charles Street 366-7191*

Westwood 02090 Temple Beth David (C) *40 Pond Street 329-1938*

Winchester Jewish Congregation 729-2988

Winthrop 02152 Congregation Tifereth Abraham (O) *283 Shirley Street 846-5063*
Temple Tifereth Israel (O) *93 Veterans Road 846-1390*

Woburn 01801 Temple Sholom Emeth (R) *14 Green Street*

Worcester 01602 Congregation Beth Israel (C) *Jamesbury Drive & Kinnicutt Road 756-6204*
Congregation Beth Judah–Young Israel (O) *889 Pleasant Street 754-3681*
Temple Emanu-El (R) *280 May Street 755-1257*
Congregation Shaari Torah East (O) *32 Providence Street 756-3276*
Congregation Shaari Torah West (O) *835 Pleasant Street 791-0013*
Temple Sinai (R) *661 Salisbury Street 775-2519*
Congregation Tifereth Israel–Sons of Jacob (O) *22 Newton Avenue 752-0904*

MIKVEHS

Brighton 101 Washington Street *(617) 782-9433*
293 Chestnut Hill Avenue *782-8340*

Brookline 1710 Beacon Street *566-9182*

Longmeadow 1104 Converse Street *(413) 567-1607*

Lynn 151 Ocean Street *(617) 595-9494 or 595-5112 or 592-9736*

Sharon 9 Dunbar Street *(617) 784-7444*

Worcester 57 Huntley Street *(617) 757-4656 or 756-8451 or 754-3681*

New Hampshire

New Hampshire was the first of the 13 colonies to declare its independence from England but was the last of the original states to grant complete political equality to Jews. Until the end of the 19th century, the history of Jews in New Hampshire was confined to scattered individuals. While there was a small Jewish settlement in Portsmouth in 1877, the first permanent Jewish community was established by immigrants from Russia and Poland who arrived in 1885. They were largely peddlers and storekeepers who came into the state via Boston.

New Hampshire's first Jewish organization, the Hebrew Ladies Aid Society, was founded in Manchester in 1896, followed the next year by Congregation Anshe Sfard, the oldest in the state. By 1905, there were 1,000 Jews scattered throughout the state. It was in that year, the height of the anti-Jewish persecutions in Russia, from which the founders of the New Hampshire Jewish community had recently fled, that witnessed a great event in Jewish history.

In the midst of the negotiations to settle the Russo-Japanese War, President Theodore Roosevelt initiated a special meeting in Portsmouth, New Hampshire. It would be a meeting between the emissaries of the Czar of Russia and leaders of American Jewry. Such personalities as Jacob H. Schiff, Adolph Lewisohn, and Oscar S. Strauss attempted to convince the Russian diplomats to halt its anti-Jewish program.

The Jewish population of New Hampshire is approximately 4,000.

BETHLEHEM

The small town of Bethlehem, located about 25 miles west of Mt. Washington, becomes a Jewish haven during the summer months. Jewish visitors have been coming to Bethlehem since the early 1900s because the town is a haven for hay fever sufferers. In the days before allergy medication, the town's elevation and lack of pollen and ragweed attracted many. Various hay fever organizations were based there, including the now-defunct Hebrew Hay Fever Association. At the height of its popularity in the 1940s and '50s, Bethlehem had 32 hotels, of which about eight were known as "Jewish" hotels. But with the development of allergy medicines, the town began to attract fewer visitors. Many old, wooden hotels burned down. Bethlehem was in decline.

About 20 years ago, the Chassidim discovered this part of New Hampshire. Apparently, Chassidim also suffer from hay fever and they prefer the natural relief to their allergies. Bethlehem also happens to be conveniently close to Montreal's large Chassidic community, had kosher hotels left from its heyday and is a pleasant contrast to the overcrowded Catskills. About five hundred Chassidim come in the summer, in addition to 200 non-Chassidic Jews.

Bethlehem, located 1900 feet above sea level in the White Mountains, is a quiet, picturesque town that boasts two glatt kosher hotels, two Chassidic shuls (shteeblech), an Orthodox (non-Chassidic) minyan, which meets in a tent on the grounds of a local motel, and the Conservative Bethlehem Hebrew Congregation, which has been located on Strawberry Hill Road since 1925. There are numerous guest houses and motels that cater to Jews, and local grocery stores carry kosher items.

MANCHESTER

TEMPLE ADATH YESHURUN
Central Street, near Maple Street

Built around the turn of the 20th century for the Reform congregation, Adath Yeshurun, this 6-story wood-frame structure stands abandoned. The Stars of David above each of the twin towers and in the center of the rose window have been carefully removed. Temple Adath Yeshurun is presently located at 678 Pine Street.

CONGREGATION ANSHE SFARD
237 Central Street

The old Anshe Sfard synagogue has been sold to an American Legion Club. Its design resembles the Eastern European *shtetl* style.

THE OLD NEIGHBORHOODS

The following list contains information about synagogues which are no longer functioning as Jewish houses of worship. These addresses are located in the old sections of the city or town. It is advisable to take extra precautions while driving through these neighborhoods.

Concord Congregation Beth Jacob *66 Downing Street*

Manchester Temple Adath Yeshurun *Central Street, near Maple Street*

Congregation Anshe Sfard *237 Central Street*

Nashua Temple Beth Abraham *Cross & Lock Streets*

The old Temple Adath Yeshurun in Manchester was built around the turn of the century.

SYNAGOGUES

[Note: All area codes 603]

Berlin 03570 Congregation Beth Israel *Exchange Place*

Bethlehem 03574 Hebrew Congregation (C) *Strawberry Hill Street* 869-5747
Congregation Machzikei Hadass (O) *Lewis Hill Road* 869-5737 (summer only)

Claremont 03743 Temple Mayer David (C) *19 High Street* 542-6773

Concord 03301 Temple Beth Jacob (R) *67 Broadway* 228-8581

Dover 03820 Temple Israel (R) *47 4th Street* 742-3976

Keene Congregation Ahavas Achim *Hastings Avenue*

Laconia 03246 Temple B'nai Israel (R) *208 Court Street* 524-7044

Manchester 03104 Temple Adath Yeshurun (R) *152 Prospect Street* 669-5650
Temple Israel (C) *678 Pine Street* 622-6171

Nashua Temple Beth Abraham (C) *4 Raymond Street* 883-8184

Portsmouth Temple Israel (C) *200 State Street* 436-4301

MIKVEHS

Bethlehem Lewis Hill Road & Main Street *(603)* 869-5737 *(summer only)*

New Jersey

Benjamin Levy, a London broker and merchant, owned three shares of the territory once known as West Jersey in 1691. He lived in London and never claimed his shares in the territory. Although there were individual Jews living in New Jersey all through the 18th century, no Jewish community developed until the 1840s.

America's first copper rolling mill was opened at Belleville in 1812 by two prominent Jews from New York City, Harmon Hendricks and Solomon Isaacs. The mill supplied the Boston firm of Paul Revere & Sons with much of its metal needs, including some copper used to build the warship, *Constitution*, and Robert Fulton's first steamboat, the *Clermont*.

The first Jewish communities were established in the 1840s and 1850s in Paterson, Newark, Trenton, and New Brunswick by immigrants from Germany, Hungary, and Bohemia.

When the first large numbers of Jews who came from Eastern Europe arrived in New Jersey in the early 1880s, they found established Jewish communities in Hoboken (1855), Jersey City (1864), Elizabeth (1864), Perth Amboy (1870), Montclair (1875), East Orange (1873), and Bayonne (1880). Before the turn of the century, there were also Jewish settlements in Passaic (1889), Atlantic City (1890), Camden (1894), and Englewood (1896).

Among the new arrivals from Eastern Europe were the pioneers who established the South Jersey farm colonies, the cradle of the Jewish agricultural movement in the United States. There were

Jewish agricultural experiments in the Dakotas, Kansas, Colorado, Nebraska, Michigan, Louisiana, Maryland, Virginia, and Washington. The only ones to survive the droughts, floods, poor land, inexperience, inadequate funding, lack of water, and poor marketing facilities, were the South Jersey agricultural colonies. Most of the Jewish farmers in New Jersey are presently involved with poultry and egg farming.

In the 1960s, the Jewish population shifted from the major cities such as Newark, Jersey City, New Brunswick, Trenton, Camden, and Paterson to such suburban communities as West Orange, Short Hills, Highland Park, Cherry Hill, Saddle Brook, Teaneck, and Wayne. The Jewish population of New Jersey is approximately 440,000.

ALLIANCE

The first South Jersey Jewish agricultural colony, Alliance, was founded in 1882 and was named for the Alliance Israelite Universelle, the Paris-based organization that aided Jews around the world. It was located on 1100 acres, 35 miles southeast of Philadelphia, near the cities of Vineland, Millville, and Bridgeton. Within the next four years, additional farm colonies were established in Rosenhayn, Norma, Carmel, and Garten Road. Some of the original synagogues in these towns are still standing, complete with synagogue furnishings, but lacking congregations. The Alliance cemetery and Chevre Kadisha (mortuary) are well maintained. The cemetery was established in 1891. The entrance post contains a marker with the names of some of the founders of the Alliance colony including Abraham Brotman (founder of Brotmanville), Nathan Bleznak, and Joseph Greenblatt. Across the road from the cemetery, at Gershel and Schiff Avenues, is the Norma Synagogue, the last surviving wood-frame synagogue in the area.

Sabbath in Brotmanville.

LAKEWOOD

Lakewood was the most famous winter resort in the east from the 1880s-1930. Before the turn of the century, few hotels admitted Jews. In 1891, however, Nathan Straus, the philanthropist, built the Lakewood Hotel. Thereafter, Lakewood became a popular resort for middle-class Jews from New York City, Newark, and Philadelphia. Other popular Jewish resorts include Elberon, Deal and Long Branch. These were known, from the 1880s-1920s, as the "Jewish Newport." The towns around Deal are today part of a growing Sephardic (Syrian) enclave, whose origins stem from Bensonhurst and Flatbush, in Brooklyn, New York.

In the 1920s, the Jewish Agricultural Society settled Jewish farmers in Toms River and Farmingdale, just south of Lakewood, on poultry and egg farms. Following World War II, many concentration camp survivors also found their way to the South Jersey poultry-raising towns.

CONGREGATION SONS OF ISRAEL
Madison Avenue and 6th Street

The oldest congregation in Lakewood, Sons of Israel, was organized around 1910. Its original building, located on Fifth and Railroad Streets, is still maintained. It is used as a senior citizen center during the week. On Sabbath, there are services held by young men and women who "walk in" to this run-down section of town.

The present (new) building of Congregation Sons of Israel, located at Madison Avenue and 6th Street, was designed in 1963 by the architectural firm of Davis, Brody, and Wisniewski. The octagonal synagogue design was inspired by the 17th century

The Holocaust Memorial in front of Lakewood's Congregation Sons of Israel.

wooden synagogues of Poland. All of those synagogues were destroyed by the Nazis during World War II. It is therefore a fitting place for a most magnificent Holocaust Memorial, located directly in front of the synagogue. The gray granite memorial stone depicts, in relief, scenes of the concentration camps and their victims.

BAIS HAMEDRASH GOVOHAH
6th Street and Private Way

The Rabbinical academy, founded by Rav Aaron Kotler, z"tl, is the center and focal point of the Orthodox Jewish community of Lakewood. The garden apartments in the vicinity of the yeshiva, house members of the Rabbinical academy (kollel) and their families.

NEWARK

The first Jew, Louis Trier, arrived in Newark in 1844. Most of the early arrivals hailed from Alsace-Lorraine and western Germany. They comprised a varied group—mostly laborers, farmers, tradesmen, and students. In 1855, there were 200 Jewish families living in Newark. Ten years later all of the leading drygoods stores in the city were owned by Jews. Louis Bamberger established the store that eventually became New Jersey's largest department store. The Ullman & Isaacs drygoods store had a young clerk by the name of Benjamin Altman, who later founded New York City's B. Altman & Company.

TEMPLE B'NAI JESHURUN
783 High Street

In 1848, Newark's first synagogue, Congregation B'nai Jeshurun, was organized. The first synagogue was a modest structure built in 1858 and was located on Washington Street. In 1914, the congregation built its second home on, then fashionable, High Street (corner Waverly). That magnificent domed-structure, with its exquisite stained glass windows depicting Biblical scenes, was sold to the Hopewell Baptist Church. All of the original stain glass windows are still intact, including their Jewish donor's names.

In 1968, Temple B'nai Jeshurun, moved to the suburban community of Short Hills. Its award-winning temple was designed by Pietro Belluschi. Temple B'nai Jeshurun follows the Reform ritual.

Newark's Market Street around the turn of the century.

CONGREGATION B'NAI ABRAHAM
Clinton and Stanley Avenues

Newark's first synagogue, Congregation B'nai Jeshurun, was largely composed of German and Bohemian peddlers and businessmen, who, speaking the language of their non-Jewish German neighbors, had managed to thrive in their enterprises. Far less prosperous were the Eastern European peddlers who spoke only Yiddish, and the general poverty kept them from organizing as early as the others. Then Abraham Newman, one of the earliest Jewish settlers and a founder of Congregation B'nai Jeshurun, left that congregation, and calling together a group of Russian and Polish Jews to conduct religious services in his house on Bank Street, helped organize them. They incorporated into a congregation in 1855, adopting the name B'nai Abraham, in appreciation of Abraham Newman's interest and generosity.

In 1861, Congregation B'nai Abraham purchased its first building, the former First Baptist Church, located on the corner of Halsey and Academy Streets. On February 22, 1897, the laying of the cornerstone of a new synagogue for the congregation was held. The 900-seat synagogue was located on the corner of High Street and 13th Avenue. As the congregation outgrew the High Street building, a new synagogue and community center was erected in the Clinton Hill section of Newark.

On September 21, 1924, the new Temple B'nai Abraham, located at Clinton and Shanley Avenues, was formally dedicated. Yossele Rosenblatt, the world-renowned cantor, officiated at this dedication ceremony. The architect, Nathan Myers, designed the impressive elliptical Neo-Classic building, complete with its copper-domed skylight.

The city of Newark at one time had a Jewish population of almost 100,000. In the 1960s, the Jewish population was less than 10,000. The majority of Newark's Jews moved to the suburbs during that decade. Congregation B'nai Abraham is presently located at 300 East Northfield Road, in Livingston, and follows the Conservative ritual.

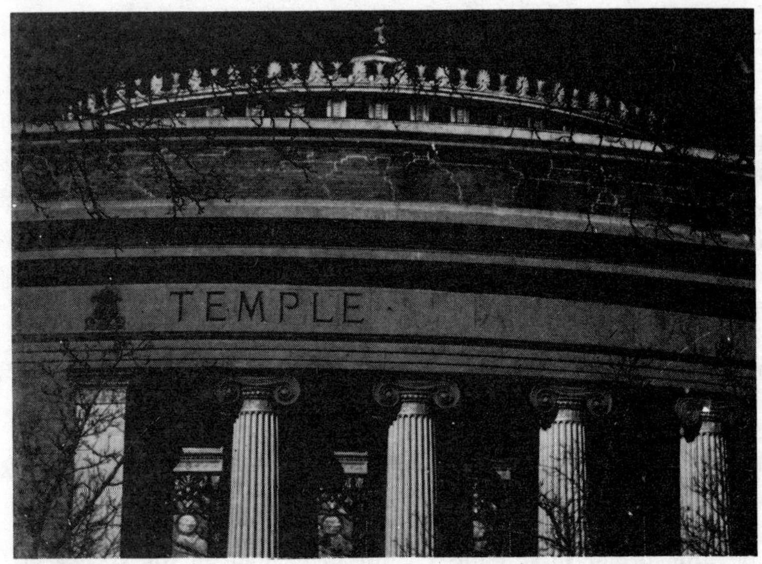

The former Temple B'nai Abraham in the Clinton Hill section of Newark.

CONGREGATION OHEB SHALOM
28 Prince Street

The third oldest congregation in Newark, Oheb Shalom, was organized in 1860 by Bohemian Jews. Their first synagogue was located at 28 Prince Street. This building is still extant but is occupied by a local church. The building, designed in the Romanesque-Revival style, is the oldest synagogue structure in the state of New Jersey. It was built during the Civil War, in 1864.

In 1911, the congregation moved to High Street. The Neo-Classical building, located at 672 High Street (near Kinney Street), was the site of many historic addresses. Woodrow Wilson, then governor of New Jersey, delivered the principal address at the dedication ceremonies. In the 1960s, Congregation Oheb Shalom moved to the suburb community of South Orange. The High Street building is still extant and is used by a local church. Congregation Oheb Shalom follows the Conservative ritual.

NEWARK MUSEUM
49 Washington Street

Louis Bamberger, the Jewish drygoods entrepreneur of the late 19th century, donated $750,000 for the building of the Newark Museum. It houses one of America's great collections of art and science.

Prince Street was the center of the Jewish section of Newark.

PATERSON

CONGREGATION B'NAI JESHURUN
(Barnert Memorial Temple)
152 Derrom Avenue

Nathan Barnert was born in Germany in 1838. In 1851, after working many years in his father's tailor shop in New York's

Lower East Side, he went out west, to California's gold rush. He returned and opened a clothing factory in New York City in 1856.

In 1858, he moved his factory to Paterson where he branched out into silk manufacturing. Nathan Barnert erected many of Paterson's large silk factories.

In 1847, New Jersey's oldest congregation, B'nai Jeshurun, was organized. Nathan Barnert donated land at the corner of Broadway and Straight Street to the congregation. In 1891, a Moorish Revival synagogue was erected. It closely resembled New York City's Temple Emanu-El in design, which was located on Fifth Avenue and East 43rd Street, except that the Paterson building only had one cupola. The congregation called their new edifice the Barnert Memorial Temple in honor of Nathan Barnert. He was elected mayor of Paterson in 1883 and donated over $1,000,000 to many Jewish philanthropies.

The Paterson Call, in its issue of April 21, 1900 reported: "The usual Saturday evening services at the Barnert Temple last night were very unusual, in the fact that a President of the Nation, the Governor of the State, and other distinguished Gentiles took part.

Former Mayor Nathan Barnert, Nathan Fleischer, and Leopold Meyer went to Carroll Hall, to conduct the Presidential party to the Temple and the delay caused the crowd outside to grow considerably larger.

The finely appointed Synagogue (of pure Moorish style with light colored brick and brown stone trim has a tower of graceful proportions rising 93 feet in the air) was brilliantly illuminated and a few palms and potted plants were placed along the front of the platform. A large flag hung outside of the Synagogue, but otherwise no preparations of an extra kind had been made.

President McKinley entered arm in arm with former Mayor Nathan Barnert. Governor Voorhees and Mayor John Hinchliffe followed. They were all in evening dress."

In commenting on President McKinley's visit, Editor Orrin Vanderhoven wrote: "It was a very graceful act on the part of the President to attend the Easter service in the Temple. It went a long way toward breaking the prejudice against the race."

The present building of Congregation B'nai Jeshurun, located at 152 Derrom Avenue, was designed in 1963 by Percival Goodman. The original Broadway building is no longer extant. The congregation follows the Reform ritual.

TEMPLE EMANU-EL
151 East 33rd Street

Temple Emanu-El was organized in 1904. Services were held, at first, wherever room could be obtained: an old church on Hamilton Street, the back of a bakery on Bridge Street, a lodge room at the Masonic Temple on Market and Church Streets. The congregation's first synagogue building was located on Van Houten Street, near Church Street. They soon outgrew that building.

In November, 1928, the contract for the erection of a new synagogue was awarded to Mr. John Ferguson, one of the foremost builders in the country. The sanctuary, dedicated in 1929, provided seating for 1250 people. Its designer, who also designed several exotic movie houses in New York City, utilized the finest marbles for the interior. The dominant style for the synagogue's exterior and interior is Art Deco. The exquisite stained glass windows depict Biblical scenes, including the seven days of Creation. There is an overwhelming stained glass skylight depicting a three-dimensional Star of David encompassed by a 40-foot circle. Temple Emanu-El follows the Conservative ritual.

ROOSEVELT

Roosevelt was built in 1935 as a cooperative agricultural-industrial community for unemployed Jewish garment workers from Philadelphia and New York City. After several aborted beginnings, at first by the garment workers themselves, then under the Department of the Interior, the Jersey Homesteads, as it was originally called, was turned over to the Agricultural Department and its chief, Rexford Guy Tugwell.

Tugwell was not going to skimp upon the lives of the garment workers. He commissioned Alfred Kastner, a product of the Swiss "Bauhaus," probably the world's most celebrated center of architecture, as architect. The town was designed with thc utmost feeling for everyday life. The houses were so modern—for that day—that they were written up in many books and magazines. The town was planned around a center "common," and each of its extensions backed upon open or wooded space set aside to provide an uncluttered and open environment for the town dweller. Each house was set in a half-acre of land, providing space for lawn and garden. Each house was identical; one level, 5-room, with a car-port and a flat poured concrete roof.

The entire town, built upon a circular plan, was surrounded by a circle of farms, hence the term, "greenbelt community." The two show-pieces of the town were the school—in its day, almost a model school—with its mural by Ben Shahn. The "Roosevelt Mural," a fresco 55 feet long and 11 feet high, shows the reception room of Ellis Island, with Albert Einstein and Charles Steinmetz arriving as immigrants. Also there is Sidney Hilman, the labor leader, who was involved in planning the community. There is a sculpture of a garment worker by Lenore Thomas and sculptured aluminum doors by Otto Wester, a German sculptor.

The factory was once another show-piece of the town. It was once a very elegant space, with hundreds of windows throughout

Ben Shahn's mural in Roosevelt.

the edifice. It was often used as a reception and party hall. Near the old factory building is a dirt road which leads to the Roosevelt cemetery.

In the early 1940s, the Jersey Homesteads project was declared an official failure. As a garment cooperative it may have failed, but as a community it prospered. When the town opened up to any sort of person who wanted to live there (since until that time garment workers were only permitted), it proved particularly attractive to artists. The world-renowned Ben Shahn settled in Roosevelt (the name of the town was officially changed after the death of Franklin D. Roosevelt) at that time.

There is a synagogue, Roosevelt Jewish Center, located at 20 Homestead Road. There are no churches in the town.

TOMS RIVER

The following is an excerpt from the "History of Pioneers—Reminiscenses and Personal Histories of the Jews of Toms River," which was edited by Jeanne Littman and Mildred Robinson in February, 1976.

The Estomin Family Story

"Coming in 1918 from New York City to the good clean air was just what the doctor ordered. My grandparents, aunts, uncles, and parents lived in the big old house on Old Freehold Road. They ran a general farm growing corn, cabbages, beets—raising cows, horses and chickens on the outside—and a boarding house on the inside. Friends and family with all their children were always coming from the City to the country.

At that time, Old Freehold Road was the main highway between Lakewood and Toms River and our house became the focal point of the Jewish community. There was no electricity in the rural areas so we had installed our own electric system. We had tremendous Delco Batteries which provided us with some of our needs.

My father continued to work in New York as a milkman for 4 years to supplement the family income. He came to Toms River every Friday night and went back every Sunday on the train from Lakewood. The trip to Lakewood by horse and buggy took longer than the train ride to New York.

Food shopping was a major outing to Lakewood to purchase flour, salt, and sugar by the 100lb. bag and then visiting Jewish friends to exchange current news. Once a week the *Shochet* came to the farms for the slaughtering of the animals for the table. Most of the food consumed was grown and canned by my mother, grandmother, and aunt. Visitors from New York brought delicacies we couldn't get here. Every Friday morning before daybreak my grandmother was preparing for Shabbas—baking her Challah, bread, pastries for the Sabbath and the rest of the week. Then followed meat, chicken and whatever else was on the menu. This was all done on a wood and coal stove which also was part of the heating system for the entire house.

Between the years 1920 and 1925 there was an influx of Jewish families. As more and more Jews settled in Toms River, there was no place large enough to meet so all the Jewish farm families got together and formed the Community of Jewish Farmers. The cornerstone was laid in 1924, the land was donated by Max Leet and the building was built by Jacob Wexler and Morris Rosenberg. Mr. Rosenberg was later one of the Gaboyim (officers) of the Congregation B'nai Israel.

The Community Center was used by all factions for all purposes—religious, political, educational, and social. Education was always uppermost in the minds of the people. There was a Jewish

Jewish farmers of New Jersey.

Shule with teachers coming from New York City to teach Yiddish speaking, reading, writing literature and history. There was a basketball team, softball team, etc.

At the beginning of World War II, I had to leave college to come home and work the farm. During the war there were very few young men left on the farms; essential work—food for the country."

You can purchase your fresh eggs from the Guttman poultry farm in Toms River.

WOODBINE

Woodbine was the largest and most successful of a number of towns established in South Jersey. It is located about 30 miles southwest of Atlantic City. It was founded in 1891 with 300 Russian and Roumanian Jews settled on a 5,300 acre estate bought by the Baron de Hirsch Fund. The aim was to establish a model agricultural community, but the difficulty of making a living from the recalcitrant land spurred, within the first year, the institution of factories for soft goods, particularly clothing.

In 1903, Woodbine was incorporated as an all-Jewish town. Jews filled all public offices and manned the police and fire departments. The principal buildings were the synagogue and the Talmud Torah. The most important civic organization was the Woodbine Brotherhood, or Agudath Achim Anshei Woodbine. It was a benevolent association which gave charity, provided relief and support for the sick and poor members, provided funerals for its members, ran the Hebrew school, and built the Woodbine Brotherhood Synagogue.

A long term associate of the synagogue was H.L. Sabsovich, the "Builder of Woodbine," who was the treasurer of the Woodbine Brotherhood. For some thirty years he managed the affairs of Woodbine, and it was he who organized and guided the model Baron de Hirsch Agricultural School, founded in 1894.

The Woodbine Brotherhood Synagogue, located at 614 Washington Avenue, was dedicated on the eve of Chanukah, November 29, 1896. It was built with the colonists themselves providing all the labor. It cost about $8,000 for the entire construction job. A loan of $2,500 from the Baron de Hirsch Fund covered some costs of materials—all of which were local. When more cash was needed, almost the entire colony turned out to work on a local road construction project, contributing their pay to the Synagogue fund. The Woodbine Brotherhood Synagogue is listed on the National Register of Historic Places and has been designated a National Historic Landmark.

Baron Maurice de Hirsch.

Woodbine, New Jersey.

Simchas Torah kiddush in Woodbine.

When you arrive in these little towns and villages in South Jersey, do not expect to find thriving Jewish communities as in Israel or in parts of New York City. Rather, you will find a few elderly retired Jewish farmers who will tell of the "good 'ol days." The present population in such towns as Brotmanville, Norma, or Woodbine is primarily black and Hispanic.

The Jewish Agricultural Society still exists. At the Society's main office in New York City, an official admits the organization does very little today to promote Jewish farming in America. The money still comes from the Baron de Hirsch Fund and most of it goes to bringing Israeli Agriculturists here to study and to support Israeli farming communities.

Perhaps the story of South Jersey's farming Jews should contain a footnote about its part in the creation of the State of Israel. The Israeli tour guide and author, Zvi Vilnay, relates how he was in the United States in 1947 trying to get weapons for the new Jewish state. "We hid the guns in chicken coops in New Jersey. There were a lot of Jewish farmers there."

THE OLD NEIGHBORHOODS

The following list contains information about synagogues which are no longer functioning as Jewish houses of worship. These addresses are located in the old sections of the city or town. It is advisable to take extra precautions while driving through these neighborhoods.

Arlington Congregation Sons of Israel *Kearny & Quincy Avenues*

Asbury Park Temple Beth El *First & Emory Streets*
Congregation Sons of Israel *Cookman & Langford Streets*
Jewish Community Center *Comstock Street & Asbury Avenue*

Atlantic City Congregation Rodef Sholom *2016 Pacific Avenue*
Congregation Amunat Israel *1714 Arctic Avenue*
Agudath Hasechtim *24 South Massachusetts Avenue*
Jewish Community Center *138 South Virginia Avenue*

Bayonne Congregation Beth Abraham *42 West 21st Street*
Congregation Ohav Sholom *39 North 20 Street*

Bloomfield Temple B'nai Zion *430 Franklin Street*
Congregation Shomer Amuno *27 Broad Street*

Bridgeton Congregation Beth Abraham *North Laurel Street*

Brotmanville Congregation B'nai Misha Anshe Astrach *Vineland Street*

Camden Congregation Adath Israel *5th & Spruce Streets*
Congregation B'nai Abraham *335 Liberty Street*
Congregation Sons of Israel *8th & Sycamore Streets*
Congregation Ahav Zedek *502 Broadway*
Temple Beth El *Park Boulevard & Belleville Avenue*
Congregation Beth Israel *331 Grand Avenue*
Jewish Center *621 Kaighm Avenue*

Carteret Brotherhood of Israel *3rd Street*

Cranford Temple Beth El *37 South Avenue W*

Dover Congregation Adath Israel *39 Orchard Street*
6 West Blackwell Street

East Orange Congregation Faith of Israel *175 Breakwood Street*
Temple Shaare Tefilo *57 Prospect Street*

East Rutherford Temple Beth El *147 Park Avenue*

Elizabeth Congregation Anshe Sfard *South 5th Street*
Congregation Holche Yosher *South Park & 5th Streets*
Congregation Ohave Zedek *408 Court Street*

Englewood Congregation Ahavath Torah *109 Englewood Avenue*
Jewish Community Center *153 Tenaly Road*
Temple Emanu-El *173 Tenafly Road*
Temple Sinai *260 Engle Street*

Englishtown Congregation Sons of Israel *Mechanic & Harrison Avenues*

Glen Ridge Congregation Guardians of the Faith *959 Bloomfield Avenue*

Greenville Congregation Ohab Sholom *46 Warner Avenue*

Hackensack Hebrew Institute *89 State Street*

Harrison Congregation B'nai Israel *223 Cleveland Avenue*

Highland Park Congregation Ahavath Achim *Richmond Street*

Hightstown Beth El Synagogue *237 Franklin Street*

Hillside Sinai Congregation *131 Maple Avenue*

Hoboken Congregation Adas Emuno *637 Garden Street*
Congregation Star of Israel *115 Park Avenue*
Congregation Beth Jacob *Clinton Avenue & Hague Street*

Irvington Jewish Center *285 Union Avenue*

Hudson City Congregation Sons of Israel *19 Cottage Street*

Jersey City Agudath Sholom *472 Bergen Avenue*
Temple Beth El *351 York Street*
Congregation Beth Hamedrash Hagadol *302 3rd Street*
Congregation Mt. Zion *Webster Avenue*
Congregation Ohab Shalom *38 Warner Avenue*
Congregation Tifereth Israel *235 5th Street*
Congregation Emanu-El *633 Bergen Street*
Jewish Community Center *604 Bergen Street*
Congregation Ohab Sholom *126 Rutgers Street*

The former Agudath Shalom, Jersey City.

Keyport United Hebrew Congregation *70 Broad Street*

Lakewood Jewish Community Center *413 5th Street*

Linden Congregation Anshe Chesed *Blanck Street & Maple Avenue*

Long Branch Congregation Achenu B'nai Israel *176 Chelsea Street*

Congregation Beth Miriam *North Bath Avenue*

Congregation Brothers of Israel *Second & Chelsea Street*

Merchantville Congregation Beth Jacob *214 North Center Street*

Metuchen Jewish Community Center *22 Center Street*

Millville Hebrew Association *19 East Main Street*

Montclair *Congregation Shomrei Emunah Highland Avenue*

New Brunswick Congregation Aava Veaha *285 Burnet Street*

Congregation Ahavath Achim *Richmond Street*

Anshe Emeth Congregation *123 Somerset Street*

Newark Congregation Adas Israel Mishnaes *32 Prince Street*

Congregation Agudath Israel *112 Custer Avenue*

Ahavas Achim Anshe Warsaw *47 Bedford Street*

Ahavas Achim B'nai Jacob *391 Avon Avenue*

Ahavas Zion *16th & Holland Streets*

Ahavath Israel *209 Wainwright Street*

Anshe Israel *104 Prince Street*

Anshe Israel Ein Jacob *28 Mercer Street*

Anshe Lubawitz *61 Barclay Street*

Anshe Ostreich Ungarin *269 Belmont Street*

Anshe Russia *220 West Kinney Street*

882 Bergen Street

Anshe Roumania *221 Prince Street*

Beth Hamdedrash Hagadol *878 Bergen Street*

Beth Samuel *47 Bedford Street*

B'nai Abraham *High Street & 13th Avenue*

Clinton and Stanley Streets

The oldest synagogue building in New Jersey is located at 28 Prince Street, in Newark.

B'nai Israel *608 Belmont Street*
B'nai Jeshurun *Washington & Market (William) Streets*
783 High Street
B'nai Joseph *198 Chadwick Street*
B'nai Judah *247 West Runyon Street*
B'nai Zion *545 West Market Street*
215 Chancellor Avenue
Ein Jacob *North 11th Street*
Kesser Torah *7 Bragaw Avenue*
Keter Torah *204 Prince*
Knesseth Israel *882 Bergen Street*
Lev Tov *249 Broome Street*
Linath Hazedek *157 Prince Street*
Newark Jewish Center *652 High Street*
Oheb (Mount Nebo) Sholom *28 Prince Street*
672 High Street

Rodfei Sholom *337 Clinton Place*
Tifereth Israel of Brisk *242 Prince Street*
Tifereth Jerusalem *68 Peshine Avenue*
Tifereth Zion *176 Clinton Avenue*
Torath Emeth *79 Jefferson Street*
Young Israel *Maple & Weequahic Streets*

New Brunswick Congregation Etz Chaim *Richmond Street*
Jewish Community Center *1 Liberty Street*
Congregation Ohav Emeth *71 New Street*

Orange Congregation Agudath Achim *Park & William Streets*
Congregation Shaarey Tefilo *Cleveland Street*
Beth Torah *270 Reynolds Terrace*

Palisades Park Congregation Sons of Israel *Broad Avenue & Edsall Boulevard*

Passaic Congregation B'nai Jacob *Washington Place*
Congregation Poali Zedek *179 3rd Street*
Congregation Adas Israel *11 Tulip Street*
Congregation Chevre Tehillim *55 Hope Avenue*
Congregation Hungarian Hebrew *71 Dayton Avenue*
Congregation Tifereth Israel *103 Madison Street*

Paterson Israel Center *115 Vreeland Avenue*
Congregation Ahavath Joseph *25 Godwin Street*
Congregation Beth Hamedrash Hagadol *1 Godwin Street*
Congregation B'nai Jeshurun *Broadway & Straight Street*
Emanu-El Temple *Van Houten & Church Streets*
United Brotherhood Congregation *92 Fair Street*

Perth Amboy Congregation Shaare Tefiloh *314 Madison Avenue*
Congregation Beth Mordecai *Hobart Street*

Plainfield Congregation Chavey Zedek Vesholom *422 West Front Street*
Congregation B'nai Israel *119 New Street*
Congregation Ohav Zedek *West 3rd Street*
Temple Sholom *Grove Street*
679 Sheridan Avenue

Congregation Ohav Sholom *Front Street*

Ringoes Hebrew Congregation

Raritan Congregation Anshe Chesed *Somerset & Thompson Streets*

Red Bank Congregation B'nai Israel *114 Wallace Street*

Rosenhayn Congregation Chevre Kadisha Anshe Ashkenaz *Morton Avenue*

Salem Congregation Oheb Sholom *Johnston Street*

Somerville Jewish Community Center *11 Park Avenue*

South Orange Congregation B'nai Jeshurun *457 Center Street*

South Amboy United Brothers Congregation *Henry Street*

Trenton Congregation Ahavath Israel *Centre Street (between Cass & Federal Streets)*

Congregation Anshei Emes *Fall & Union Streets*

Congregation Hachino B'nai Israelites *316 Union Street*

Temple Har Sinai *Stockton & Front Streets*

Jewish Community Center *18 South Stochton Street*

Union Hill Temple Emanu-El *Kossuth Street*

Vineland Ahavas Achim Congregation *300 South 3rd Street*

Beth Israel Congregation *7th & Elmer Streets*

West Englewood Congregation Beth Sholom *359 Rutgers Street*

Waverly Congregation Ahavas Achim *Ham Street (between 6th Street & Boulevard)*

Westwood Temple Emanu-El *111 Washington Avenue*

Woodbury Congregation Beth Israel *25 Hopkins Street*

Center and Harrison Streets

Riverside Congregation Kneseth Israel *45 Hancock Street*

Roselle Congregation Beth David *1101 Frank Street*

Congregation Emanu-El *159 East 9th Street*

Rutherford Temple Beth El *147 Park Avenue*

South River Congregation Anshe Emeth *Whitehead Street*

Springville Congregation Agudas Achim *Springville Road & Mount Laurel Road*

Trenton Congregation Brothers of Israel 316 *Union Street*
Congregation People of Truth 22 *Atterbury Avenue*

Ventnor Congregation Beth Judah 2 *North Troy Avenue*

West Cranford Congregation Beth El 37 *South Avenue*

KOSHER RESTAURANTS

Atlantic City International Restaurant/Pacific & South Chelsea Avenues *(609) 344-7071*

Bayonne Goodwill Deli *815 Broadway (201) 339-2392*
Reitner's Deli *908 Broadway 437-1594*

Cherry Hill Kosher Market *907 West Marlton Pike (609) 428-6663*
Max Barr Deli *1400 Plaza, Kings Highway 795-9590*
Pastry Palace *190 Barclay Center 429-3606*

Clifton The Village II Kosher Deli *389 Piaget Avenue (201) 772-5387*

Deal Jerusalem II Pizza *106 Norwood Avenue 531-9837*

East Brunswick The Kosher Deli *300 Route 18 390-0880*
Betty's Cakery *312 Rues Lane 257-6155*

East Windsor Quality Kosher *405 Mercer Street 448-1277*

Elizabeth Kosher Paradise *155 Elmora Avenue 354-0448*

Englewood Gourmet Gallery Bake Shop *10 South Dean Street 569-2704*

Fair Lawn Pizza & Stuff *14-20 Plaza Road 796-1494*
Ben-Daid International Foods Emporium *24-28 Fair Lawn Avenue 794-7740*
Temptations *1413 Plaza Road 791-0470*

Haddonfield Bennett's Kosher Meats *63 Ellis Street 428-1393*

Highland Park Jerusalem Pizza *231 Raritan Avenue 828-9687*
The Meating Place *229 Raritan Avenue 846-3444*
Dan's Meats *515 Route 27 572-2626*

Hoboken Deli King *425 Raritan Avenue 545-8595*

Lake Hiawatha Singer's Kosher Meats *59 North Beverwyck Avenue 263-3220*

Lakewood Kosher Experience *Route 9 & Kennedy Boulevard 370-0707*
R & S Kosher Deli *416 Clifton Avenue 363-6688*
Estherdale's *200 Clifton Avenue 363-0840*
Gelbstein's Bakery *415 Clifton Avenue 363-3636*

Linden County Kosher *1170 Saint George Street 925-4050*

Long Branch Club Deli & Restaurant *628 Ocean Avenue 229-2211*

Margate Kosher Market *11 North Washington Avenue 822-2580*

Matawan Ken's Deli *Route 34 583-1111*

New Brunswick Chabad House *8 Sicard Street 828-7374*

Old Bridge Goldberg's Kosher Meats *Route 516 679-2266*

Parsippany Arlington Deli *744 Route 46W 335-9400*

Passaic Brook Kosher Market *222 Brook Avenue 773-1910*

Teaneck Greenspan's Market *206 Plaza 837-8110*
Ma'adan Take Out Food *456 Cedar Lane 692-0192*
Tofutti *492A Cedar Lane*
Hunan Teaneck *515 Cedar Lane (201) 692-0099*
Jerusalem Pizza *496 Cedar Lane 836-2120*
Phibbleberry's Bakery *312 Queen Anne Road 836-8063*

Tenafly Center Court Eatery (JCC On the Palisades) *411 East Clinton Avenue* 569-7900

Vineland Nunberg's Deli *746 North Chelsea Avenue* (609) 692-3502

Wayne The Village II Kosher Deli *11 Wayne Hills Mall* 633-0757

West Orange Cafe Deborah (YMHA) *760 Northfield Avenue* 736-3200
Reuben's Deli *500 Pleasant Valley Way* 731-6351

Westwood Bader's East Side Deli *463 Broadway* 358-1200

SYNAGOGUES

Note: All area codes are 201 except 609 where indicated

Aberdeen Temple Beth Ahm (C) *550 Lloyd Road 583-1700*
Temple Shalom (R) *5 Ayrmont Lane 566-2621*

Asbury Park 07712 Congregation Sons of Israel *412 Asbury Avenue 775-1964*

Atlantic City 08401 Congregation Beth Jacob Amunath Israel (O) *506 Pacific Street (609) 345-1946*
Chelsea Hebrew Congregation (C) *4001 Atlantic Avenue 345-0825*
Community Synagogue Beth Kehillah (C) *901 Pacific Avenue 345-3282*
Congregation Rodef Shalom (O) *4609 Atlantic Avenue 345-4580*

Avenel 07001 Congregation Sons of Jacob *Lord Street*

Bayonne 07002 Temple Beth Am (R) *111 Avenue B 858-2020*
Temple Emanu-El (C) *735 Kennedy Boulevard 436-4499*
Congregation Ohav Shalom (O) *1022 Avenue C 858-9618*
Congregation Oheb Zedek *912 Avenue C*
Congregation Talmud Torah *41 North 20th Street*
Uptown Synagogue *Avenue C & 49th Street*

Belleville 07109 Congregation Ahavath Achim (C) *125 Academy Street*

Belmar 07719 Congregation Sons of Israel (O) *505 11th Avenue 681-3200*

Bergenfield 07621 Bergenfield-Dumont Jewish Center (C) 165 North Washington Avenue 384-3911
Congregation Beth Abraham *338 South Prospect Avenue* 384-2567

Bloomfield 07003 Temple Ner Tamid (C) *936 Broad Street* 338-6482

Boonton 07005 Congregation Adath Israel (C) *200 Overlook Avenue* 334-6044
Temple Beth Sholom (C) *110 Harrison Street* 334-2714

Bordentown 08505 Congregation B'nai Abraham (C) *58 Crosswick Street*

Bound Brook 08805 Congregation Kneseth Israel (C) *229 Mountain Avenue*

Bradley Beach 07720 Congregation Agudath Achim (O) *301 McCabe Avenue* 774-2495
Magen David Congregation (O) *101 Fifth Avenue*

Bricktown 08723 Temple Beth Or (C) *200 Van Zile Road* 458-4700

Bridgeton 08302 Congregation Beth Abraham (C) *Fayette Street & Belmont Avenue* (609) 451-7652

Burlington Hebrew Congregation *212 High Street*

Caldwell 07006 Congregation Augdath Israel of West Essex (C) 20 Academy Road 226-3600

Cedar Grove 07009 Temple Sholom (R) *760 Pompton Road* 239-1321

Cherry Hill 08034 Congregation Beth El (C) *2901 West Chapel Avenue* (609) 667-1300
Temple Emanu-El (R) *Cooper River Parkway & Donahue Street* 665-0888
Congregation Sons of Israel (O) *720 Cooper Landing Road* 667-9700

Cinnaminson 08077 Temple Sinai (C) *New Albany Road & Route 130* (609) 829-0658

Clark 07066 Temple Beth Or (C) *111 Valley Road* 381-8403

Clayton 08312 Congregation Sons of Israel (C) *East Center Street (609) 881-2267*

Cliffside Park 07010 Temple Israel (C) *207 Edgewater Road 945-7310*

Clifton 07011 Temple Beth Sholom (R) *733 Passaic Avenue 773-0355*

Clifton Jewish Center (C) *18 Delaware Street 772-3131*

Daughters of Miriam Synagogue (O) *155 Hazel Street 772-3700*

Closter 07624 Temple Beth El of Northern Valley (R) *221 Schraalenburgh Road 786-5112*

Colonia 07067 Temple Ohev Sholom (C) *220 Temple Way 338-7222*

Cranford 07016 Temple Beth El (C) *338 Walnut Avenue 276-9231*

The Sephardic Synagogue in Deal serves the Syrian Jewish community.

Deal 07723 Synagogue of Deal (O) *128 Norwood Avenue* 531-3200
Ohel Yaacob Congregation (O) *4 Ocean Avenue* 531-0217

Dover 07801 Congregation Adath Israel (C) *18 Thompson Avenue* 366-0179

East Brunswick 08816 East Brunswick Jewish Center (C) *511 Ryders Lane* 257-7070
Young Israel (O) *195 Dunhams Corner Road* 257 8349

East Windsor 08520 Beth El Synagogue (C) *50 Maple Stream Road* (609) 443-4454

Edgewater Temple Beth Am (R) *1276 River Road*

224-0335

Edison 08817 Congregation Beth El (C) *91 Jefferson Boulevard* 985-7333
Temple Emanu-El (R) *100 James Street* 549-4442
Congregation Ohr Torah (O) *2 Harrison Street* 572-7181

Elberon 07740 Temple Beth Miriam (R) *180 South Lincoln Avenue* 222-3754
Congregation Brothers of Israel (O) *250 Park Avenue* 222-6666

Elizabeth 07202 Congregation Adath Jeshurun (O) *200 Murray Street* 355-6723
Congregation Bais Yitzchok–Chevra Tehilim (O) 153 Bellevue Street 354-4789
Temple Beth El (R) *1374 North Avenue* 354-3021
Temple B'nai Israel (C) *1005 East Jersey Street* 354-0400
Elmora Hebrew Center (O) *420 West End Avenue* 353-1740
Jewish Educational Center Synagogue (O) *330 Elmora Avenue* 353-4446
1391 North Avenue 354-6058

Elmwood Park 07407 Elmwood Park Jewish Center (C) *100 Gilbert Avenue* 797-7320

Emerson 07630 Emerson Jewish Center (C) *53 Palisade Avenue* 265-2272

Englewood 07631 Congregation Ahavath Torah (O) *240 Broad Street 568-1315*
Temple Emanu-El (C) *147 Tenafly Road* 567-1300
Congregation Shomrei Emunah (O) *89 Hugenot Street* 567-9420

Englishtown 07726 Temple Shaari Emeth (R) *Craig Road* 462-7795
Congregation Sons of Israel (O) *Gordons Corner Road* 446-3000

Fair Lawn 07410 Congregation Ahavath Achim (O) *18-19 Saddle River Road 797-0502*
Temple Avoda (R) *10-10 Plaza Road 797-9716*
Temple Beth Sholom (C) *40-25 Fair Lawn Avenue 797-9321*
Congregation B'nai Israel (C) *Pine Avenue & 30th Street 797-9735*
Fair Lawn Jewish Center (C) *10-10 Norma Avenue 796-5040*
Congregation Shomrei Torah (O) *19-10 Morlot Avenue 791-7910*

Flanders 07836 Temple Hatikvah (C) *Pleasant Hill Road 584-0212*

Flemington 08822 Jewish Community Center (C) *Hopewell & East Main Streets 782-6410*

Florham Park Suburban Jewish Community Center of Morris County (C) *165 Ridgedale Avenue 377-6020*

Fort Lee 07024 Jewish Community Center (C) *1449 Anderson Avenue 947-1735*
Young Israel (O) *1610 Park Avenue 592-1518*

Franklin 07416 Congregation Sons of Israel *Oak Street*

Freehold 07728 Congregation Agudath Achim (O) *Broad & Stokes Streets 431-8666*

Garfield 07026 Jewish Community Center (C) *537 Harrison Avenue*

Glen Rock 07452 Glen Rock Jewish Center (C) *682 Harristown Road 652-6624*

Hackensack 07601 Temple Beth El (C) *280 Summit Avenue 342-2045*

Haddon Heights 08035 Temple Beth Sholom (C) *White House Pike & Green Street (609) 547-6113*

Hammonton 08037 Temple Beth El (C) *642 Bellevue Avenue*

Highland Park 08904 Congregation Etz Chaim (O) *230 Dennison Street 247-3839*
Highland Park Conservative Temple (C) *201 South 3rd Street 545-6482*
Congregation Ohav Emeth (O) *415 Raritan Avenue 247-3038*

Hillside 07205 Hillside Jewish Center (O) *1550 Summit Avenue 923-6191*
Temple Shomrei Torah (C) *910 Salem Avenue 351-1945*
Congregation Sinai Torah Chaim (O) *1531 Maple Avenue 923-9500*

Hoboken 07030 United Synagogue of Hoboken (C) *830 Hudson Street 659-2614*

Hopatcong 07843 Lake Hopatcong Jewish Community Center (C) *15 Durban Road 398-8700*

Howell 07731 Jewish Community Center (C) *Windler Road 367-1677*

Irvington 07111 Congregation Agudath Israel (O) *1125 Stuyvesant Avenue 372-1780*
Temple B'nai Israel (C) *706 Nye Avenue 372-9656*
Congregation Chevre Anshe Lubavitch (O) *74 Mill Road 399-1199*
Congregation Ahavath Achim Bikur Cholim (O) *644 Chancellor Avenue*
Congregation Chevre Tehillim Tifereth Israel (O) *745 Chancellor Avenue 371-6699*

Jackson 08527 Jewish Community Center *Whitesville section*

Jersey City 07305 Congregation Agudath Achim (O) *2456 Kennedy Boulevard 432-8379*

Congregation Ahavas Achim (O) *79 Audobon Avenue 434-7604*
Temple Beth El (C) *2419 Kennedy Boulevard 333-4229*
Congregation B'nai Jacob (C) *176 West Side Avenue 435-5725*
Congregation Mount Sinai (O) *128 Sherman Avenue 659-4267*
Congregation Sons of Israel (O) *35 Cottage Street 798-0172*
294 Grove Street 332-3212

Kearny 07032 Congregation B'nai Israel (C) *780 Kearny Avenue 998-3813*

Lake Hiawatha 07034 Jewish Center (C) *20 Lincoln Avenue 334-0959*

Lakewood 08701 Congregation Ahavath Sholom (C) *Forest Avenue & 11th Street 363-5190*
Temple Beth Am (R) *Madison & Carey Streets 363-2800*
Beth Hamedrash Gevoha (O) *617 Private Way 363-1233*
Congregation Sons of Israel (O) *Madison Avenue & 6th Street 364-2230*
Ridge Avenue & Railroad Street

Lawrenceville 08648 Young Israel (O) *25 Texas Avenue (609) 883-8833*

Leonia 07605 Congregation Adas Emuno (R) *254 Broad Avenue 592-1712*
Congregation Sons of Israel (C) *150 Grand Avenue 944-3477*

Linden 07036 Congregation Anshe Chesed (O) *Orchard Terrace & Saint George Avenue 486-8616*
Temple Mekor Chayim (C) *Deerfield Road & Academy Terrace 925-2283*

Suburban Jewish Center (C) *Kent Place & Deerfield Terrace*

Livingston 07039 Temple Beth Sholom (C) *193 East Mount Pleasant Avenue 992-3600*
Temple B'nai Abraham (C) *300 East Northfield Road 994-2290*
Temple Emanu-El (R) *264 West Northfield Road 992-5560*

Suburban Torah Center (O) *85 West Mount Pleasant Avenue* 994-0122

Long Branch 07740 Congregation B'nai Sholom (C) *213 Lenox Avenue* 229-2700
Congregation Brothers of Israel (O) *250 Park Avenue* 222-6666

Lyndhurst 07071 Lyndhurst Hebrew Center (C) *333 Valley Brook Road*

Mahwah Temple Beth Havarim (R) *59 Masonicus Road*

327-4333

Maplewood 07040 Congregation Ahavath Zion (O) *421 Boyden Avenue* 761-5444
Congregation Beth Ephraim-B'nai Zion (O) *520 Prospect Street* 762-5722
Congregation Anshe Russia (O) *14 Hauseman Court*

McKee City Jewish Farmers Congregation(O) *English Creek Road*

Manalapan Temple Sholom *Freehold-Englishtown Road* 446-1200
Temple Shaari Emeth (R) *Craig Road* 462-7744

Margate 08402 Temple Beth El (C) *500 North Jerome Avenue* (609) 823-2725
Congregation Beth Israel(R) *8401 Ventnor Avenue* 823-4116
Temple Emeth Sholom (R) *8501 Ventor Avenue* 822-4343

Matawan 07747 Temple Beth Ahm (C) *550 Lloyd Road* 583-1700
Congregation Beth Tefilah (O) *479 Lloyd Road* 583-6262
Temple Shalom (R) *5 Ayrmont Lane* 566-2621

Maywood 07607 Temple Beth Israel (C) *34 West Magnolia Avenue* 845-7550

Merchantville 08109 Congregation Beth Jacob (C) *109 East Maple Avenue* (609) 662-4509

Metuchen 08840 Temple Neve Sholom (C) *250 Grove Avenue* 548-2238

Congregation Beth Jacob-Beth Israel (C) *109 East Maple Avenue 662-4509*

Millburn 07041 Congregation B'nai Israel (C) *160 Millburn Avenue 379-3811*

Millville 08332 Temple Beth Hillel (C) *3rd & Oak Streets*

Montclair 07042 Congregation B'nai Keshet (Rec.) *87-89 Valley Road 746-4889*

Congregation Shomrei Emunah (C) *67 Park Street 746-5031*

Morganville Temple Rodef Torah 536-4454

Morristown 07960 Congregation Ahavath Yisroel (O) *9 Cutler Street 267-4184*

Temple B'nai Or (R) *Overlook Road 539-4539*

Jewish Community Center (C) *177 Speedwell Avenue* 538-9292

Lubavitch Rabbinical College (O) *226 Sussex Avenue* 267-9404

Mount Freedom 07970 Hebrew Congregation *Sussex Turnpike 895-2100*

Mount Holly 08060 Temple Har Zion (C) *High & Ridgeway Streets (609) 267-0660*

New Brunswick 08902 Anshe Emeth Temple (R) *222 Livingston Avenue*

Congregation B'nai Tikvah (C) *1001 Finnegans Lane* 297-0696

Chabad House (O) *8 Sicard Street 828-7374*

Congregation Poale Zedek (T) *145 Neilson Street*

New Milford 07646 Jewish Center (C) *435 River Road* 261-4847

Mount Laurel 08054 Congregation Mekor Shalom *Church & Fellowship Roads*

Newark 07106 Congregation Ahavas Sholom (O) *145 Broadway 485-2609*

Congregation Ahavas Achim *125 Academy Boulevard* 759-9394

Beth David Jewish Center (C) *828 Sanford Avenue 372-9360*

Mount Sinai Congregation(O) *250 Mount Vernon Place 372-9360*
Congregation B'nai Moshe *19-29 Ross Street*

Newton 07860 Jewish Center of Sussex County (C) *13 Washington Street 383-4570*

Norma 08347 Norma Congregation Brotherhood (O) *Wallace & Almond Streets (609) 691-4740*

North Bergen 08047 Temple Beth Abraham (O) *8410 4th Avenue 869-2426*
Temple Beth El (C) *7501 Hudson Avenue 869-9149*

Nutley 07110 Temple B'nai Israel (C) *192 Center Street 667-3713*

Oakhurst 07755 Temple Beth El (C) *301 Monmouth Road 531-0300*
Congregation Magen David (O) *395 Deal Road 531-3220*

Oakland 07436 Jewish Community Center (C) *192 Ramapo Valley Road 337-5569*

Ocean 07712 Temple Beth Torah (C) *1200 Roseld Avenue 531-4410*

Old Bridge 08857 Congregation Beth Ohr (C) *300 Route 516 257-9867*

Paramus 07652 Congregation Beth Tefillah (O) *241 Midland Avenue 265-4100*
Jewish Community Center (C) *Spring Valley Road & Midland Avenue 262-7691*

Park Ridge 07656 Temple Beth Sholom (C) *32 Park Avenue 391-4620*

Parlin 08859 Temple Ohave Sholom (C) *3018 Bordentown Avenue 727-4334*

Parsippany 07054 Congregation Ahavath Torah (O) *1180 Route 46 335-3636*
Temple Beth Am (R) *870 South Beverwyck Road 887-0046*

Passaic 07055 Congregation Adas Israel (O) *565 Broadway 773-7272*

Passaic Park Jewish Center (O) *181 Van Houten Avenue 777-5929*
Congregation B'nai Jacob (O) *112 Washington Place 473-2164*
Congregation Chevre Tehillim (O) *132 Spring Street 473-0263*
Temple Emanu-El (C) *185 Lafayette Avenue 777-9898*
Congregation Tifereth Israel (O) *180 Passaic Avenue 773-2552*
Young Israel (O) *200 Brook Avenue 778-7117*

Paterson 07504 Temple B'nai Jeshurun (R) *152 Derrom Avenue 279-2111*
Community Synagogue (C) *660 14th Avenue 742-9345*
Temple Emanu-El (C) *151 East 33rd Street 684-5565*

Penns Grove 08069 Congregation Shaari Zedek (C) *99 North Broad Street*

Perrineville 08520 Jewish Center (O) Hightstown Road 446-6116

Perth Amboy 08862 Congregation Beth Mordecai (C) *224 High Street 442-9697*
Congregation Shaarey Tefiloh (O) *15 Market Street 826-2977*

Pine Brook 07058 Jewish Center (C) *Change Bridge Road 227-3520*

Plainfield 07060 Temple Beth El (C) *225 East 7th Street 756-2333*
Temple Sholom (R) *815 West 7th Street 756-6447*

Pleasantville 08232 Congregation B'nai Israel (C) *West Jersey Avenue & Franklin Boulevard*

Pompton Lakes 07442 Congregation Beth Sholom (C) *21 Passaic Avenue 835-9785*
Jewish Community Center (C) *525 Wanaque Avenue*

Princeton 08540 Jewish Center (C) *457 Nassau Street (609) 921-0100*

Rahway 07065 Temple Beth Torah (C) *1365 Bryant Street 574-8432*

Red Bank 07701 Congregation Beth Sholom (O) *186 Maple Avenue 741-1657*

Ridgefield Park 07660 Temple Emanu-El (C) *120 Park Street 342-0050*

Ridgewood 07450 Temple Israel (C) *475 Grove Street 444-9320*

River Edge 07661 Temple Sholom (R) *385 Howland Avenue 489-2463*

Rockaway 07866 White Meadow Temple (C) *153 White Meadow Road 627-4500*

Roosevelt 08555 Jewish Center (T) *20 Homestead Lane (609) 448-2526*

Rumson 07710 Congregation B'nai Israel (C) *Hance & Ridge Roads 842-1800*

Rutherford 07070 Temple Beth El (C) *185 Montross Avenue 438-4931*

Salem 08079 Oheb Shalom Synagogue (C) *240 Grant Street*

Scotch Plains 07076 Temple Israel (C) *1920 Cliffwood Street 889-1830*

Short Hills 07078 Congregation B'nai Jeshurun (R) *1025 South Orange Avenue 379-1555*

Somerset 08873 Temple Beth El (C) *1495 Amwell Road 873-2325*

Somerville 08876 Temple Beth El (R) *67 Route 206 South 722-0674*

South Orange 07079 Congregation Beth El (C) *222 Irvington Avenue 763-0111*
Congregation Oheb Sholom (C) *170 Scotland Road 762-7067*
Congregation Sharey Tefilo-Israel (R) *432 Scotland Road 763-4116*

South River 08882 Congregation Anshe Emeth (C) *88 Main Street 257-4190*

Spotswood Jewish Center (R) *251-1119*

Springfield 07081 Temple Beth Ahm (C) *60 Temple Drive 376-0539*
Congregation Israel (O) *339 Mountain Avenue 376-6806*
Temple Shaarey Shalom (R) *78 South Springfield Avenue 379-5387*

Succasunna 07876 Temple Sholom (R) *215 South Hillside Avenue 584-5666*

Summit 07901 Jewish Community Center (C) *67 Kent Place Boulevard 273-4921*
Temple Sinai (R) *208 Summit Avenue 273-4921*

Teaneck 07666 Congregation Beth Aaron (O) *950 Queen Anne Road 836-6210*
Congregation Beth Am (R) *510 Claremont Avenue 836-5752*
Congregation Beth Sholom (C) *Rugby Road & Rutland Avenue 833-2620*
Congregation B'nai Yeshurun (O) *641 West Englewood Avenue 836-8916*
Temple Emeth (R) *1666 Windsor Road 833-1322*
Jewish Center of Teaneck (C) *70 Sterling Place 833-0515*
Congregation Rinat Yisrael (O) *389 West Englewood Avenue 837-2795*

Tenafly 07670 *Temple Sinai (R) 1 Engle Street 568-3035*

Tinton Falls Monmouth Reform Temple (R) *332 Hance Avenue 747-9365*

Toms River Congregation B'nai Israel (C) *1488 Old Freehold Road 349-1244*

Trenton 08618 Adath Israel Congregation (C) *715 Bellevue Avenue (609) 599-2591*
Congregation Ahavath Israel (C) *1130 Lower Ferry Road 882-3092*
Congregation Brothers of Israel (C) *499 Greenwood Avenue 695-3479*
Har Sinai Temple (R) *491 Bellevue Avenue 392-7143*

Congregation People of Truth (O) *1201 West State Street 396-4343*

Twin Rivers Sholom Hebrew Institute (O) *639 Abingdon Drive (609) 443-4877*

Union 07083 Congregation Beth Sholom (C) *2046 Vaux Hall Road 686-6773*

Temple Israel (C) *2372 Morris Avenue 687-2120*

Union City 07087 Congregation Beth Jacob (O) *325 4th Street 863-3114*

Temple Israel Emanu-El (O) *33rd Street & New York Avenue 866-6656*

Kehilas Sanz Yeshiva (O) *34th Street & New York Avenue*

Ventnor 08406 Congregation Beth Judah (C) *6725 Ventnor Avenue (609) 822-7116*

Verona 07044 Congregation Beth Am (C) *56 Grove Avenue 239-0754*

Vineland 08360 Congregation Beth Israel (C) *1015 Park Avenue (609) 691-0852*

Congregation Sons of Jacob (O) *321 Grape Street 691-9818*

Wanamassa Congregation Sons of Jacob (O) *Logan Road & Park Boulevard 775-1964*

Warren Moutain Jewish Center (C) *104 Mount Horeb Road 356-8777*

Wayne 07470 Temple Beth Tikvah (R) *950 Preakness Avenue 595-6565*

Wayne Conservative Synagogue *30 Hinchman Avenue 696-2500*

Westfield 07090 Temple Emanu-El (R) *756 East Broad Street 232-6770*

Rabbinic Center Synagogue (R) *128 East Dudley Avenue 233-0419*

West Caldwell 07006 Young Israel (O) *1 Henderson Drive 762-6260*

West New York 07093 Congregation Talmud Torah (O) *5308 Palisade Avenue 867-6859*

West Orange 07052 Congregation Ahavath Achim (O) *700 Pleasant Valley Way 736-1407*
Congregation Daughters of Israel (O) *1155 Pleasant Valley Way 731-5100*
Congregation B'nai Sholom (C) *300 Pleasant Valley Way 731-0160*
Congregation Plaza (O) *750 Northfield Avenue 325-9192*
Young Israel (O) *567 Pleasant Valley Way 731-3383*

Westwood 07675 Temple Beth Or (R) *56 Ridgewood Road 664-7422*

West Marlboro Congregation Ohev Sholom (O) *103 School Road*

Wildwood 08260 Beth Judah Synagogue (C) *Spencer & Pacific Avenues (609) 522-7541*

Willingboro 08046 Congregation Beth Torah (C) *Beverly Rancocas Road (609) 877-4214*
Temple Emanu-El (R) *JFK Way 871-1736*

Woodbine 08270 Woodbine Brotherhood Synagogue (O) *614 Washington Avenue (609) 861-2554*

Woodbridge 07095 Congregation Adath Israel (C) *424 Amboy Avenue 634-9601*

Woodbury Heights 08097 Congregation Beth Israel (C) *High & Warner Streets (609) 848-7272*

Woodcliff Lake 07675 Temple Emanu-El (C) *87 Overlook Drive 391-0801*

Wyckoff Temple Beth Rishon *585 Russel Avenue 891-4466*

MIKVEHS

Cherry Hill 720 Cooper Landing Road *(609) 667-9700 or 779-2815 or 667-3515*

Elizabeth 35 North Avenue (201) 352-5048

Highland Park 112 First Avenue South *(201) 249-2411 or 846-5256*

Lakewood 705 Madison Avenue *(201) 370-8909*

Norma Peach Street *(609) 691-7191 or 692-7176*

Oakhurst 201 Jerome Avenue *(201) 531-1712*

Passaic High & Van Houten Streets *(201) 778-7117*

Perth Amboy 15 Market Street *(201) 826-2977*

Teaneck 1726 Windsor Road *(201) 837-8220*

West Orange 717 Pleasant Valley Way *(201) 731-1427*

New York

In the 1650s, Holland was a world power, with colonies in North and South America. In 1654, the Jewish community of Recife, Brazil was expelled by the Portuguese regime which had just captured the city. The Jews were members of the Dutch West India Company, an international trading concern with headquarters in Amsterdam, Netherlands and branch colonies in Brazil, Surinam, Curaçao, St. Martin, and St. Eustatius.

These Jewish refugees set sail for lands offering religious freedom. Some of these wandering Jews landed in the Caribbean islands of Jamaica and Barbados. One ship fleeing this Recife Expulsion, carrying twenty-three Jewish men, women, and children, wasn't as fortunate in its search for freedom. Their ship, heading for Amsterdam, was captured in the Caribbean Sea by Spanish pirates. A French galleon, the St. Catherine, came to their rescue. This ship was heading for Montreal, Canada and dropped off its Jewish castaways in the Dutch colony of Nieuw Amsterdam (now New York).

The St. Catherine docked in the harbor of New Amsterdam in September, 1654. The twenty-three Jewish refugees were greeted by the anti-Semitic governor of the colony, Peter Stuyvesant. He did not want any Jews in his colony who would be a "burden on the colony." Afterall, these people arrived penniless. They were placed under arrest until orders were received from Amsterdam. Many of the shareholders of the Dutch West India Company in Amsterdam were Jewish. Pressure was applied on

Governor Stuyvesant, and he was ultimately forced to let these Jews into the colony. The conditions for entry were on the condition that the Jews care for themselves, and not be a burden upon the colony. This was the first official Jewish settlement in North America.

The Jews were granted permission to travel, trade, and buy real estate throughout New Netherland. The first trader to take advantage of these rights was Asser Levy. He owned real estate in Oyster Bay, Bruecklen (Brooklyn), and at Fort Orange, the first permanent settlement at what is now Albany.

The first synagogue in North America was organized by the twenty-three Jews who arrived in New Amsterdam in September, 1654. They called their congregation, *Shearith Israel,* because they felt that they actually were the "remnants of Israel." The congregation followed the (Western) Sephardic ritual, similar to their "mother" congregation in Amsterdam—the Great Portuguese Synagogue (Esnoga).

The first synagogue in North America was located on Mill Street (today's South William Street, located near Wall Street) and was built in 1730. That structure is no longer extant. The congregation is, however, still functioning. It is presently located on Central Park West and West 70th Street (the Upper West Side).

New York's second oldest congregation, B'nai Jeshurun, was organized as an offshoot from Congregation Shearith Israel (Spanish and Portuguese Synagogue) in 1825. It was the first Ashkenazic congregation, organized by Jews who had come from Germany and Poland.

Jewish communities were established in towns and cities along the Erie Canal and on both sides of the Hudson River during the 1830s and 1840s. The oldest existing Jewish community north of New York City is in Albany, where Congregation Beth El, now part of Temple Beth Emeth, was founded in 1838. Most of the Jews who came to Albany were from Bavaria where the repressions following the Napoleanic Wars were the most severe in all of Europe.

The 1840s witnessed the creation of Jewish communities in Syracuse, Rochester, Buffalo, Utica, Poughkeepsie, and

Plattsburgh. Most of the German Jewish immigrants were involved in dry goods and peddling. Many Jewish settlers were tailors and founded Rochester's ready-to-wear mens clothing industry in the 1850s. During the Civil War, they made uniforms for the Union Army.

Two of America's earliest Reform congregations were founded in New York; Temple Emanu-El (New York City), organized in 1845 and Congregation Beth El (Albany), organized in 1850.

During the Eastern European Jewish immigrations of the 1880s, existing Jewish communities were enlarged and new settlements were founded in such cities as Binghamton, Suffern, Spring Valley, Lake Placid, Yonkers, Mount Vernon, Hempstead, Sag Harbor, and Lindenhurst.

Some of these Eastern European Jewish settlers were founders of Jewish farming communities in Sullivan and Ulster Counties and were assisted with the aid of the Baron de Hirsch Fund and the Jewish Agricultural Society. Some of the farmers failed to provide enough income for their families from farming so they took in boarders from New York City into their farmhouses. Some of these boarding houses developed into the now-famous Jewish hotels of the Catskills such as Grossinger's, the Nevele, and Kutscher's.

The 1960s was the decade in which thousands of people shifted from the established inner city Jewish communities to the suburbs. New towns were incorporated by several Chassidic sects who had lived in overcrowded apartments in Williamsburg, Brooklyn. They created new all-Jewish towns or *shtetls* in Rockland County such as New Square and Kiryas Joel.

The Jewish population of New York is approximately 2.7 million, of which 1.7 reside in New York City.

ALBANY

CONGREGATION BETH EMETH
100 Academy Road

The first Jewish community in New York's State Capital arrived in the 1830s from Bavaria. Congregation Beth El was the first synagogue and was organized in 1838. In 1846, Rabbi Issac Mayer Wise arrived from Bohemia and became Albany's first rabbi. Initially, the congregation followed the Orthodox ritual. By 1850, Rabbi Wise had become outspoken in his advocacy of Reform. Rabbi Wise had introduced a number of changes at Beth El that were not universally popular. He insisted upon a more orderly and dignified worship service. He introduced a mixed choir that sang German and English hymns. He shortened some prayers and eliminated others. He participated in disputations in other cities attacking Orthodoxy. He criticized local slaughtering practices and questioned publicly the piety of at least one synagogue official. Opposition became bitter and tension within the congregation mounted until physical violence of Rosh Hashanah, September 7, 1850, was inevitable. Police were summoned to quell the fist-fights and the synagogue was closed.

The following month, a group broke away from Beth El and organized Anshe Emeth, a Reform congregation. Rabbi Wise was the spiritual leader. This congregation became the fourth Reform Jewish congregation in America, being preceded only by Beth Elohim of Charleston, South Carolina in 1841, Har Sinai of Baltimore in 1842, and Temple Emanu-El of New York City in 1845. The congregation ratified the use of family pews, constituting the first instance of such usage in a Jewish house of worship—a reform to be adopted later by all congregations of American Reform. In 1854, Rabbi Issac Mayer Wise became the rabbi of Cincinnati's Congregation B'ne Jeshurun. In 1885, Beth El merged with Beth Emeth. A new building was designed by a member of the congregation, architect Adolph Fleischmann. The consulting architect was Isaac G. Perry, architect and superintendent of the State Capital, then under construction. The magnificent fieldstone Romanesque Revival temple was dedicated in 1889 and was located at Lancaster, Swan, and Jay Streets. The building, located just west of the new capital complex, is still extant but it is now used as a Baptist church.

In 1957, Temple Beth Emeth dedicated its present synagogue building, located at 100 Academy Road. It was designed by architect Percival Goodman.

CONGREGATION BETH EL JACOB

In 1841, several members of Congregation Beth El, Albany's first congregation, organized Beth El Congregation. The last location of the synagogue was at 90 Herkimer Street. In the 1960s, the Jews moved to the suburbs because of the deteriorating section. Recently, the neighborhood has experienced a renaissance and many of the old residential buildings have undergone rehabilitation. The old Beth El Jacob synagogue building has also been restored, however, it is no longer used as a Jewish house of worship.

BINGHAMTON

BETH DAVID SYNAGOGUE
39 Riverside Drive

This Orthodox congregation commissioned architect Werner Seligman to design its new synagogue in 1960. He created a work of art. As you enter at street level you are enclosed by a courtyard

Beth David Congregation front elevation.

which has a daily chapel on one side, a multi-purpose space on another side, and the synagogue office and rabbi's study on yet another side. The main sanctuary seems to float in space. It is located upstairs, on the roof. There are floor to ceiling windows and skylights. In the spring and summer the worshipper becomes one with nature, sitting within the tree-scapes. The architect has also designed another modern and sculptural synagogue in the city of Cortland, New York.

BUFFALO

GRAND ISLAND

The second largest city in the state, Buffalo, was totally destroyed during the War of 1812. In 1825, Mordecai Manuel Noah, a well-known politician, playwright, journalist, Sheriff of New York, and leader in the Jewish community, wanted to create a city of refuge for all the Jews. The site was to be on Grand Island, New York, located between Buffalo and Niagra Falls. The plan invited all Jews of the world to come to "Ararat" as a way station on the

Mordecai Manuel Noah.

road to Zion where they could acquire skill in agriculture in preparation for a new life in Palestine. An important element in this scheme was that Noah would become the governor and judge of Israel.

A cornerstone made of Ohio sandstone was inscribed with the Hebrew passage "*Shema Yisrael*, (Hear O Israel, etc.)—Ararat, a City of Refuge for the Jews founded by Mordecai Manuel Noah in the Month of Tishri September, 1825 and in the Fiftieth Year of American Independence."

On September 15, 1825, Noah, the only Jew at the time in Buffalo, led the processional dressed in his special robes of a "Judge of Israel." The marching bands played, the canons fired, and the fireworks exploded. This fantastic pageant and spectacle was all part of Noah's proclamation of the creation of Ararat. The Jewish communities of Europe and America condemned this ridiculous scheme. The concept of Ararat was soon forgotten. The sandstone cornerstone, however, is still extant! It is located on the lower level of the Grand Island Town Hall, located on Baseline Street. Mordecai Manuel Noah is buried in New York City's Spanish and Portuguese cemetery, located on West 21st Street, just west of 6th Avenue.

TEMPLE BETH EL
151 Richmond Avenue

The first Jewish settlement in Buffalo occurred in 1847 when Congregation Beth El was organized. The first synagogue was a converted schoolhouse on Pearl Street, near Eagle Street which was purchased in 1850. Its 1910 building at 151 Richmond Avenue is a brick structure with limestone trim and a massive copper dome. That building is now used by a local church. The congregation is presently located in the suburban town of Tonawanda, at 2368 Eggert Road.

TEMPLE BETH ZION
805 Delaware Avenue

The first Reform congregation in Buffalo, Beth Zion, was founded in 1850. Services were conducted in the massive stone structure which was located at 805 Delaware Avenue until the devastating fire in 1961 which totally destroyed it.

In 1967, Temple Beth Zion completed its new synagogue on the same site. It was designed by the architectural firm of Harrison and Abramovitz, designers of the Brandeis University Chapel and the West Point Chapel. The monumental precast concrete structure consists of two arc shaped walls, joined at the ends by stained glass windows designed by artist Ben Shahn. The arc walls are scalloped and slant upward, resulting in increased structural strength. The massive reinforcing tension cables are exposed at either end of the structure.

No secular activities are housed in the sanctuary structure. There are extensive administrative, educational, and social activities in harmonious, but stylistically unrelated buildings linked to the rear of the sanctuary. The two massive Ten Commandment Tablets flanking the Ark are decorated with gold mosaic tiles designed by Ben Shahn. The 10 foot high menorah in front of the Ark was sculpted from one massive quartz crystal.

The original Temple Beth Zion.

Temple Beth Zion in Buffalo.

CONGREGATION AHAVATH SHOLOM
Jefferson Avenue near William Street

Built in 1890 by Eastern European Jews, Congregation Ahavath Sholom's design is unique. There is one central bulbous dome above the brick structure. There is also a rose window on the front façade. The neighborhood changed in the 1960s and the congregation disbanded. The building is still extant and was sold to a church.

THE CATSKILLS

SHOLAM COLONY

On the wall in the lobby of the Ezrath Israel Synagogue in Ellenville there is a memorial plaque honoring the Sholam Colony. In 1838, the first Jewish agricultural colony in the United States was established. In 1837, a small group of New York City Jews purchased about 500 acres from Edmund Bruyn, sight unseen. They named their colony Sholam, peace. They found barren land, but no peace. Unable to farm due to the rocky soil conditions, they nevertheless cleared the land, built roads, erected eight frame houses on stone foundations, set aside a burial ground, and built a small synagogue. They tried manufacturing fur caps and goose quill pens, cobbling, tailoring, and peddling used clothing they acquired in New York City. Starvation faced them. Mortgages were foreclosed. Most returned to the city by 1842. There is absolutely nothing left of their homes or the synagogue, which was later used as a dance hall. There is, however, a sign post which reads, "Sholam Road." The site of the Sholam Colony is located eleven miles north of Ellenville, along Route 55A, on the northeast side of the Rondout Reservoir.

The Catskill Mountains were the summer vacation spots for the upper middle-class German Jews in the 1880s and 1890s. They were "restricted" from vacationing in such resorts as Saranac Lake, Lake Placid, and Saratoga Springs. At the turn of the century Eastern European Jews were removed from the big cities such as New York City and Philadelphia and were resettled in Jewish farming communities in Sullivan and Ulster Counties. They were assisted with the aid of the Baron de Hirsch Fund and the Jewish Agricultural Society. Many of these Jewish farmers were unable to make a living from agriculture alone. They supplemented their

The little red schoolhouse served the children of the Jewish farmers near Ellenville. It is located on the golf course of the Nevele Country Club.

The original Grossinger's Hotel.

incomes by renting-out some of their rooms in the farmhouse to boarders during the summer season.

This is how Joseph Slutsky started in 1903. His Nevele Country Club in Ellenville emerged. The name "Nevele" is derived from Slutsky's eleven children—eleven spelled backwards is "Nevele!"

In 1914, an Austrian immigrant, Selig Grossinger, was ordered by his doctors to leave the bad climate of New York City. He bought a 50-acre farm near Liberty, New York. They soon took in boarders at $9 a week. This was the beginning of Grossinger's Hotel. Many movie and television stars got their first break into show business while entertaining audiences in such Catskill resort hotels as Grossinger's, Brown's, Kutscher's, and the Concord. In the 1920s, there were hundreds of Jewish hotels in the Catskills. The fastest way to get to them was by railroad. The New York, Ontario and Western Railroad left Pennsylvania Station in New York City and stopped in such towns as Ellenville, Monticello, Mountaindale, Centerville (Woodridge), South Fallsburg, Hurleyville, Ferndale, Liberty, and Fleischmanns. Most of the early hotels have been demolished. Some have been purchased by religious camps or by bungalow colonies. Grossinger's Hotel has just gone "Co-op." The old railroad was torn-up in the 1950s. The right-of way is now used as a hiking and snowmobile trail.

The earliest synagogues in the Catskills served the Jewish farming communities. Many of these are still in use and now serve the year-round permanent Jewish communities as well as the summer resort vacationers. There are synagogues in Ellenville, Glen Wild, Harris, Hunter, Fleischmanns, Jeffersonville, Liberty, Livingston Manor, Loch Sheldrake, Monticello, Mountaindale, Parksville, Port Jervis, South Fallsburg, Swan Lake, Tannersville, Keuneonga Lake, Woodbourne, and Woodridge. There were synagogues in the following towns also: Granit, Kerhonksen, East Mountaindale, Briggs Highway (Ellenville), Spring Glen, Dairyland, Ulster Heights, and Greenfield Park.

The resort towns of Fleischmanns, Hunter, and Tannersville are frequented by the German Jewish community of Washington

Heights, in New York City. They are part of the Breuer Kehillah. Fleischmanns is named for the inventor of compressed yeast cakes, Charles Fleischmann, who built summer homes in the town.

For further information about hotels in Sullivan County, please call the Sullivan County Tourist Information Center at (914) 794-3000.

The original Congregation Ezrath Israel in Ellenville was organized in 1907 by Jewish farmers.

The synagogue and adjoining Talmud Torah on the Minnewaska Trail, Kerhonksen.

The Hebrew Congregation of Mountaindale with its adjoining mikveh.

CHAPPAQUA

TEMPLE BETH EL
220 South Bedford Road

Set in the woods on land which originally was owned by Horace Greeley, Temple Beth El is the only synagogue which was designed by the late architect Louis I. Kahn. It was designed in 1972 in the style of the 17th century wooden synagogues of Poland. The concrete and wooden structure houses a series of classrooms which surround the main sanctuary. During High Holy Day services, the walls of the classrooms are opened up, creating a much larger space. The 30-foot clerestory above the sanctuary has been compared to a modern version of a baldachino or canopy which was common in the Polish wooden synagogues of the 17th century. Temple Beth El follows the Reform ritual.

GLOVERSVILLE

Nathan Littauer was a peddler who settled in Gloversville in the 1840s. He later opened a glove factory. His son Lucius N. Littauer inherited the business and expanded it. He was elected to Congress and established the first chair in Judaica at Harvard University. He later donated over 12,000 volumes of rare Hebrew books and manuscripts to Harvard. Half of the public buildings in Gloversville are named in honor of Lucius N. Littauer.

Louis Kahn's only synagogue was built for Temple Beth El in Chappaqua. Its design resembles a 17th century Polish wooden synagogue.

KIRYAS JOEL

The world headquarters of the Satmar Chassidim is located in Williamsburg, Brooklyn. Many of the chassidic families are very large, with an average of eight or ten children. The old apartments in Williamsburg are not very large. Much more space was required. In the 1960s, the chassidim purchased one square mile of land near Monroe, New York, in Rockland County, about 50 miles from New York City. Large single-family homes were built. There are presently about 800 families in Kiryas Joel. The town is named after the last Satmer Rebbe, Joel Teitelbaum.

The main synagogue is the largest and tallest structure in the town. The main sactuary has an exquisite marble Ark and several lavish crystal chandeliers. There are several smaller prayer rooms adjoining the main sanctuary.

The Great Synagogue in Kiryas Joel.

There are about 6,000 children in Kiryas Joel who attend the four schools; two for boys and two for girls. There is a medical center, Hatzalah—medical emergency ambulance service, and shopping mall, complete with its own kosher pizza shop.

The plaza in front of the main synagogue also serves as the central bus terminal. There are buses leaving for the City and for nearby Jewish communities of Monsey and Spring Valley every hour. Most of the residents are employed in the Diamond Center in New York City. There is separate seating for men and separate seating for women on all buses. Sometimes prayers are recited on the buses, necessitating the use of a *mechitzah* or partition, usually a curtain which blocks the views between the men's and women's sections. The bus actually becomes a mobile synagogue.

Kiryas Joel is located along Route 17 (the Quickway), at exit 130—Monroe. It is, in essence, a modern-day *shtetl*.

LONG ISLAND

There were Jewish merchants on Long Island as early as the 1660s. Asser Levy, one of the first twenty-three Jews to arrive in New Amsterdam, owned real estate in Oyster Bay.

The earliest Jewish community was organized in Sag Harbor in 1883. The oldest synagogue on Long Island, Temple Adas Israel, was built in 1898. Other early congregations were organized in Glen Cove (1897), East Setauket (1893), Greenport (1890), Huntington (1900), Patchogue (1903), Rockville Centre (1907), Hempstead (1908), Riverhead (1911), and Great Neck (1912).

The Jewish Agricultural Society brought Jewish settlers to Kings Park, Farmingdale, Riverhead, Center Moriches, and East Islip in 1905. During World War I, many Jewish men received their military training at Camps Yaphank and Upton, near Patchogue. Some of the soldier's families settled in nearby towns for the duration of the war.

Following World War II, Abraham Levitt converted Long Island potato farms into a large-scale housing development. He built mass-produced or production-line houses. All of the houses were exactly the same and were therefore very inexpensive. Thousands of returning veterans, who had limited incomes, were able to afford to buy a basic 4-room house for $6,990 or to rent one at $60 a month. Levitt built 18,000 single-family houses on 4,000 acres. This was the beginning of Levittown. Land for the Levittown Israel Community Center was donated by the Levitts.

The Five Towns communities of Cedarhurst, Lawrence, Hewlett, Woodmere, and Oceanside as well as Long Beach were orginally summer resort areas. In the 1920s, these towns became permanent, year-round, communities.

MAMARONECK

WESTCHESTER DAY SCHOOL
856 Orienta Avenue

Founded in 1948, the Westchester Day School was the first Hebrew all-day school in the county. The school is situated on a 27-acre estate originally owned by Edwin Weatherbee and Amy Henrietta Constable, daughter of Arnold Constable, the department store heirs. The estate overlooks the Long Island Sound at Orienta Point. The classes range from nursery to eighth grade. This is a traditional Hebrew Day School with courses in Hebrew, Bible, and Talmud. There are additional subjects such as math, science, language arts, computer science, dance, drama, and journalism. There are three tennis courts and two swimming pools.

The school chapel functions as the Orthodox synagogue for the Jewish community of Mamaroneck on the Sabbath and Jewish holidays. The administrative offices are housed in the original 1890 mansion. It is a pleasure to be "sent to the principal's office" in this school. It is located in the old Drawing Room and contains all of its original hand-carved mahogany paneling on the walls, exposed ceiling timbers, and fireplace.

NEWBURGH

GOMEZ HOUSE
Millhouse Road

This stone house was built in 1720 by Lewis Gomez, a Sephardic Jew who was a wealthy merchant who traded with Indian tribes and British military forces. This is the oldest structure built and occupied by Colonial Jews in North America and is still standing. It is located on Millhouse Road—about 100 feet south of the Ulster County line on Route 9W. The building is presently occupied by Mildred Starin. Tours of the Gomez House are available by calling (914) 236-3126. On old maps of the area the small brook next to the Gomez House is referred to as "Jew's Creek."

The Gomez House was built by a Colonial Sephardic Jew, Lewis Gomez, in 1720.

NEW ROCHELLE

BETH EL SYNAGOGUE—CENTER
Northfield Road and North Avenue

The sculpture entitled "The Living Star of David" was designed by Israeli artist Yaakov Agam, hangs in the main foyer. The Menorah near the Ark is a replica of the Menorah in the Second Temple in Jerusalem, as depicted in the Arch of Titus in Rome. A magnificent bronze sculpture by Luise Kaisch entitled "The Wall of Martrys" symbolizes Jewish martyrdom throughout the Diaspora.

NEW YORK CITY

CONGREGATION SHEARITH ISRAEL
8 West 70th Street

The oldest Jewish congregation in North America, Shearith Israel, was organized in the Dutch settlement of New Amsterdam in 1654. The first structure built expressly as a synagogue for the congregation was erected in 1730 on Mill Street (now South William Street, in the Wall Street area). The synagogue was enlarged on the same site in 1818. The congregation moved uptown as the neighborhood became an industrial and commercial zone. It moved to Crosby Street, between Broome and Spring Streets (in the Soho District) in 1834. In 1860, the congregation moved to 5 West 19th Street and moved once again to its present location at Central Park West and West 70th Street, in the Upper West Side. The present building was designed in 1897 by the Jewish architect Arnold Brunner in the Classical Revival style.

Although all of the former synagogue buildings are no longer extant, the original furnishings and religious ornaments, including the reading table *(Tebah)*, Holy Ark *(Heychal)*, and even the floorboards have been removed and incorporated into the present building. This adheres to the Rabbinical law which stipulates that the sanctity *(kedushah)* of a synagogue remains in that structure forever. The congregation actually dismantled all of its prior structures in fear that they might be sold to or be used by churches.

The little Synagogue, used for daily services, is a replica of the original Mill Street building. Among the many Torah scrolls that are kept in the Ark, three have been rescued from destruction by the Nazis coming from the Sephardic congregation in the Hague, Netherlands. A pair of silver bells crowning the scrolls bears the name of Myer Myers (1723-1795), a notable New York silversmith in his day. The four silver candlesticks represent an *Havdalah* set, consisting of a candleholder, wine goblet, and spice

box—designed to lift apart during the *Havdalah* ceremony (marking the conclusion of the Sabbath day). Made of Spanish brass, the candlesticks may date from the Spanish Inquisition of the 15th century. The *Marranos* or secret Jews had to camouflage their religious practices for fear of being killed. These candlesticks were designed to appear as simple sources of light, but to the secret Jews of Spain they were actually used for their religious service.

The Eternal Light *(Ner Tamid)* has been in continuous use since 1818. Some of the benches (bancas) are from the Mill Street and Crosby Street synagogue buildings. The stained glass windows in both the Little Synagogue and the main sanctuary were designed by Louis Comfort Tiffany.

The reading platform *(Tebah)* in the main sanctuary was intended to be finished in marble, similar to the Holy Ark. The congregation ran out of sufficient funds after it completed the building. A ship's carpenter was commissioned and designed the reading platform in wood, using the shape of the stern of a boat as its model. The congregation was very pleased with the "temporary" design of the reading platform and decided not to replace it with marble.

There are twelve (gas-lit) candlesticks surrounding the reading platform, symbolic of the twelve tribes of Israel. The original Mill Street Synagogue floorboards have been incorporated into the floor of this reading platform. When a member of the congregation is called to the Torah he literally stands on the same floorboards that his Sephardic ancestors stood upon.

Congregation Shearith Israel, also known as the Spanish and Portuguese Synagogue, is an official New York City Historic Landmark. The congregation follows the Western Sephardic (Orthodox) ritual. For information about services and tours of the facilities, please call (212) 873-0300.

Interior view of the Spanish & Portuguese Synagogue.

SPANISH AND PORTUGUESE CEMETERY
St. James Place near Chatham Square (Chinatown)

The first Jewish cemetery in the United States was consecrated in 1656. The exact site of that cemetery is unknown. The remains of that cemetery were moved to Chatham Square. It was acquired in 1682. Benjamin Bueno de Mesquita, who died in 1683, was the first person to be buried there. The cemetery played a part in the American defense of New York in 1776. It was fortified by the patriots as one of the defenses of the city. Among the graves in the cemetery are those of 18 Revolutionary soldiers and patriots. These include Hayman Levy, Isaacs Moses, and Gershom Mendes Seixas, minister of Congregation Shearith Israel, who closed the synagogue and removed the Torahs to Stratford, Connecticut, when British forces occupied New York.

There are two additional Jewish cemeteries which belong to the Spanish and Portuguese Synagogue. One is located on West 11th Street, just east of Sixth Avenue. The other is located on West 21st Street, just west of Sixth Avenue. Mordecai Manuel Noah, the playwright, politician, and colorful character who attempted to found a Jewish agricultural colony on Grand Island in the Niagra River (see Buffalo, New York), was one of the last persons to be buried in the 21st Street cemetery. There are also three soldiers of the American Revolution buried in this cemetery.

On Memorial Day, members of Congregation Shearith Israel decorate the graves of the Revolutionary soldiers and patriots with the American flag, in all three cemeteries.

CENTRAL SYNAGOGUE
Lexington Avenue and East 55th Street

Organized by Bohemian Jews in 1839, Congregation Shaaray Hashomayim merged with Congregation Ahavath Chesed to create the Central Synagogue. The first buildings of the congregation were located in the Lower East Side. In 1872, the present structure was built. It was designed by the first Jewish architect in America, Henry Fernbach. The design is Moorish Revival and is an exact replica of the Dohany utca Synagogue, in Budapest, Hungary. That is the largest synagogue in Europe with a seating capacity of 3300 and was constructed in 1859.

The Central Synagogue has a seating capacity of over 1300. The cornerstone of the Central Synagogue was laid in 1870 by Rabbi Isaac Mayer Wise, whose son later became rabbi of the congregation. The Central Synagogue follows the Reform ritual. It is an official New York City, New York State, and National Historic Landmark. It is the oldest synagogue building in continuous use by one congregation.

For information about services and tours of the Central Synagogue, please call (212) 838-5122.

The Central Synagogue was built in 1872.

CASTLE CLINTON
Battery Park

This fortress was built in 1807 as the West Battery and was designed to protect New York harbor against possible invasion. The building was later converted into a concert hall, in which P.T. Barnum introduced a Swedish opera star, Jenny Lind, in 1850. The building later housed the New York Aquarium, before its move to the Bronx Park and finally to Coney Island, in Brooklyn.

Between 1855 and 1890, that building was known as Castle Garden, also known in Yiddish as "Kessel Garten." This was the Immigrant Landing Depot, where over seven million new Americans were processed. It was closed down in 1890 because of political scandals. Castle Clinton is today a National Historic Landmark. It has been restored as a fortress. This monument is part of the Gateway National Park.

ELLIS ISLAND
Upper New York Bay

Ellis Island, opened in 1892, served as the immigration center after Castle Garden was closed down. The immigrants arrived by steamships, usually in the steerage compartment since they had less than $5 in their pockets, and docked in Lower Manhattan or in Hoboken, New Jersey. They were transferred onto ferries which shuttled them to Ellis Island.

The immigrants were given a tag which had their name, number, and country of origin. They carried their heavy baggage up four flights of stairs before they were processed. This was not a harsh or inhumane treatment. Rather, it was part of the medical examination process. Doctors stood on every stair landing looking for certain symptoms such as heavy breathing. The doctors would mark an "L" for lung disease or "H" for heart ailment with a piece of chalk on the immigrant's clothing. As the immigrants reached the top of the stairs they would be given more thorough medical examinations. The most dreaded exam was for Trachoma, an eye disease.

The immigrants were seated in the Main Hall, in cubicles, almost like cattle. Yet, the vast majority of the immigrants arriving at Ellis Island were processed within a day or two.

The immigrants were able to purchase railroad tickets to any city in America. Many times, the immigrants were told in the "old country" to buy a train ticket to "Springfield, America." If you look at a map of the United States you will see that there are no less than fifteen "Springfields" throughout the country! This is how many Yiddish-speaking East European immigrants would end up in Springfield, Illinois, Missouri, Massachusetts, and South Carolina.

Ellis Island is part of the Gateway National Park. It is being restored and will reopen in 1988. Tours of the facilities are given by the park rangers. The only access to Ellis Island is by ferry which depart from Battery Park, in New York.

STATUE OF LIBERTY
Upper New York Bay

Liberty Island is the island on which the Statue of Liberty stands. It is a monument and symbol of freedom and hope for millions of immigrants. The statue was constructed in 1876 and presented by France to the United States as a gift in honor of its Centennial anniversary. It took an additional ten years to complete the pedestal upon which the statue stands. The dedication was in October, 1886.

The Statue of Liberty was designed by Frederic Bartholdi and engineered by Gustav Eifel, the designer of the Eifel Tower in Paris. At the base of the statue is a plaque bearing the sonnet "The New Colosus" by the Jewish poetess, Emma Lazarus. Emma Lazarus was a descendant of the Reverend Gershom Mendes Seixas, minister of the Spanish and Portuguese Synagogue.

The sonnet is recognized by its key phrase, "Give me your tired, your poor, your huddled masses yearning to breathe free."

The Museum of Immigration is housed at the base of the Statue of Liberty. There are daily boat tours to Liberty Island leaving from Battery Park.
For further information about ferry schedules to Liberty Island and Ellis Island, please call (212) 269-5755.

ELDRIDGE STREET SHUL
14 Eldridge Street

Built by Eastern European immigrants in 1886, the Eldridge Street Shul, Congregation Kahal Adas Jeshurun Anshei Lubz, is an official New York City and National Historic Landmark. It was the first Orthodox synagogue built specifically as a Jewish house of worship in the Lower East Side. Other major congregations simply purchased former churches and renovated them into synagogues (e.g. Bialystoker Synagogue, Roumanian-American Synagogue, and the Bais Hamedrash Hagadol). The Eldridge Street synagogue was designed by the architectural firm of the Herter Brothers. They were better known as interior decorators for such fashionable clients as the Vanderbilts.

The façade of the building is eclectic; incorporating Romanesque, Gothic, and Moorish elements. The main sanctuary has not been used since the 1930s. It is an immense and opulent room with elaborate brass chandeliers with Victorian glass shades hanging in the midst of a huge, barrel-vaulted space. The Ark was designed in Italian walnut.

The Eldridge Street Shul is presently undergoing a major rehabilitation project. When completed, there will be daily and Sabbath services and also a major Jewish museum on the premises, similar to the Alt-Nue Shul in Prague, Czechoslovakia, where after morning services, the synagogue is opened up to the public for viewing.

For further information about the Eldridge Street Project and tours of the synagogue, please call (212) 219-0888.

Exterior view of the landmark Eldridge Street Synagogue, built in 1886.

CONGREGATION ANSHE SLONIM
172 Norfolk Street (Lower East Side)

This Gothic Revival structure was built in 1849 by the Reform Congregation Anshe Chesed. It was designed by architect Alexander Saeltzer and had a seating capacity of 1500. Anshe Chesed, not to be confused with the present-day Ansche Chesed, a Conservative congregation on the Upper West Side, was organized in 1828, sold the building in 1874 to the Orthodox Congregation Oheb Zedek, and eventually merged with Temple Emanu-El. In 1921, the building was purchased by Congregation Anshe Slonim. It occupied the structure until 1975 when its membership began to dwindle because of the changing neighborhood. At that point, the building was abandoned. The city had plans to demolish the structure. In 1986, however, a Spanish sculptor, Angel Orensanz, purchased the former synagogue for $500,000. He has plans to use part of the building as his studio, convert other parts of the space into artists' lofts, and convert the basement into a community center.

The building has recently been declared an official New York City Historic Landmark. The front façade, therefore, cannot be altered. This is the oldest synagogue structure in New York State.

YESHIVA UNIVERSITY MUSEUM
2520 Amsterdam Avenue (West 185th Street)

Located on the Washington Heights campus of Yeshiva University, the Yeshiva University Museum is housed in the lower floors of the modern library building. If one has visited the Beit Hatefutsot—Museum of the Diaspora in Tel Aviv, Israel, one will recall the magnificent scale models of the synagogues from all around the world. The Yeshiva University Museum houses those original scale models. Some of the scale models on permanent display include: Florence, Prague, Worms, Venice, China, and Elkins Park (Frank Lloyd Wright).

There are exhibitions which interpret Jewish life and history through traditional and contemporary art and artifacts.

The Yeshiva University Museum is open to the public Tuesday-Thursday from 11:00 a.m. to 5:00 p.m. and on Sunday from 12:00 noon to 6:00 p.m. For further information about the museum and guided tours, please call (212) 960-5390.

The former Congregation Anshe Slonim in the Lower East Side is the oldest synagogue structure in New York.

Temple Emanu-El, Fifth Avenue & 43rd Street, circa 1868.

TEMPLE EMANU-EL
Fifth Avenue and East 65th Street

Organized in 1845, Temple Emanu-El is New York's first Reform congregation. Its first location was in the Lower East Side. In 1868, Temple Emanu-El built its lavish twin-tower Moorish Revival synagogue on Fifth Avenue and East 43rd Street. It was designed by the architectural firm of Leopold Eidlitz and Henry Fernbach. The New York Times described the structure as the "architectural sensation of the city." This building's design inspired other Reform congregations to design their new temples in a similar motif. Some of these structures include: The Barnert Memorial Temple in Paterson, New Jersey (built in 1892 but demolished in the 1950s); Temple Emanu-El in Kingston, New York (built in 1892 but now used as a church); Emanu-El Congregation in Willemstad, Curaçao (built in 1867 but now used as a social hall). Temple Emanu-El's Fifth Avenue and 43rd Street structure was demolished in the 1920s.

In 1929, Temple Emanu-El built the world's largest Reform temple in the world. It is located on the corner of Fifth Avenue and East 65th Street, on the site of the old Vincent Astor mansion. The temple's vestibule walls and floors are Siena travertine; the ceiling is walnut. The walls of the building are actually bearing or self supporting. The main body of the auditorium is 77 feet wide, 150 feet in length, and 103 high. The seating capacity is 2,500.

The Sanctuary (Ark area) is 30 feet in depth and just over 40 feet wide, with a marble floor and marble (and mosaic) wainscot on the sides. Below the massive arch is the Ark, with columns of French Benou Jaume marble. The Ark doors are bronze, and the frame of the opening is of Siena marble with mosaic insets. The columns are crowned with small bronze tabernacles.

Twenty five feet above the Sanctuary is the choir loft, cut off by a pierced railing surmounted by marble columns of varied colors. The great organ, located above the chancel, is four manual, having 116 speaking stops, 50 couplers, 7,681 speaking pipes, 32 bell chimes, and 61 celestia bars.

The rose window, Gothic in design, is located above the main entrance on Fifth Avenue. The stained glass was designed in England. The twelve petals are symbolic of the twelve tribes of Israel. There are four stained glass windows in the main auditorium which depict historic synagogues. The former temple building, at Fifth Avenue and East 43rd Street and Temple Beth El, which merged with Temple Emanu-El in 1927 and was located on Fifth Avenue and East 76th Street, are portrayed at the southwest corner window (at eye level). The Alt-Nue Shul in Prague, Czechoslovakia and the Rashi Shul in Worms, West Germany are portrayed in stained glass at the northeast corner windows (about 15 feet above the floor).

The Beth El Chapel adjoins the main auditorium of Temple Emanu-El. It is named for Temple Beth El which merged with Emanu-El in 1927. This exquisite chapel is designed in the Byzantine motif. It is used for small weddings, and Bar and Bat Mitzvahs. The two domes of the chapel are supported by six columns of pink Westerly granite, while the side walls rest on arches springing from columns of Breche Oriental marble. Verdello marble is used for the wainscots.

The Sanctuary arch, in which blue is the dominant color, has a golden brown mosaic background with the Ten Commandments inscribed in blue, against which the Ark of wrought steel is set. The stained glass windows above the Ark, depicting the Holy Land, was designed by Louis Comfort Tiffany.

For information about services and tours of Temple Emanu-El, please call (212) 744-1400.

THE JEWISH MUSEUM
Fifth Avenue and East 92nd Street

Under the auspices of the Jewish Theological Seminary of America, the Jewish Museum has become the repository of the largest and most comprehensive collection of Jewish ceremonial objects in the world. The museum's notable items include: panels of the famous frescoes of Dura Europos, Syria; mosaics from ancient synagogues in Israel; several ancient Torah Arks and Torah curtains; and an exquisite collection of medieval Chanukah menorahs.

The Jewish Museum is housed in the old Warburg mansion. The museum is open to the public: Monday-Thursday from 12:00 noon to 5:00 p.m. and on Sunday from 11:00 a.m. to 6:00 p.m. For further information about exhibits, lectures and special events, please call (212) 860-1888.

Interior view of the landmark Park East Synagogue.

CONGREGATION ZICHRON EPHRAIM (PARK EAST SYNAGOGUE)
163 East 67th Street

Organized in 1888, its 1890 Moorish Revival building was designed by Schneider and Herter. (The Herter Brothers designed the Eldridge Street Synagogue in 1886.) This synagogue was founded by Jews from south Germany as an Orthodox congregation. It is one of the few synagogues still owned by the same congregation which built it. It is an official New York City landmark. It is located directly across the street from the Russian Mission to the United Nations and is the scene of many anti-Soviet rallies.

TEMPLE BETH EL OF BOROUGH PARK
4802 15th Avenue

Organized as a surburban community at the turn of the century, Borough Park has today been referred to the "Jerusalem of America." It has the largest concentration of Jews in the metropolitan area. There are approximately 100,000 Jews living in Borough Park. It is the world headquarters of many Chassidic groups including the Bobover, Munkacher, Gerer, and Belzer. The neighborhood has become the home of many recent Russian immigrants. On Sundays, 13th Avenue becomes a shopper's marketplace.

Temple Beth El, the first congregation in the area, was organized in 1902. Its first location was at 4022 12th Avenue. That building now houses Congregation Anshe Lubawitz. In 1920, Beth El moved to its present location. It is housed in a spectacular Moorish structure on 15th Avenue, at 48th Street. The structure was designed by the architectural firm of Shampan & Shampan and is said to possess near-perfect acoustics. Notable spiritual leaders include Rabbi Dr. Israel Schorr, and cantors Herschman, Moshe Kousevitzki, and Moshe Stern.

Temple Beth El of Borough Park was built in 1920.

LUBAVITCH CHASSIDIC WORLD HEADQUARTERS
770 Eastern Parkway

The simple brick building on Eastern Parkway, in the Crown Heights section of Brooklyn, houses the world headquarters of the Lubavitch Chassidic Movement. Its spiritual leader, Rabbi Menachem M. Schneerson, is known to his followers as the "Rebbe." The Lubavitch Movement was the pioneering force in establishing the Jewish Day School system in the United States. These Chabad Lubavitch centers cater to the needs of the respective Jewish communities. Its numerous centers and activities throughout the world reach out to Jews of all backgrounds. The Lubavitch Movement is involved in assisting newly-arrived Jewish immigrants from Russia and Iran. The Movement has an outreach program which involves the use of mobile vans, known as "Mitzvah Tanks." The "Tanks" travel throughout the world and help Jews perform mitzvahs (commandments of Jewish law).

The immediate area around 770 Eastern Parkway is an oasis of Jewish life. On certain anniversary dates, the Lubavitcher Rebbe delivers public addresses, called "Fabrengens," where thousands of his Chassidic followers gather to celebrate. The singing and dancing is interspersed with messages delivered by the Rebbe. The Fabrengens are televised live on cable television networks and are transmitted live via telecommunication satellites to radio stations throughout the world.

Notable dates of special Fabrengens occur, as per the Jewish calendar, on the 6th of Tishri, 19th of Kislev, 10th of Shevat, 11th of Nissan, 12th of Tamuz, and on the 18th of Elul.

There are exact replicas of the front façade of 770 Eastern Parkway in Kfar Chabad, in Israel and in Westwood (Los Angeles), California. For further information about the Lubavitch Movement and tours of the Lubavitch World Headquarters, please call (718) 774-4000 or (718) 778-4270.

770 Eastern Parkway is the world headquarters of the Lubavitch Chassidic Movement.

CONGREGATION DERECH EMUNAH
199 Beach 67th Street

The oldest functioning synagogue in continuous use in Queens, Congregation Derech Emunah, was designed by architect William A. Lambert in 1905. He is said to have modelled the synagogue after the famous Touro Synagogue of 1763 in Newport, Rhode Island, the oldest extant synagogue in the country. The Georgian character of Derech Emunah synagogue relates somewhat to the Touro Synagogue, but the main massing of the two buildings is quite different. The shingle-sided Congregation Derech Emunah synagogue is representative of what the prominent architectural historian, Vincent Scully, has termed the "shingle style." Popular in resort towns such as Newport and Nantucket during the late 19th century, the shingle style characterized many seaside residences and was typical of the Colonial Revival architecture of the period. The synagogue combines the use of shingles with a variety of elegant neo-Georgian details, creating a distinctive and handsome building which is reminiscent of American colonial architecture.

Congregation Derech Emunah is an official Historic Landmark.

This synagogue is an impressive reminder of the importance of this section of the Rockaways during the early twentieth century, when the area was a stylish Jewish summer-resort colony known as Arverne-by-the-Sea. The building has been declared an official New York City Historic Landmark.

INTERNATIONAL SYNAGOGUE
John F. Kennedy International Airport

Located in the middle of Kennedy International Airport (Chapel area), the International Synagogue was designed in 1963 by the architectural firm of Bloch & Hesse. Designed as a sculptural abstraction, this synagogue blends in well with its environment, where architectural masterpieces have been assembled as a showcase for the international traveller. Some of the architects represented at Kennedy Airport include, I.M. Pei, Eero Saarinen, and Skidmore, Owings & Merrill.

The interior rendition of the Ten Commandments on bronze plaques was designed by world-renowned artist Chaim Gross. The stained glass windows flanking the Ark were designed by the Israeli artist, Ami Shamir. The spatial design of the interior closely resembles that of North America's first synagogue, the Mill Street Synagogue, in Lower Manhattan. Under the auspices of the New York Board of Rabbis, the synagogue is intended to serve the needs of the approximately 3,000 Jewish workers at the airport. There were plans to demolish all three chapels (Jewish, Catholic, and Protestant) and move them within a new structure which would also house administrative offices as well as additional parking facilities. Those plans were put on hold after community protests were voiced.

Adjoining the Jewish Chapel is an exquisite Jewish Museum. There are religious artifacts which were donated by Jewish communities from all parts of the globe. There is a portable Holy Ark which was used in the battlefields of Europe during World War

II by the United States Army. The three small Torahs housed in that small Ark have each witnessed a dramatic period of Jewish history. One Torah was used in Ellis Island by newly-arrived immigrants. Another was buried in the Berlin Jewish cemetery during the rule of the Nazi Party in Germany. The third Torah was tossed atop a chandelier in a Roumanian synagogue in the process of a game the Nazis were playing. They had a "game of catch" with the sacred objects of the synagogue! The Torah sat up in the chandelier for the duration of the war.

For information about tours of the International Synagogue, please call (718) 656-5044.

The Ark in the International Synagogue at Kennedy Airport was designed by Chaim Gross.

PORT CHESTER

CONGREGATION KNESES TIFERETH ISRAEL
575 King Street

Architect Philip Johnson decided that his synagogue should be built for the maximum appreciation of the entire congregation. He created a rectangular sanctuary lit by lance-like stained glass windows, covered by a tent-like falsework vault and partitioned during normal services with a seven foot screen. For High Holy Day services, the screen is removed, and the room functions as the religious environment. Spatial hierarchy was a concern for Johnson in this building, as demonstrated by the small, oval-shaped lobby which not only dramatizes the entrance to the religious space, but provides a permanent juxtaposition to the severe rectangular sanctuary.

Rather than compromise the spartan effect of the rectangle and oval on their small knoll, Johnson dispensed with the offices underground and behind the sanctuary—thus preserving the monumental aesthetic. Executed in the Bauhaus style, the Port Chester synagogue building is remarkably similar in appearance to Johnson's famous glass house in New Canaan, Connecticut. As such, it has been widely discussed as one of the architect's pivotal early designs and as the first International Style synagogue.

PORT JERVIS

CEJWIN CAMPS
Route 209

One of the earliest Jewish camps in the Catskills, Cejwin was organized in 1919. Its synagogue building contains an exquisite mural depicting the establishment of the State of Israel in 1948. Due to economic difficulties, Cejwin was forced to sell about two thirds of its 600-acre camp. Part of the former D & H (Delaware & Hudson) Canal with its tow path, used by mule teams to pull barges alongside the canal, was located within the Cejwin Camp grounds. If you follow the old canal bed, you will see the suspension bridge designed by John Roebling, of Brooklyn Bridge fame, at Minisink Ford. At that location, the D & H Canal actually crossed the Delaware River via the suspension bridge!

ROCHESTER

TEMPLE B'RITH KODESH
2956 Elmwood Avenue

Located in the suburb community of Brighton, Temple B'rith Kodesh is the oldest congregation in the Rochester area. It was organized in 1848, the year of a revolution in France and turmoil in Germany, where a democratic movement was being crushed. It was the year of the Gold Rush, the year that women's rights champions held a meeting in Rochester, and the year the gaslight era began in the city.

The first synagogue for the congregation was built in 1876 and was located on St. Paul Street. Originally, the congregation followed the Orthodox ritual. In 1883, the Temple introduced a new ritual almost entirely in English. It was one of the first congregations in the United States to adopt this practice. In 1897, a new temple was constructed on the corner of Gibbs and Grove Streets. It was designed as a fielstone Romanesque Revival structure.

In 1962, Temple B'rith Kodesh dedicated its present building which was designed by Pietro Belluschi. The synagogue is roofed

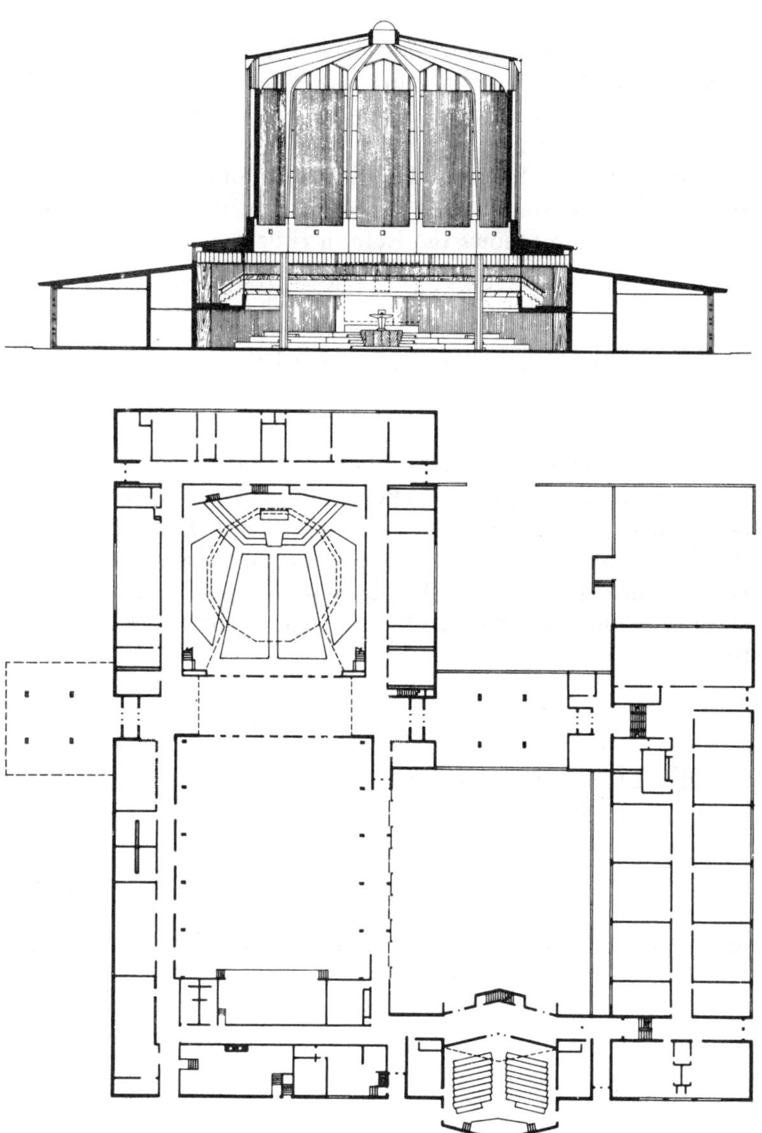

Rochester's Brith Kodesh, elevations and plans.

by a twelve-sided drum dome which is part of a flexible plan complex centered around a courtyard. The main sanctuary is detailed with redwood and brick reminiscent of the early works of Frank Lloyd Wright.

The exquisite Ark was designed by Louise Kaisch and is a sculptural manifestation, cast in bronze, depicting Biblical scenes. The congregation follows the Reform ritual.

CONGREGATION KIPEL VOLLIN
472 Ormond Street

This synagogue was originally located on a different site. It was transported intact to this location but appears to have been put down backwards! The front façade faces the back yard. Apparently, this Orthodox congregation insisted on having the Ark face in an easterly direction as prescribed by Jewish law. The front of the synagogue building was therefore turned around to accommodate these requirements.

LEOPOLD STREET SHUL
30 Leopold Street

This synagogue dates from 1866, making it the oldest synagogue structure in New York State, outside of New York City. It is presently used by the Black Hebrews. The building has been designated a National Historic Landmark.

SCHENECTADY

ADATH ISRAEL CONGREGATION

The original location of Adath Israel Congregation was at 872 Albany Street. That 1926 structure now houses a furniture warehouse. The Hebrew name entablature above the front entrance is still visible. Inside the building there is wall-to-wall furniture. However, one can still see where the old Ark stood and the women's gallery is still untouched. The second location of Adath Israel was at 816 State Street. That 1937 structure is now used by the Schenectady Light Opera Company.

SYRACUSE

TEMPLE SOCIETY OF CONCORD
501 University Avenue

This is the second oldest congregation in the state, outside of New York City. It was founded in 1839. The Classical Revival building was built in 1910. Proceed down the hill and you will discover two former synagogues.

TEMPLE ADATH JESHURUN
601 South Crouse Avenue

This Conservative congregation is presently located in the suburbs, at 450 Kimber Road and is housed in a 1970 pyramidal structure designed by Percival Goodman. The original downtown building is still extant and is used as the Syracuse University Playhouse. Continue down the hill to the next corner...

TEMPLE BETH EL
601 Irving Place

All Judaic traces on the front façade have been carefully eradicated. The building, originally built for Temple Beth El, is now used as a church.

TROY

TEMPLE BERITH SHOLOM
167 Third Street

This Romanesque Revival structure was built in 1870. It is the second oldest synagogue structure still used as a Jewish house of worship in the state, outside of New York City. The two wide doors on the street level, at one time, served as the stables for the horses and carriages.

Temple Berith Sholom was built in 1870.

WESTCHESTER

There were Jewish merchants as early as 1715 in Rye, New Rochelle, and Pleasantville. The permanent Jewish congregations were organized in Yonkers—Hebrew Benevolent Society (1890) and Congregation Oheb Zedek (1903), Mount Vernon—Congregation Brothers of Israel (1891), Ossining—Congregation Sons of Israel (1891), Port Chester (1892), and Tarrytown (1893).

WEST POINT

JEWISH CHAPEL

The United States Military Academy at West Point was established in 1802. One of the first graduate Corps of Cadets was Simon Levy. Samuel Noah, West Point's thirtieth graduate, joined Captain Benjamin Dunning's company defending Brooklyn during the War of 1812. During the Civil War, Confederate General Abraham Myers served as Quartermaster General in Richmond while Union General Alfred Mordecai, Jr. fought galliantly in the field. Both men had been cadets. Nearly one hundred Jewish West Pointers commanded units during World War I. Jewish West Pointers served in World War II, Korea, and Vietnam.

The Jewish Chapel was dedicated in May, 1984. It was designed by Max Abramovitz, of the architectural firm of Abramovitz-Harris-Kingsland. This firm was also responsible for such projects as the United Nations, Lincoln Center, Brandeis University Chapel, and Temple Beth Zion (Buffalo, New York). New Hampshire granite and limestone are used throughout and create a modern structure in the military gothic tradition. The gallery and museum displays the contribution Jews have made to America and its military forces. The Jewish Chapel is open weekdays; Monday-Friday from 9:00-4:30 p.m. and on weekends and holidays from 12:00 noon - 4:00 p.m.

The Jewish Chaplain, Rabbi M.A. Abramowitz, will be happy to greet all visitors. For further information, please call (914) 446-7706 or (914) 938-4106.

The West Point Jewish Chapel was dedicated in 1984.

GRAVE OF MICKEY MARCUS

Colonel David "Mickey" Marcus graduated from West Point in 1924. He was born in Brownsville, Brooklyn. Before Israel's War of Independence in 1948, he was smuggled into Palestine by the Jewish Agency. He dictated the first military manuals which were published in Hebrew. He set up officers' training schools and advised the Hagannah on the purchase and use of arms. Mickey Marcus was, in effect, one of the creators of the Israeli Defense Forces. While commanding Israeli troops he was killed by "friendly fire," when he did not know the correct password requested by a Hebrew speaking Israeli soldier.

Colonel David "Mickey" Marcus is buried alongside his wife in the West Point Cemetery. The location of the gravestones are just behind the Post Chapel (non-sectarian), about 50 feet to the left, just off the paved road. There is a bronze plaque which was presented by the State of Israel honoring this "soldier for all humanity"—in recognition for his sacrifice for the establishment of the State of Israel.

The grave of Colonel David "Mickey" Marcus in the West Point Cemetery.

THE OLD NEIGHBORHOODS

The following list contains information about synagogues which are no longer functioning as Jewish houses of worship. These addresses are located in the old sections of the city or town. It is advisable to take extra precautions while driving through these neighborhoods.

Albany Congregation Ahavath Sholom *173 Sherman Avenue*
Congregation Beth El Jacob *Herkimer & Franklin Streets*
Temple Beth Emeth *Lancaster & Swan Streets*
Jewish Community Center *111 Washington Avenue*
Congregation Sons of Abraham *74 South Ferry Street*

Alden Terrace Jewish Community Center *417 Hendricson Street*

Amityville Beth Sholom Center *39 Greene Avenue*

Amsterdam Congregation Sons of Israel *19 Liberty Street*

Auburn Congregation B'nai Israel *18 Seminary Avenue*

Babylon Congregation Beth Sholom *George Street*

Batavia Congregation Shomrei Emunah *232 South Liberty Street*

Binghamton Hebrew Brothers' Association *145 Susquehanna Street*
Hebrew Reform Society *Merlord Building*
Congregation Sons of Israel *12 Water Street*
Jewish Community Center *155 Front Street*
Temple Israel *18 Exchange Place*

Brooklyn Ahavath Scholom Beth Aron *98 Scholes Street*
Congregation Emanuel *Fourth Avenue & 49th Street*
Congregation B'nai Sholom *327 Ninth Street* *401 Ninth Street*

B'nai Jacob *136 Prospect Avenue*
Congregation Shaare Zedek *Kingston Avenue & Park Place, 767 Putnam Avenue*
Congregation Ahavat Chesed *742 Jefferson Avenue*
Congregation Tiferes Israel *Willoughby & Throop Avenues*
Chevre Kadische Congregation *93 Moore Street*
Temple Petach Tikvah *Lincoln Place & Rochester Avenue*
Congregation Mount Sinai *305 Schermerhorn Street*
Other Locations *(without congregation names)*

691 Lafayette Avenue
569, 665, 730 Willoughby Avenue
476 Koskiusko Street
298 Howard Avenue
726 Gates Avenue
136 Stanhope Street

188 Stockton Street
928 DeKalb Avenue
592 Marcy Avenue
16 Putnam Avenue
52 Stuyvesant Avenue
60 Woodbine Street

Lenox Road & East 55th Street
407 East 53rd Street
2059 Beford Avenue
153 Ocean Avenue
810 East 49th Street
724 Driggs Avenue
904 Bedford Avenue

151 Woodruff Avenue
2310 Cortelyou Road
672 Lefferts Avenue
35 East 52nd Street
777 Schenectady Avenue
888 East 56th Street
211 Ocean Avenue

954 Jefferson Avenue
Sumner & Van Buren Avenues
1372 Gates Avenue
Clermont & Willoughby Avenues

305 East 21st Street
347 East 49th Street
955 Manhattan Avenue

Buffalo Congregation Ahavath Achim *833 Fillmore Street*
Congregation Ahavath Sholom *407 Jefferson Avenue*
Congregation Anshe Lubavitch *Pratt Street*
Congregation Beth Achim *851 Fillmore Street*
Beth El Temple *151 Richmond Avenue*
Congregation Beth Jacob *Clinton & Walnut Streets*
Temple Beth Zion *599 Delaware Avenue*
Congregation Brith Sholom *171 Pine Street*
1052 Hertel Avenue

Temple Israel, located at Bedford & Lafayette Avenues, in Brooklyn's Bedford-Stuyvesant section served as a traffic court before its demolition in the 1960s.

Temple Emanu-El *383 Colvin Avenue*
Congregation Brith Israel *Hickory Street (between William & Clinton Streets)*

Centerville (now Woodridge) Congregation Anshe Centerville

Catskill Temple Israel *Main Street*

Cohoes Congregation Beth Jacob *294 Remsen Street*

Chappaqua Temple Beth El *Broadway & Locust Street*

College Point (Queens) *Congregation Agudas Achim*

21st Avenue & 124th Street

Croton-on-Hudson Temple Israel *Glengary Road*

Elmira Congregation B'nai Israel *High Street*
Congregation Shomrei Hadath *Orchard Street*
Talmud Torah *Sullivan Street*

Fulton Congregation Tifereth Israel *First Street*

Glen Cove Congregation Tifereth Israel *Continental Place & Henderson Avenue*

Fort Washington Temple Beth Israel *138 Bayview Avenue*

Glens Falls Congregation Shaare Tefila *10 Jay Street*

Gloversville Congregation Knesseth Israel *114 East Fulton Street*
Jewish Community Center *28 East Fulton Street*

Greenport Tifereth Israel Congregation *4th & Front Streets*

Harlem Adath Jacob Anshe Slabodka of Harlem *18 West 114th Street*
Agudath Israel *1 West 113th Street*
Temple Ansche Chesed *1881 Seventh Avenue*
Chevre Beth Hamedrash D'Sfardim D'Harlem *(8) 41 West 113th Street*
Talmudical Institute of Harlem *56 West 114th Street*
Temple Israel of Harlem *Lenox Avenue & 120th Street*
Mount Zion Congregation *67 East 113th Street*
Nachlath Zvi *170 East 114th Street*
Adath Jeshurun *112 East 110th Street*
Anshe Chesed *160 East 112th Street*
Melakai Sholaum *170 East 114th Street*
Khol Adath Kurland *25 West 115th Street*
Chevre Bikur Cholim of Harlem *80 East 110th Street*
Chevre B'nai Solomon Anshei Zaimel *22 West 114th Street*
Chevre Etz Chaim *41 West 113th Street*
Khal Adath Jeshurun of Harlem *63 East 113th Street*
Kol Israel Anshei Poland *24 West 114th Street*
Beth Hakneseth Mishkan Israel *85 East 110th Street*
Congregation Mleah Sholom *170 East 114th Street*
Mount Nebo Congregation *562 West 150th Street*
Chevre Shaarei Tephila *78 East 11th Street*

Shaarei Zedek of Harlem *23 West 118th Street*
Congregation Shearith B'nai Israel *22 East 113th Street*
Kehila Kedosha Shearith Israel Mi-Turkey *132 East 111th Street*
First Hungarian Congregation Ohab Zedek *18 West 116th Street*
Chevre B'nai Adam *100 West 116th Street*
Society B'nai Elijah Anshei Zagar *107 West 116th Street*

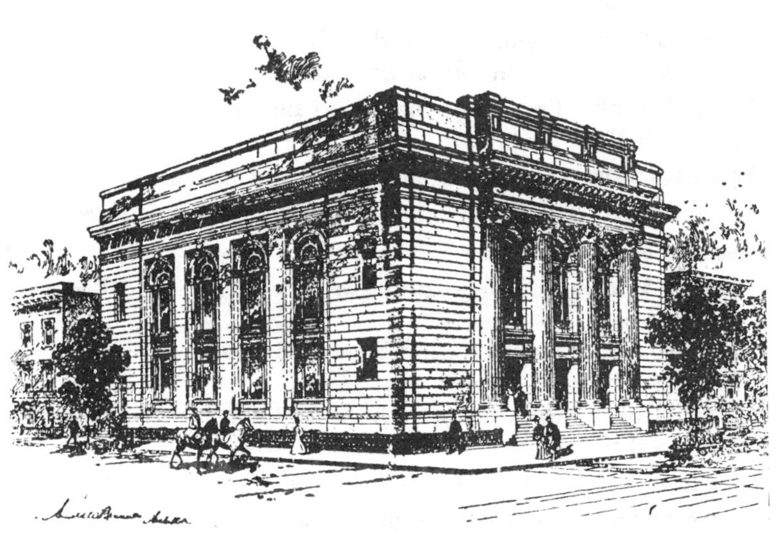

Temple Israel of Harlem was organized in 1875.

Haverstraw Congregation Sons of Israel *37 Clove Street*

Hempstead Congregation Beth David *94 Fulton Street*
Nassau Community Temple *165 Woodfield Road*

Hoosick Falls Congregation Ohav Sholom *Classic Street*

Hudson Congregation Anshe Emeth *4 Warren Street*
Congregation Tiferes Israel *South 1st Street*

Kings Park Kings Park Synagogue *135 Main Street*

Kingston Congregation Agudas Achim *24 West Union Street*
Congregation Ahavath Israel *72 Broadway*
72 Wurts Street
Jewish Community Center *265 Wall Street*
Temple Emanu-El *50 Abeel Street*

Lake Placid Lake Placid Synagogue *418 Main Street*

Liberty Ferndale Synagogue *Liberty Gardens A3*
Hebrew Congregation *West Broadway*

Lindenhurst Congregation Beth Jacob *74 John Street*
Hebrew Congregation *West Broadway*

Long Beach East End Synagogue *East Park Avenue & Roosevelt Boulevard*

Middletown Hebrew Congregation *13 Linden Avenue*

Monticello Jewish Community Center *196 Broadway*

Mount Kisco Hebrew Congregation *Stewart Avenue*

Mount Vernon Congregation Brothers of Israel *10 South 8th Street*
Congregation Emanu-El *203 Summit Avenue*
120 East Prospect Avenue
Jewish Community Center *230 South Columbus Avenue*
Fleetwood Synagogue *11 East Broad Street*

Nanuet Hebrew Center *Main Street*

Newburgh Congregation Agudas Achim *Montgomery & 4th Streets, 259 Grand Street*
Congregation Sons of Israel *25 William Street*
Temple Beth Jacob *90 South Street*

New Rochelle Temple Israel *36 Banks Street,*

456 Webster Avenue
Congregation Anshei Sholom *Bonnafoy Place*

Niagra Falls Temple Beth Israel *Cedar Avenue & 4th Street*

Oceanside Jewish Center *90 Brower Street*

Ogdensburg Congregation Anshe Zophen *Ford Street*

Olean Hebrew Congregation *133 North Union Street*

Ossining Congregation Sons of Israel *61 Durston Avenue, 18 Waller Avenue*

Peekskill Congregation of Peekskill *10 Union Avenue*

Plattsburgh Congregation Beth Israel *Oak Street*

Port Chester Congregation Kneses Israel *Willet Avenue*
Lake Street Synagogue
Congregation Tifereth Israel *Traverse Avenue*

Port Jervis Congregation Agudath Achim *Seward & Ball Streets*

Poughkeepsie Congregation Brethren of Israel *Vassar & Mill Streets*
Congregation B'nai Israel *39 South Bridge Street*
Jewish Community Center *54 North Hamilton Street*
Congregation Shomrei Hadat *52 Noxon Street, 16 South Bridge Street*
Temple Beth El *12 Montgomery Street*

Riverhead Congregation Agudas Achim *Union Street*

Rochester Congregation Agudas Achim Nusach Ari *171 Chatham Street, 27 Morris Street*
Congregation Anshe Poland *34 Pryor Street*
Congregation Atz Chaim *84 Herman Street*
Temple Berith Kodesh *117 Gibbs Street*
Congregation Beth El *Park Avenue & Meigs Street*
Cong Beth Hakneses Hachodosh *168 Chatham Street, 408 Ormond Street*
Beth Hamedrash Hagadol *30 Hanover Street*

Congregation Beth Israel *30 Leopold Street*
Beth Joseph Center *1150 Saint Paul Street*
Chatham Congregation *202 Chatham Street*

Rome Congregation Adas Israel *109 South James Street, 705 Hickory Street*

Saranac Lake Jewish Community Center *13 Church Street*

Schenectady Congregation Agudas Achim *165 Nott Terrace*
Jewish Community Center *300 Germania Avenue*
Congregation Ohev Zedek *506 Hamilton Street*
Congregation Shaare Shomayim *12 North College Street*

Spring Valley Congregation Ohev Sholom *34 Henrietta Place*
Temple Beth El *15 Madison Avenue*

Syracuse Congregation Adath Israel *816 South State Street*
Congregation Adath Yeshurun *711 South State Street*
601 South Crouse Avenue
Congregation Anshe Sfard *815 Orange Street*
Beth Hamedrash Hagadol *907 Orange Street*
Congregation Beth Israel *721 Grape Street*
Congregation Chevre Shas *Harrison & State Streets*
Congregation Poale Tzedek *817 Almond Street*
Congregation Tifereth Isarael *727 South State Street*
Temple Beth El *601 Irving Avenue*

Tarrytown Hebrew Congregation *Valley Street*

Troy Congregation Shaare Tefila *9 Division Street*
Temple Beth El *1713 5th Avenue*
Jewish Community Center *87 1st Street*

Tuckahoe Genesis Hebrew Center *Crestwood Station*
Midchester Jewish Center *236 Grandview Boulevard*

Tupper Lake Cong Beth Joseph *Lake Street*

Utica Congregation House of David *120 Broadway*
Congregation House of Israel *Whitesboro & Washington Streets*

Congregation House of Jacob *29 Seneca Street, 14 Clinton Place*
Congregation Shomre Shabbes *310 Liberty Street*
Congregation Union of Brothers *Broadway*
Temple Emanu-El *219 Hillcrest Manor Court*
Congregation Tifereth Zvi *313 James Street*

Watertown Congregation Degel Israel *Prospect Street*

White Plains Temple Israel *Fischer & Lexington Avenues*
Hebrew Free School *74 Martin Avenue*

Woodmere Woodmere Minnionaires *29 Woodmere Boulevard*

Yonkers Congregation Agudath Achim *25 Hudson Street*
Congregation Ohav Zedek *9 Prospect Street*
Congregation Anshe Zedek *7 Ingraham Street*
Jewish Community Center *122 South Broadway*
Congregation Sons of Israel *155 Elliott Avenue*
Temple Emanu-El *63 Hamilton Avenue*

KOSHER RESTAURANTS

Albany Kosher Pizza *483 Washington Avenue (518) 465-5638*
Hagelu Kosher Grocery *544 Delware Avenue 434-3354*
Kagan Grocery *448 Madison Avenue 449-7961*
Capitol Bakery *1028 Broadway 465-1561*

Baldwin Ben's Deli *933 Atlantic Avenue (516) 868-2072*
Mazur Kosher Meats *909 Atlantic Avenue 623-8252*

Bellmore Sammy's Kosher Pizza *2492 Merrick Avenue (516) 783-8193*

Binghamton Kosher Market *14 Conklin Avenue (914) 723-5331*

Buffalo Chabad House *3292 Main Street*
2501 North Forest Road (716) 668-1642
Silverstien's Deli *677 Niagra Boulevard 836-0762*

Cedarhurst Burger Nosh *530 Central Avenue (516) 569-6183*
Delicious Kosher Dairy Restaurant *698 Central Avenue 569-6725*
Jacob's Ladder *83 Spruce Street 569-3373*
King David Deli *550 Central Avenue 569-2890*
Sabra Pizza *560 Central Avenue 569-1563*

Commack Pastrami-N-Friend *110A Commack Road (516) 499-9537*
Commack Kosher Meats *132 Jericho Turnpike 543-2300*

East Meadow Brodie's Deli *1518 Front Street*

Franklin Square Rosebrook Caterers *366 Dogwood Avenue (516) 483-3361*

Great Neck Ari's Take-Out *31 North Station Place (516) 466-2565*
Gel of Great Neck *503 Middle Neck Road 487-5886*

Kingston Deising Bakery *109-117 North Front Street (914) 338-7503*

Lawrence Super Sol Market *330 Central Avenue (516) 295-3300*

Value Plus Kosher Market *290 Burnside Avenue 239-5458*

Long Beach S & S Bagel Cafe *76 West Park Avenue (516) 431-5789*

Pick-N-Save *Kosher Foods 172 East Park Avenue 889-2828*

Malverne Malverne Kosher Meats *370 Hempstead Avenue (516) 599-1070*

Merrick Long Island Kosher Meats *1984 Merrick Road (516) 378-6463*

Monsey Kosher Delight *82 Route 59 (914) 356-9555*

Meal Mart *41 Main Street 352-9008*

Ram Caterers *20B Robert Pitt Drive 352-0733*

Mount Kisco Kosher Deli *41 South Moger Avenue (914) 666-6600*

Kosher Grocery *Pines Bridge Road 666-8629*

Mount Vernon The Pelhams *675 East Lincoln Avenue (914) 667-1116*

Westchester Glatt Kosher Market *25 West Grand Street 664-4313*

Saber's Cake Nook *33 West Grand Street 664-5796*

Newburgh Katz's Bakery (c/o Shop Rite) *North Plank Road (914) 561-0073*

New Rochelle Kosher Konnection *1284 North Avenue (914) 636-5636*

New York City (Manhattan) Benjamin of Tudela *307 Amsterdam Avenue (212) 496-5018*

Bernsteins-on-Essex *135 Essex Street 473-3900*

Cafe Masada *1239 1st Avenue 998-0950*

Cheers Kosher Italian Restaurant *120 West 41st Street 840-8810*

Dairy Planet *182 Broadway* *227-8252*
Famous Dairy Restaurant *222 West 72nd Street* *595-8487*
Greener Pastures *117 East 60th Street* *832-3212*
La Kasbah *70 West 71st Street* *769-1690*
Levana's *141 West 69th Street* *877-8457*
Maccabbeem *147 West 47th Street* *575-0226*
Jerusalem II *1375 Broadway* *819-1891*
Marrakesh West *149 Bleeker Street* *777-8911*
Edible Pursuits *325 5th Avenue* *686-5330*
Madras Palace *104 Lexington Avenue* *532-3314*
Moshe Peking *40 West 37th Street* *594-6500*
Ratner's Dairy Restaurant *138 Delancey Street* *677-5588*
Lou G. Siegel's *209 West 38th Street* *921-4433*
Verve Naturelle *157 West 57th Street* *265-2255*

NEW YORK CITY - BROOKLYN

Carmel Restaurant *523 Kings Highway (718) 339-0172*
Edna's Restaurant *125 Church Avenue 438-8207*
Famous Dairy Restaurant *4818 13th Avenue 435-4201*
Glatt Chow *1204 Avenue J 692-0001*
The Gourmet Cafe *1622 Coney Island Avenue 338-5825*
Kings Deli *924 Kings Highway 336-7500*
Kosher Castle *5006 13th Avenue 871-2100*
Kosher Delight *1223 Avenue J 377-6873*
4600 13th Avenue 435-8500
Little Jerusalem *502 Avenue M 376-9831*
Me "V" Me Restaurant *1521 Kings Highway*
Shang Chai Rstaurant *2189 Flatbush Avenue 377-6100*
Sparkling Night *1416 Avenue J 253-7440*
Tacos Olé *1932 Kings Highway 339-1116*
Tel Aviv Restaurant *1121 Avenue J 258-9583*
Yunkee *1424 Elm Avenue 627-0072*
New York Steak House *5908 Avenue N 531-1783*

NEW YORK CITY - QUEENS

Burger Nosh *69-74 Main Street (718) 793-6927*
Golan Restaurant *97-28 63rd Road 897-7522*
Tain Lee Chow *72-24 Main Street 268-0960*
The Flame Lapid *97-04 Queens Boulevard 275-1403*
Sholom Japan *67-05 Main Street*

NEW YORK CITY - BRONX

Dexter's Restaurant *5652 Mosholu Avenue (212) 548-0440*

Oceanside Hunki's Pizza *3300 Long Beach Road (516) 766-3666*

Orangeburg Palisade Kosher Deli *6 Orangetown Shopping Center (914) 359-4880*

Patchogue Deli King *85 West Main Street (516) 475-3364*

Plainview Kosher Meat Farm *365A South Oyster Bay Boulevard (516) 931-6446*
Pearl Bakery *26 Manetto Hill Mall 935-5225*

Rochester Fox's Deli *3000 Winton Road South (716) 427-8200*
Jewish Community Center *1200 Edgewood Avenue* 461-2000
Israel's Bakery *1248 North Clinton Avenue* 342-6060
Malek's Bakery *1795 Monroe Avenue* 461-1720

Ronkonkoma Ben's Kosher Restaurant *135 Alexander Avenue (516) 979-8770*

Roslyn Heights Bon Apetit *444 Willis Avenue (516) 621-0402*

Sayville Bagels de Lox *372 Montauk Highway (516) 563-2716*

Schenectady New Mount Pleasant Bakery *941 Crane Street (518) 374-7577*

Smithtown Phil's Kosher Chinese Restaurant (516) 360-8490

Spring Valley Gartner's Inn *Hungry Hollow Road (914) 356-0875*
Oneg Pizza *33 Maple Avenue 356-3560*

Suffern Glatt Stop *191 Route 59 (914) 357-9594*

Syracuse Martin's & Tenenbaum's *2914 East Genesee Street (315) 446-3254*

Syracuse Pickles Unlimited *4469 Eat Genesee Street 445-1294*

Valley Stream Parkmore Kosher Meats *951 Rosedale Road (516) 791-3086*

West Hempstead Hunki's Pizza *338 Hempstead Avenue (516) 538-6655*

White Plains Ken-Mar Kosher Market *333 Mamaroneck Avenue (914) 761-8046*

Woodmere Pizza Pious *1063 Broadway (516) 295-2050*

SYNAGOGUES

Albany 12208 Congregation Beth Emeth (R) *100 Academy Road (518) 436-9761*
Congregation B'nai Sholom (R) *420 Whitehall Road 482-5283*
Chabad House (O) *122 South Main St. 482-5781*
Temple Israel - Knesseth Israel (C) *600 New Scotland Avenue 483-7858*
Congregation Ohav Sholom (C) *New Krumkill Road 489-4706*
Congregation Shomray Torah (O) *463 New Scotland Avenue*

Amenia 12501 Congregation Beth David (R) *Main Street*

Amherst 14226 Temple Sinai (R) *50 Alberta Drive (716)834-0708*

Amityville 11701 Beth Sholom Center (C) *79 County Line Road*

Amsterdam 12010 Congregation Songs of Israel (C) *355 Guy Park Avenue (518) 842-8690*
Temple of Israel (R) *8 Mohawk Place*

Atlantic Beach 11509 Jewish Center (O) *Nassau Avenue & Park Street (516) 371-0972*

Auburn 13021 Congregation B'nai Israel (C) *8 John Smith Avenue (315) 253-6675*

Babylon 11702 Congregation Beth Sholom (C) *441 Deer Park Avenue (516) 587-5650*

Baldwin 11510 Jewish Center (C) *885 East Seaman Avenue 223-8688*
South Baldwin Jewish Center (C) *2959 Grand Avenue 223-8688*

Batavia 14020 Temple Emanu-El (C) *124 Bank Street*

Bay Shore 11706 Temple Beth Am (C) *28 6th Avenue*
Bay Shore Jewish Center (C) *34 North Clinton Avenue (516) 665-1140*
Sinai Reform Temple (R) *39 Brentwood Road 665-5755*

Beacon 12508 Beacon Hebrew Alliance (C) *55 Fishkill Avenue (914) 831-2012*

Bedford Hills 10507 Yeshiva Ohel Shmuel (O) *Haines Road (914) 241-2700*

Bellmore 11710 Bellmore Jewish Center (C) *2550 South Centre Avenue (516) 781-3072*
Temple Beth El (C) *1373 Bellmore Road 781-2650*
East Bay Reform Temple (R) *2569 East Merrick Road 781-5599*

Bethpage 11714 Jewish Community Center (C) *600 Broadway (516) 938-7909*

Binghamton 13903 Congregation Beth David (O) *39 Riverside Drive (607) 722-1793*
Temple Concord (R) *9 Riverside Drive 723-7355*
Temple Israel (C) *Deerfield Place 723-7461*

Brewster 10509 Temple Beth Elohim (R) *Route 22 (914) 279-4585*

Briarcliff Manor 10510 Congregation Sons of Israel (C) *1666 Pleasantville Road (914) 762-2700*

Buffalo 14221 Ahavas Achim Lubavitch Synagogue (O) *345 Tacoma Avenue (716) 877-5790*
Congregation Bais Kneses Hagadol (O) *50 Starin Avenue 835-4139*
Congregation Beth Abraham (O) *1073 Elmwood Avenue*
Temple Beth Am (R) *4660 Sheridan Drive 663-8877*
Temple Beth Zion (R) *805 Delaware Avenue 886-7150*
Congregation Brith Israel - Anshe Emes (O) *1237 Hertel Avenue*
Congregation Brith Sholom (O) *787 Delaware Avenue 885-7848*

Catskill 12414 Temple Israel (R) *Spring Street (518) 943-5758*

Cedarhurst 11516 Bais Medrash (O) *504 West Broadway (516) 569-1971*
Temple Beth El (C) *Broadway & Locust Avenue 569-2700*
Sephardic Temple (C) *Branch Boulevard & Haley Drive 295-4644*
Young Israel (O) *8 Spruce Street 569-3324*

Center Moriches 11934 Jewish Center (C) *North Ocean Avenue (516) 878-0388*

Chappaqua 10514 Temple Beth El (R) *220 South Bedford Avenue (914) 238-3928*

Cold Spring Harbor 11724 Congregation Kehillath Sholom (Rec) *58 Goose Hill Road (516) 234-0548 Avenue*

Commack 11725 Temple Beth David (R) *100 Hauppauge Road (516) 499-0915*
Commack Jewish Center (C) *83 Shirley Court 543-3311*
Lubavitch Congregation (O) *65 Valleywood Road 462-6640*
Young Israel (O) *40 Kings Park Road 543-1441*

Croton-on-Hudson 10520 Croton Jewish Center (C) *52 Scenic Drive (914) 271-2218*

Deer Park 11729 Suffolk Jewish Center (C) *330 Central Avenue (516) 667-7695*

DeWitt 13214 Congregation Beth Sholom Chevre Shas (C) *5205 Jamesville Road (315) 446-9570*

Dobbs Ferry 10522 Greenburgh Hebrew Center (C) *515 Broadway (914) 693-4260*

Dunkirk 14048 Temple Beth El (C) *507 Washington Avenue*

East Hampton 11937 Jewish Center of Hamptons (R) *44 Woods Lane (516) 324-9858*

East Northport 11731 Jewish Center (C) *328 Elwood Road (516) 368-6474*
Young Israel (O) *547 Larkfield Road 368-5880*

East Rockaway 11518 Jewish Center (C) *295 Main Street (516) 599-2634*

East Meadow 11554 East Meadow Jewish Center (C) *1400 Prospect Avenue (516) 483-4205*
Temple Emanu-El (R) *123 Merrick Avenue 794-8911*
Suburban Park Jewish Center (C) *400 Old Country Road 796-8833*

Ellenville 12428 Congregation Ezrath Israel (O) *Rabbi Eisner Square (914) 647-4450*

Elmira 14905 Temple B'nai Israel (R) *900 West Water Road (607) 734-7735*
Congregation Shomrei Hadath (C) *Cobbles Park 732-7410*

Elmont 11003 Temple B'nai Israel (R) *Elmont Road & Baylis Avenue (516) 354-1156*
Elmont Jewish Center (C) *500 Elmont Road 488-1616*

Endicott 13760 Temple Beth El (C) *119 Jefferson Avenue 785-3840*

Farmingdale 11735 Farmingdale Jewish Center (C) *425 Fulton Street (516) 694-2343*

Fleischmannns 12430 Congregation B'nai Israel (C) *Wagner Avenue*

Florida 10921 Temple Beth Sholom (C) *Roosevelt Avenue*

Franklin Square 11010 Jewish Center (C) *Pacific & Lloyd Streets (516) 354-2322*

Freeport 11520 Congregation B'nai Israel (C) *91 North Bayview Avenue (516) 623-4200*

Garden City 11530 Jewish Center (R) *168 Nassau Boulevard (516) 248-9180*

Geneva 14456 Temple Beth El (R) *755 South Main Street (315) 789-2945*

Glen Cove 11542 North Country Reform Temple (R) *Crescent Beach Road (516) 671-4760*
Congregation Tifereth Israel (C) *Hill Street & Landing Road 676-5080*

Glen Wild 12738 Hebrew Congregation (O)

Glens Falls 12801 Temple Beth El (R) *3 Marion Avenue (518) 792-4364*

Congregation Shaaray Tefila (C) *68 Bay Street 792-4364*

Gloversville 12078 Knesseth Israel Congregation (C) *34 East Fulton Street (518) 725-0649*

Great Neck 11024 Temple Beth El (R) *5 Old Mill Road (516) 487-0900*
Temple Emanu-El (R) *150 Hicks Lane 482-5701*
Great Neck Synagogue (O) *26 Old Mill Road 487-6100*
Temple Isaiah (R) *35 Bond Street 487-8709*
Temple Israel (C) *108 Old Mill Road 482-7800*
Young Israel (O) *236 Middle Neck Road 487-5190*

Harrison 10528 Jewish Community Center (C) *Union Avenue (914) 835-2850*

Hastings-on-Hudson 10706 Temple Beth Sholom (R) *740 North Broadway (914) 478-3833*

Hauppage 11787 Temple Beth Chai (C) *870 Townline Road (516) 724-5807*

Haverstraw Congregations Sons of Jacob *37 Clove Avenue*

Hempstead 11550 Congregation Beth Israel (C) *141 Hilton Avenue (516) 489-1818*

Henrietta 14467 Temple Beth Am (C) *3249 East Henrietta Road (716) 334-4855*

Herkimer 13350 Temple Beth Joseph (C) *327 North Prospect Street (315) 866-4270*

Hewlett 11557 Congregation Beth Emeth (C) *36 Franklin Avenue (516) 374-9220*
Congregation Toras Chaim (O) *1170 William Street 374-7363*

Hicksville 11801 Congregation Shaare Zedek (O) *Old Country & New South Roads (516) 938-0420*
Hicksville Jewish Center (C) *6 Maglie Drive 931-9323*

Hornell 14843 Temple Beth El (C) *12 Church Street*

Hunter 12442 Congregation Anshei Kol Israel (O) *Main Street*

Hudson 12534 Congregation Anshe Emeth (C) *240 Joslen Boulevard (518) 828-6848*

Huntington 11743 Temple Beth El (R) *660 Park Avenue (516) 421-5835*
Huntington Jewish Center (C) *510 Park Avenue 427-1089*

Huntington Station 11747 South Huntington Jewish Center (C) *2600 New York Avenue (516) 421-3224*

Hurleyville 12747 Congregation Anshe Hurleyville (O) *141 South Aurora Street*

Island Park 11558 Congregation Beth Emeth (C) *191 Long Beach Road (516) 432-6706*

Ithaca 14850 Temple Beth El (C) *Court & Tioga Streets (518) 273-5775*
Hillel Congregation (O) *Anabel Taylor Hall Cornell University 256-4227*
Young Israel (O) *106 West Avenue 272-5810*

Jamestown 14701 Temple Hesed Abraham (R) *215 Hall Avenue*

Jeffersonville Hebrew Congregation

Jericho 11753 Jericho Jewish Center (C) *North Broadway (516) 938-2540*
Temple Or Elohim (R) *18 Tobie Lane 822-1019*

Jericho Gardens 11590 Temple Beth Torah (C) *243 Contiague Rock Road (516) 334-7979*

Kings Park 11754 Congregation Etz Chaim (O) *44 Meadow Road (516) 269-9666*
Kings Park Jewish Center (C) *Route 25-A 269-1133*

Kingston 12401 Congregation Agudas Achim (O) *254 Lucas Avenue (914) 331-1176*
Congregation Ahavath Achim (C) *100 Lucas Avenue 338-4409*
Temple Emanu-El (R) *243 Albany Avenue 338-4271*

Kiryas Joel 10950 Congregation Yetev Lev (O)

Lake Grove 11755 Lake Grove Jewish Center *821 Hawkins Avenue (516) 585-9710*

Lake Peekskill 10537 Temple Israel (C) *Lake Drive (914) 528-2305*

Lake Placid 12946 Lake Placid Synagogue (T) *30 Saranac Avenue (518) 523-3876*

Lake Success 11020 Jewish Center (C) *354 Lakeville Road (516) 466-0569*

Larchmont 10538 Congregation Beth Emeth (C) *2111 Boston Post Road (914) 834-2543*
Larchmont Temple (R) *75 Larchmont Avenue 834-6120*

Lawrence 11559 Congregation Beth Sholom (O) *390 Broadway (516) 569-3600*
Congregation Kol Yisroel Chaverim (O) *124 Richmond Place 239-1033*
Temple Israel (R) *140 Central Avenue 239-1140*
Congregation Shaaray Tefila (O) *25 Central Avenue 239-2444*
Temple Sinai (R) *131 Washington Avenue 569-0267*

Levittown 11756 Israel Community Centre (C) *3235 Hempstead Turnpike (516) 731-2580*

Liberty 12754 Congregation Ahavath Israel (O) *39 Chestnut Street (914) 292-8843*

Lido Beach 11561 Lido Beach Synagogue (O) *1 Fairway Road (516) 889-9650*

Livingston Manor 12758 (O) Congregation Agudas Achim

Lindenhurst 11757 Lindenhurst Hebrew Congregation *225 North 4th Street (516) 226-2022*

Long Beach 11561 Temple Beth El (O) *570 West Walnut Street (516) 432-1678*
Congregation Beth Sholom (C) *700 East Park Avenue 432-7464*
Temple Emanu-El (R)455 Neptune Boulevard 431-4060
Temple Israel (O) *305 Riverside Boulevard 432-1410*
Sephardic Congregation *161 Lafayette Boulevard 432-9224*
Temple Zion (O) *62 Maryland Avenue 432-5657*
Congregation Bachurei Chemed (O) *210 Edwards Boulevard*
Young Israel (O) *158 Long Beach Boulevard*

Lynbrook 11563 Congregation Beth David (C) *188 Vincent Avenue (516) 599-9464*
Temple Emanu-El (R) *Ross Plaza 593-4004*

Mahopac 10541 Temple Beth Sholom (C) *Route 6 & Croton Falls Road (914) 628-6133*

Malverne 11565 Malverne Jewish Center (C) *1 Norwood Avenue (516) 593-6364*

Mamaroneck 10543 Westchester Jewish Center (C) *Rockland & Palmer Avenues (914) 698-2960*
Westchester Day School Synagogue (O) *856 Orienta Avenue 698-8900*

Manhasset 11030 Temple Judea (R) *3333 Searingtown Road (516) 621-8049*

Massapequa 11758 Congregation Beth El (C) *99 Jerusalem Avenue (516) 541-0740*
Temple Judea (R) *Jerusalem & Central Avenues 798-5444*
Temple Sinai (R) *270 Clock Boulevard 795-5015*

Mastic Beach 11951 Mastic Beach Hebrew Center *Neighborhood Road*

Merrick 11566 Temple Beth Am (R) *Merrick & Kirkwood Avenues (516) 378-3477*
Temple Israel of South Merrick (C) *2655 Clubhouse Road 378-1963*
Merrick Jewish Center (C) *225 Fox Boulevard 379-8650*
Congregation Ohav Sholom (O) *145 South Merrick Avenue 378-1988*

Middletown 10940 Temple Sinai (C) *75 Highland Avenue (914) 343-1862*

Monroe 10950 Temple Beth El (R) *314 North Main Street (914) 783-7756*
Congregation Etz Chaim *251 Spring Street 783-7424*

Monsey 10952 Congregation Ayshel Abraham (O) *15 Monsey Boulevard (914) 352-0630*
Congregation Bais Torah (O) *36 Carlton Road 578-9515*

Community Synagogue (O) *15 Cloverdale Lane 356-2720*
Congregation Hadar (O) *70 Highview Road 357-1515*
Monsey Jewish Center (C) *101 Route 306 352-6444*
Congregation K'hal Torath Chaim (O) *Phyllis Terrace*
Congregation Machzikei Torah (O) *3 Ralph Boulevard*

Monticello 12701 Temple Sholom (R) *Port Jervis & Dillon Roads (914) 794-8731*
Congregation Tifereth Israel (O) *18 Landfield Avenue 794-8470*

Mount Kisco 10549 Congregation Bet Torah (C) *60 Smith Avenue (914) 666-7595*
Congregation Beth Medrash Chemed (O) *Pines Bridge Road 666-8629*

Mount Vernon 10552 Congregation Brothers of Israel (O) *116 Crary Avenue (914) 664-8945*
Emanu-El Jewish Center (C) *261 East Lincoln Avenue 667-0616*
Fleetwood Synagogue (O) *11 East Broad Street 664-7643*
Free Synagogue of Westchester (R) *500 North Columbus Avenue 664-1727*
Sinai Temple (R) *132 Crary Avenue 668-9471*

Mountaindale 12763 Hebrew Congregation (O)

Nanuet 10954 Nanuet Hebrew Center (C) *34 South Middletown Road (914) 623-3735*

Newburgh 12550 Congregation Agudas Israel (O) *290 North Street (914) 562-5604*
Temple Beth Jacob (R) *344 Gidney Avenue 562-5516*

New City 10956 Temple Beth Sholom (R) *228 New Hempstead Road (914) 638-0770*
New City Jewish Center (C) *Old Schoolhouse Road 634-6140*

New Hyde Park 11040 Temple Emanu-El (R) *3315 Hillside Avenue (516) 746-1120*
Jewish Community Center (C) *100 Lakeville Road 354-7583*
Young Israel (O) *264-15 77th Avenue 343-6509*

New Paltz 12561 Congregation Ahavath Achim (C) *1 Main Street*

New Rochelle 10804 Congregation Anshe Sholom (O) *50 North Avenue (914) 632-9220*
Congregation Beth El (C) *Northfield Road & North Avenue 235-2700*
Temple Israel (R) *1000 Pinebrook Boulevard 235-1800*
Young Israel (O) *1228 North Avenue 636-8215*

New Square 10977 Congregation Zemach David (O) *13 Truman Avenue (914) 354-9736*

Note: There are over 1,000 congregations in New York City. People interested in obtaining the list of congregations should refer to Oscar Israelowitz's "Guide to Jewish New York City." Those interested in acquiring information about services should call one of the following telephone numbers:
Orthodox - (212) 563-4000 or (212) 929-1525
Conservative - (212) 533-7800
Reform - (212) 249-0100
Reconstructionist - (212) 724-7000

Niagra Falls 14301 Temple Beth El (R) *720 Ashland Avenue (716) 282-2717*
Temple Israel (C) *College & Madison Avenues 285-9894*

North Bellmore 11710 Young Israel (O) *2428 Hamilton Road (516) 826-0048*

Norwich 13815 Norwich Jewish Center (R) *72 South Broad Street*

Nyack 10960 Congregation Sons of Israel (C) *300 North Broadway*

Oakdale 11769 B'nai Israel Reform Temple (R) *67 Oakdale Bohemia Road (516) 563-1660*

Oceanside 11572 Temple Avodah (R) *3050 Oceanside Road (516) 766-6809*
Congregation Darchei Noam (O) *Skillman & Waukema Avenues 764-0800*
Oceanside Jewish Center (C) *2860 Brower Avenue 764-4213*

Congregation Shar Hashamayim (O) *3309 Skillman Avenue 764-6888*
Young Israel (O) *150 Waukema Avenue 764-1099*

Ogdensburg 13669 Congregation Anshe Zophen (C) *416 Greene Street (315) 393-3787*

Olean 14760 B'nai Israel Congregation (C) *127 South Barry Street 372-3431*

Oneonta 13820 Temple Beth El (C) *83 Chestnut Street (607) 432-5522*

Orangeburg 10962 Orangeburg Jewish Center (C) *Independence Avenue (914) 359-5920*

Oswego 13126 Congregation Adath Israel (C) *35 East Oneida Street*

Oyster Bay 11771 Oyster Bay Jewish Center (C) *Berry Hill Road (516) 922-6650*

Palisades 10964 Congregation Gemilas Chesed *Oak Tree Road 923-8700*

Parksville 12768 Congregation Tifereth Israel Anshei Parksville *Route 17*

Patchogue 11772 Temple Beth El (C) *45 Oak Street (516) 475-1882*
Young Israel (O) *28 Mowbray Street 654-0882*

Pearl River 10965 Beth Am Temple (R) *60 East Madison Avenue (914) 735-3845*

Peekskill 10566 First Hebrew Congregation (C) *1821 East Main Street (914) 739-0500*
813 Lower Main Street

Pelham Manor 10803 Pelham Jewish Center (C) *451 Esplanade*

Plainview 11803 Temple Beth Elohim (R) *926 Round Swamp Road (516) 694-4544*
Manetto Hill Jewish Center (C) *244 Manetto Hill Road 935-5454*
Plainview Jewish Center (C) *95 Floral Drive 938-9610*

Plainview Synagogue (O) *255 Manetto Hill Road 433-6590*
Young Israel (O) *132 Southern Parkway 433-4811*

Plattsburgh 12901 Temple Beth Israel (R) *Bowman Street & Marcy Lane 563-3343*

Pomona 10970 Pomona Jewish Center (C) *106 Pomona Road*

Port Chester 10573 Congregation Kneses Tifereth Israel (C) 575 King Street (914) 939-1004

Port Jefferson 11776 North Shore Jewish Center (C) 385 Old Town Road (516) 928-3737

Port Jervis 12771 Temple Beth El (C) *88 East Main Street*

Port Washington 11050 Temple Beth Israel (C) *Temple Drive (516) 767-1708*
Community Synagogue (R) *150 Middle Neck Road 883-3144*

Potsdam 13676 Congregation Beth El (C) *81 Market Street*

Poughkeepsie 12603 Temple Beth El (C) *118 Grand Avenue (914) 454-0570*
Congregation Shomre Israel (O) *18 Park Avenue 454-2890*
Vassar Temple (R) *140 Hooker Avenue 454-2570*

Putnam Valley 10579 Reform Temple (R) 528-7550

Riverhead 11901 Temple Israel (C) *490 Northville Turnpike (516) 727-3191*

Rochester 14618 Temple Beth David (C) *3200 Saint Paul Boulevard (716) 266-3223*
Temple Beth El (C) *139 South Winton Road 473-1770*
Temple Beth Hamedrash–Beth Israel (C) *1369 East Avenue 244-2060*
Beth Joseph Center (O) *1150 Saint Paul Street 423-0030*
Congregation Beth Sholom (O) *1161 Monroe Avenue 473-1625*
Temple Brith Kodesh (R) *2131 Elmwood Avenue 244-7060*
Temple Emanu-El (R) *2956 Saint Paul Boulevard 266-1978*
Congregation Light of Israel (Sephardic) (O) *206 Norton Street 544-1381*
Temple Sinai (R) *363 Penfield Road 381-6890*

Congregation Ahavas Achim (O) *703 Joseph Avenue*
Congregation Beth Hakneses (O) *19 Saint Regis Drive 271-5390*
Congregation B'nai Israel (O) *692 Joseph Avenue*
Congregation Tifereth Israel (O) *271 Dartmouth Street*

Rockville Center 11570 Temple B'nai Sholom (C) *100 Hempstead Avenue (516)764-4100*
Central Synagogue (R) *430 DeMott Avenue 766-4300*

Rome 13440 Congregation Adas Israel (C) *705 Hickory Street 337-3170*

Ronkonkoma Jewish Center (C) *821 Hawkins Avenue (516) 585-0521*

Roslyn Heights 11577 Temple Beth Sholom (C) *Roslyn Road & Northern State Parkway (516) 621-2288*
Reconstructionist Synagogue (Rec) *1 Willow Street*
Shelter Rock Jewish Center (C) *Searington & Shelter Rock Roads 741-4305*
Temple Sinai (R) *425 Roslyn Road 621-6800*

Rye 10580 Community Synagogue (R) *200 Forest Avenue (914) 967-6262*
Congregation Emanu-El (R) *Westchester Avenue & Kenilworth Road 967-4382*

Sag Harbor 11963 Temple Adas Israel (R) *Elizabeth Street & Atlantic Avenue (516) 725-0904*

Saratoga Springs 12866 Congregation Shaarei Tefilah (O) *260 Broadway*
Temple Sinai (R) *509 Broadway (518) 584-8730*

Sayville 11782 Temple Sholom (T) *225 Greeley Avenue (516) 567-3207*

Scarsdale 10583 Scarsdale Synagogue (R) *2 Ogden Road (914) 725-5175*
Westchester Reform Temple (R) *255 Mamaroneck Road 723-7727*
Young Israel (O) *1313 Weaver Street 636-8686*

Schenectady 12309 Congregation Adath Israel *872 Albany Street*

Congregation Agudath Achim (C) *2117 Union Street (518) 393-9211*
Congregation Beth Israel (O) *2195 Eastern Parkway 377-3700*
Congregation Gates of Heaven (R) *852 Ashmore Avenue 374-8173*

Sharon Springs Hebrew Congregation (O)

Smithtown 11787 Temple Beth Sholom (C) *Edgewood Avenue & River Road (516) 724-0424*

South Fallsburg 12270 Hebrew Association (O) *(914) 434-9675*

Spring Valley 10977 Congregation Ayshel Avrohom (O) *111 South Madison Avenue (914) 352-0630*
Temple Beth El (R) *415 Viola Road 356-2000*
Congregation B'nai Yechiel (O) *80 Washington Avenue*
Jewish Community Center (C) *250 North Main Street 356-3710*
Congregation Ohev Sholom (O) *14 Linden Avenue*
Congregation Shaarey Tfiloh (C) *972 South Main Street 356-2225*
Congregation Sons of Israel (C) *80 Williams Avenue 352-6767*
Young Israel (O) *Pascack Road 352-8654*

Stony Brook 11790 Temple Isaiah (R) *1404 Stony Brook Road (516) 751-8518*

Suffern 10901 Reform Temple (R) *70 Haverstraw Road (914) 357-5872*
Congregation Sons of Israel (O) *Suffern Place 357-9827*

Swan Lake 12783 Congregation Ahavas Sholom (O)

Syosset 11791 East Nassau Hebrew Congregation (O) *310-A South Oyster Bay Road (516) 921-1800*
Midway Jewish Center (C) *330 South Oyster Bay Road 938-8390*
North Shore Synagogue (R) *83 Muttontown Road 921-2282*

Syracuse 13210 Temple Adath Yeshurun (C) *450 Kimber Road (315) 445-0002*
Congregation Anshe Sfard (O) *3528 Genesee Street*
Congregation Ner Tamid (C) *5061 West Taft Road 458-2022*

Sephardic Congregation(O) *119 Doll Parkway 446-0760*
Temple Society of Concord (R) *910 Madison Street 475-9952*
Young Israel (O) *4313 East Genesee Street 446-6194*

Tannersville Hebrew Congregation (O) *South Main Street*

Tarrytown 10591 Temple Beth Abraham (R) *25 Leroy Street (914) 631-1770*

Tonawanda 14150 Temple Beth El (C) *2368 Eggert Road 836-3762*

Troy 12180 Temple Berith Sholom (R) *167 3rd Street (518) 272-8872*
Congregation Beth El (C) *411 Hoosick Street 272-6113*
Congregation Beth Israel Bikur Cholim *27 Centerview Drive*
Congregation Beth Tephila (O) *82 River Street 272-3182*

Tuckahoe 10707 Genesis Hebrew Center (C) *25 Oakland Avenue 961-3766*

Uniondale 11553 Uniondale Jewish Center (C) *760 Jerusalem Avenue*

Upper Nyack 10960 Temple Beth Torah (C) *Route 9W (914) 358-2248*

Utica 13501 Temple Beth El (C) *1607 Genesee Street (315) 724-4751*
Temple Emanu-El (R) *2710 Genesee Street 724-4177*
Congregation Zvi Jacob (O) *110 Memorial Parkway 724-8357*

Valley Stream 11580 Congregation Beth Sholom (O) *550 Rockaway Avenue (516) 561-9245*
Temple Gates of Zion (C) *322 North Corona Avenue 561-2308*
Temple Hillel (C) *1000 Rosedale Road 791-6344*
Congregation Tree of Life (C) *502 North Central Avenue 825-2090*

Walden 12586 Congregation Beth Hillel (O) *20 Pine Street*

Wantagh 11793 Wantagh Jewish Center (C) *3710 Woodbine Avenue (516) 785-2445*
Suburban Temple (R) *2900 Jerusalem Avenue 221-2370*

Watertown 13601 Congregation Degel Israel (C) *557 Thompson Boulevard*

Waverly 14892 Congregation Beth Israel (C) *339 Broad Street*

Westbury 11590 Temple Beth Torah (C) *243 Cantiague Road (516) 334-7979*
Community Reform Temple (R) *712 Plain Road 333-1839*
Temple Sholom (C) *675 Brookside Court 334-2800*
Westbury Hebrew Congregation (C) *221 Old Westbury Road 333-7977*

West Hempstead 11552 Congregation Anshe Sholom (O) *472 Hempstead Avenue (516) 489-8112*
Jewish Community Center (C) *711 Dogwood Street 481-7448*
Nassau Community Temple (R) *240 Hempstead Avenue 485-1811*
Young Israel (O) *630 Hempstead Avenue 481-9429*

White Plains 10607 Congregation Beth Am Sholom (Rec) *295 Soundview Avenue*
Hebrew Institute (O) *20 Greenridge Avenue (914) 948-3095*
Temple Israel Center (C) *280 Old Mamaroneck Road 948-2800*
Jewish Community Center (R) *252 Soundview Avenue 949-4717*
Woodlands Community Temple (R) *50 Worthington Road 592-7070*
Lincoln Park Jewish Center (C) *311 Central Park Avenue 365-7119*
Midchester Jewish Center (C) *236 Grandview Boulevard 779-3660*
Northeast Jewish Center *11 Salisbury Road 337-0268*
Congregation Ohab Zedek (O) *63 Hamilton Avenue 963-1951*
Congregation Sons of Israel (O) *105 Radford Avenue 969-4453*

Woodbourne Hebrew Congregation (O)

Woodmere 11598 Congregation Ohr Torah (O) *410 Hungry Harbor Road (516) 791-2130*
Congregation Sons of Israel (C) *111 Irving Place 374-0655*
Young Israel (O) *859 Peninsula Boulevard 295-0150*

Woodridge 12789 Congregation Ohav Sholom (O)
Yonkers 10710 Temple Emanu-El (R) *306 Rumsey Road (914) 963-0575*
Greystone Jewish Center (O) *600 North Broadway 963-8888*
Yorktown Heights 10598 Temple Beth Am (R) *Church Street (914) 962-7500*
Jewish Center (C) *2966 Crompond Road 245-2324*

MIKVEHS

Bedford Hills 165 Haines Road *(914) 666-4391*
Albany 190 Elm Street *(518) 434-0603 or 489-6155*
Binghamton 39 Riverside Drive *(607) 722-1793*
Buffalo 1248 Kenmore Avenue *(716) 632-1531 or 875-8451 or 877-0769*
Cedarhurst 504 West Broadway *(516) 569-1971*
Ellenville Rabbi Eisner Square *(914) 647-8740*
Fleischmanns (914) 254-4595 *(summer only)*
Great Neck 26 Old Mill Road *(516) 487-2726*
Hewlett 1156 Peninsula Boulevard *(516) 569-5514*
Liberty 37 Lincoln Place *(914) 292-6677 (summer only)*
Long Beach Scharf Manor *274 West Broadway (516) 431-7758*
Monroe 20 Quickway Road *(914) 783-3451 or 782-8261*
Monsey Maple Leaf Road *(914) 356-1000*
Monticello 16 North Street *(914) 794-6757 or 794-8470*
Mount Kisco Pines Bridge Road *(914) 666-5321*
Mountaindale (914) 434-9192 or 434-4963

New York City (Manhattan) 313 East Broadway (212) 475-8514
234 West 78th Street 799-1520
Broadway & West 186th Street 923-1100
Oceanside 3397 Park Avenue (516) 766-3242
Poughkeepsie 18 Park Avenue (914) 454-4078
Rochester 27 Saint Regis Drive North (716) 244-4888
Huntington Station 2600 New York Avenue (516) 421-3224
Scarsdale 1313 Weaver Street (914) 961-6971 *or* 636-8686
Spring Valley 33 Truman Avenue (914) 354-6578
Syracuse 2200 East Genesee Street (315) 446-5735 *or* 472-8411
Tannersville Thompkins Street (518) 589-5830 *(summer only)*
Troy 2306 15th Street (518) 274-5572
Utica 110 Memorial Parkway (315) 724-8357 *or* 733-0125
West Hempstead 775 Hempstead Avenue (516) 489-9358
Woodridge East Pond Road (914) 434-9726
Pennsylvania

Pennsylvania

The first Jewish settler in Pennsylvania, Nathan Levy, arrived in Philadelphia in 1735. There were Jewish traders in the state, however, in the late 17th century. Nathan Levy, a merchant and shipper, purchased a small piece of ground for a cemetery after the death of his child in 1740. This plot was located on the north side of Walnut Street, between 8th and 9th Streets. The wooden gate at the entrance of the cemetery has marks of British bullets. It was the custom of the British army during the Revolutionary War to execute deserters at the gates of Jewish cemeteries.

In 1738, David and Moses Franks, nephews of Nathan Levy, arrived in Philadelphia from New York City. They had extensive shipping interests and did regular business with London firms. It was on one of their vessels, the *Myrtilla,* that the Liberty Bell, built in England, arrived in 1752.

Barnard Gratz arrived from Germany in 1753 and was involved in international shipping: sending furs, grains, lumber, and cattle overseas in exchange for money and consumer goods. His niece was the noted Rebecca Gratz, founder of the Female Hebrew Benevolent Society and the first Sunday Hebrew school in the country.

The first synagogue in Pennsylvania was organized in Philadelphia in 1773. Kahal Kodesh Mikveh Israel followed the (Western) Sephardic ritual and was associated with New York City's Shearith Israel Congregation (Spanish and Portuguese Synagogue).

During the Revolutionary War Jews were engaged in privateering against British shipping and provided blankets, rifles, bullets, and other essential supplies for the troops. Haym Salomon, the noted patriot and financier, was responsible for lending money to the Continental Congress for the duration of the American Revolution. There were Jews with George Washington in Valley Forge.

The first synagogue in the state was built in 1782 for Congregation Mikveh Israel of Philadelphia. It was located on the north side of Cherry Street, midway in the block from 3rd Street to Sterling Alley. The Reverend Gershom Mendes Seixas, minister of New York's Shearith Israel Congregation, who had fled to Philadelphia during the British occupation of New York, became Mikveh Israel's first rabbi. The first president of the congregation was Barnard Gratz.

Most of the congregants were refugees; Jews who had fled the onslaught of the British invasions of New York, Savannah, and Charleston. After the Revolutionary War, the Jews returned to their respective cities, leaving Mikveh Israel in danger of having to close its doors. A public appeal was made to all Philadelphians, of all religious persuasions, to help save the building. Benjamin Franklin was among those who contributed.

In 1795, Philadelphia's first Ashkenazic synagogue, Rodeph Shalom, was organized by German Jews. In 1820, there were about 500 Jews in Philadelphia. By the Civil War, the Jewish population reached 8,000. The immigration wave during this period consisted of Jews who had been influenced by westernized education and the spirit of "scientific" Reform Judaism in Germany which sought to adapt Judaism to the demands of contemporary life. In 1841, a third synagogue, Kneseth Israel, became Philadelphia's first Reform congregation.

In 1859, Colonel E.L. Drake struck oil in Titusville. This was the world's first oil well. Jewish merchants soon moved into the oil towns. They provided goods and services for the "black gold" rushers. Synagogues were organized in the oil towns of Titusville and Oil City. Other Jewish merchants settled in the coal mine towns such as Carbondale, Pottsville, Shenadoah, and Shamokin.

The first Jewish settlers in Pittsburgh arrived in 1749 when it was still called Fort Pitt, a British post. They were Jewish traders who were travelling in the wilderness of the Alleghenies and brought sundries for the Indians. The first major Jewish settlement was established in Pittsburgh in the 1840s. The first congregation was organized in 1846 and was called Etz Chaim. The second congregation was created out of a quarrel over ritual between the German and Polish Jews. This was Congregation Rodef Shalom and was organized in 1854. Rodef Shalom built Pittsburgh's first synagogue in 1861. It was located on Hancock Street (now 8th Street). The first East European congregation, Beth Hamedrash Hagadol, was organized in 1871.

The Jewish population of Pennsylvania is approximately 420,000.

Rebecca Gratz

AARONSBURG

This is the first town in the United States founded by and named for a Jew, Aaron Levy. He was an Indian trader, land speculator, merchant, and soldier. Levy purchased 334½ acres in Penns Valley, located about 30 miles southwest of Wiliamsport, in 1779. He laid out streets 50 feet wide with the main thoroughfares called "Aaron's Square" and "Rachel's Way," after his wife.

ALIQUIPPA

Located in the heart of the steel mills, many of which have recently closed down, Aliquippa is situated 20 miles northwest of Pittsburgh. Congregation Agudath Achim's first location was at 501 Church Street (up the hill). That brick building now stands abandoned. The congregation moved to Main and 21st Street in the 1950s. That building no longer houses the congregation. It has been remodelled and now is the site of an office complex. It is still possible to distinguish where the original round main sanctuary was located within the complex.

ALLENTOWN

The old Congregation Sons of Israel, at 6th and Tilghman Streets, was built in 1905 in the Gothic style. Several years ago it was sold to a Greek Orthodox church. Today, there are bright gold Greek crosses atop the spires. There are still, however, Stars of

David atop each of the three front doors of this monumental fieldstone structure.

BANGOR

The Bangor Jewish Community Center, located on 4th Street, is no longer a functioning Jewish house of worship. The building was sold to the municipality of Bangor and, as stipulated in the bill of sale, cannot be used for commercial or industrial purposes. There is a plaque on the front façade indicating that this building was once a synagogue.

BEAVER FALLS

The original building for Congregation Agudath Achim was located at Fifth Street and 6th Avenue and was built in 1914. The area is now zoned for the city's industrial district. The building is presently used as a kitchen cabinet factory.

CARBONDALE

Congregation Agudath Sholom, located at 51½ Pike Street, was built in 1907. It served the Jewish community of this small coal-mining town. Several years ago the 3-story brick synagogue structure encountered structural damage. The walls actually started caving-in! What remains of the synagogue today is the fieldstone foundation with its original cornerstone indicating the congregation's name and date of construction. A new pitched roof sits directly on the building's foundation. Services have been held therefore, in the synagogue's basement.

EASTON

Temple Covenant of Peace was founded in 1839. Its original synagogue was built in 1842 and was located at 38 South 6th Street. The design is Moorish-Revival and has been compared to a miniature version of the Great Synagogue of Florence, Italy.

Nearby, at 126 South 6th Street, stands the remains of the original building of Congregation B'nai Abraham, built in 1908. That building is presently used as a P.A.L. (Police Athletic League) Center.

Both congregations are still functioning but are located in other sections of the city.

ELKINS PARK

The first home of Congregation Beth Sholom was in Philadelphia, at Broad and Cortland Streets. That 1920 building was sold to the American Meat Cutters Union and served as its meeting headquarters. The structure was recently sold to an Oriental church.

In 1954, the congregation moved north to Elkins Park and commissioned Frank Lloyd Wright to design its new synagogue. Wright was the son of a Unitarian minister and had a profound knowledge of the Bible. He designed "An American Synagogue for Jews to worship in."

Congregation Beth Shalom was designed by Frank Lloyd Wright.

The building, in its general appearance, derives from 17th and 18th century Polish synagogues. The central feature is a corrugated glass roof (which was later replaced with plastic due to heavy vibrations from low-flying aircraft), which is supported by a tripod faced in stamped aluminum, which in turn rests on prow-like concrete buttresses. Like many of Wright's buildings, Beth Shalom has a unifying geometric device, in this case a triangle (in his Guggenheim Museum in New York, Wright's ideé fixe was the circle). From room to chandelier to lecturn, the triangular motif is carried through to produce an effect not far removed from that of Art Deco.

With his tripod roof, Frank Lloyd Wright hoped to suggest both Mount Sinai and the tent tabernacles of the ancient Hebrews. The building has been described as a "Mount Sinai in modern materials." The wandering of the Jews in the wilderness (desert) for 40 years is suggested in the undulating floor levels in the main sanctuary, symbolic of sand dunes. The carpeting also reflects the desert in its buff color.

The building was completed in 1956. The congregation follows the Conservative ritual.

Section view of Congregation Beth Shalom.

GREENSBURGH

Congregation B'nai Israel was organized in 1893. Its original synagogue building, located at Ludwick Street and North Hamilton Avenue, is still extant but no longer in use. Its Holy Ark was designed following Eastern European motifs and is hand-carved solid oak.

A striking feature in this synagogue is the use of natural light. Opposite the Ark, which aligns the east wall, there is a rose window. During the High Holy Days, the western rose window permits the sun's rays to fall directly onto the Holy Ark during the N'eelah prayers. That prayer is chanted towards the end of the Yom Kippur service, marking the conclusion of that holiest of days. The Ark is literally aglow during this service.

HONESDALE

Honesdale is located in the coal-mining district of northeastern Pennsylvania. The Jewish community approached the town elders for permission to erect a synagogue in 1849. They were granted permission to build their synagogue only on the condition that the structure resemble all of the other churches in the town. Specifically, this "Jewish Church" was required to have a "steeple!" The Jews were dumbfounded. They had to comply with these anti-Semitic demands. The results are evident in the only synagogue in the United States which was built with a steeple. But resting proudly above that steeple is a little Star of David! Beth Israel Synagogue is a small white clapboard structure located at 7th and Court Streets. The congregation follows the Reform ritual.

Beth Israel Synagogue in Honesdale.

McKEESPORT

The beautiful Ark in Congregation Gemilas Chesed, located at 1400 Summit Street (White Oak), was removed from a former synagogue which closed down several years ago.

MIDDLETOWN

The small red brick synagogue of Congregation B'nai Jacob, located at Water and Nisley Streets, is situated in the vicinity of the Three-Mile-Island nuclear reactor.

OIL CITY

Oil was discovered in Titusville, 15 miles north of Oil City, in 1859. The world's first oil well was drilled by "Colonel" Edwin L. Drake. Jewish merchants soon followed and provided goods and services for the "black gold" rushers. Congregation B'nai Gemilas Chesed was located in Titusville at North Martin Street. That congregation is no longer functioning.

Congregation Etz Chaim was Oil City's first synagogue. Its first building was located at Plum and Center Streets. It was built around 1900, is still extant, but stands abandoned. Its present one-story modern brick synagogue building is located at 316 West 1st Street and was built in 1960.

The first oil well in the world was drilled in Titusville.

PHILADELPHIA

MIKVEH ISRAEL CONGREGATION
44 North 4th Street

Organized in 1740, Mikveh Israel is the second oldest congregation in the United States. The first services were conducted in a house in Sterling Alley. In 1782, the first synagogue in Pennsylvania was built. It was located on Cherry Street, between 3rd Street and Sterling Alley. In 1825, a second Cherry Street synagogue was built to accommodate Philadelphia's growing Jewish population. The congregation moved again, in 1909, to its even larger edifice at Broad and York Streets. It sold that structure in the 1960s to Dropsie University and moved back to Downtown Philadelphia, near Independence Hall, where it was first organized.

The first minister of Mikveh Israel was the Reverend Gershom Mendes Seixas of New York's Congregation Shearith Israel. He had fled New York rather than stay in British occupied territory and arrived in Philadelphia in 1780. From 1829-1850 the Reverend Isaac Leeser was Mikveh Israel's spiritual leader. He organized the Hebrew Sunday School Society with Rebecca Gratz in 1843. He also established the Maimonides College, the first American rabbinical school.

Plans for the present synagogue were designed by the late architect, Louis Kahn, in 1963. He was concerned with the play of natural light on walls of brick and exposed concrete. The effects of sunlight are crucial, since most of the important rituals take place during the day.

Though never built, Louis Kahn's sanctuary appeared as a massive fortress-like brick octagon, with towers marking the corners. These were pierced with round headed arches for light. The sanctuary stood independent of the remainder of the complex, though its towers were mirrored in the adjacent chapel and social hall. (You can see Louis Kahn's Richards Medical Research Building in the University of Pennsylvania, in Philadelphia)

The present building was designed by the architectural firm of H2L2 in 1976. The main sanctuary contains the beautifully detailed marble reading platform *(Tebah)* and a hand-carved wood Chair of Elijah, which is used during circumcision ceremonies. These treasures were removed from earlier synagogue buildings of the congregation.

The Museum of American Jewish History adjoins the Mikveh Israel Congregation. Note the exquisite tapestry on the wall near the entrance which portrays the history of the congregation. For information about museum hours and synagogue services, please call (215) 922-5446 or 923-3811.

The history of Congregation Mikveh Israel is portrayed on the tapestry in the synagogue lobby.

The Chair of Elijah in Congregation Mikveh Israel.

MIKVEH ISRAEL CEMETERY
Spruce Street, between 8th and 9th Streets

This cemetery is owned by Mikveh Israel Congregation. It was purchased by Nathan Levy in 1740. The cemetery is surrounded by an old brick wall. The historic plaque outside the cemetery states: "Notables buried here include Nathan Levy, whose ship brought the Liberty Bell to America; Haym Salomon, Revolutionary War patriot and financier; the Gratz family; and Aaron Levy, founder of Aaronsburg." There are also 33 Revolutionary War soldiers buried in this cemetery.

ENTEBBE MEMORIAL
Mikveh Israel Plaza

The Entebbe Memorial, located in front of Philadelphia's Congregation Mikveh Israel, was prepared by the Museum of American Jewish History. The memorial was dedicated in memory of Jonathan "Yoni" Netanyahu who was the only Jew killed during the rescue raid on Entebbe on July 4, 1976. The four white marble slabs were designed by the Israeli sculptor, Buky Schwartz.

The statue "Religious Liberty" which stands just to the left of congregation Mikveh Israel, was relocated from Fairmont Park.

Mikveh Israel's cemetery.

CONGREGATION RODEPH SHALOM
615 North Broad Street

Organized in 1795 as Philadelphia's second synagogue, Rodeph Shalom was the first Ashkenazic congregation in the United States. This 1928 structure has an exquisite mosaic-tiled front façade and houses the Philadelphia Museum of Judaica. There is a suburban branch to this congregation, located at 8201 High School Road, in Elkins Park.

Around 1868 the congregation's Juliana Street synagogue was found inadequate, ground was purchased at the southeast corner of Broad and Mount Vernon Streets. The architectural firm of Frazer, Furness, and Hewitt was commissioned to design a new synagogue. The building was dedicated in 1870.

Marcus Jastrow of Posen, the minister of Rodeph Shalom, introduced several reforms within this Orthodox congregation. Women occupied seats on one side and men on the other side of the main hall. The installation of an organ was decided upon from the outset. The reader's stand was turned around so that he would face the worshippers instead of the Ark. The congregation did not completely break with Orthodoxy until 1901. Although strongly Romanesque in plan and elevation, the decoration was Moorish, with horeshoe arches of alternating light and dark voussoirs. The asymmetrical façade, with a tower on one corner only, was characteristic of the general trend toward picturesqueness. The tower served as a stair-block and was capped with a flattened bulbous dome. The mixture of styles was carried into the interior where lavish Islamic decoration contrasted with an English hammerbeam roof. The building was demolished in the 1920s.

The Pennsylvania Academy of Fine Arts, located at the corner of Broad and Cherry Streets, was designed by the same architectural firm in the same Moorish motif. The original Rodeph Shalom consisted of a sanctuary only. That building was demolished and was replaced with the present temple structure which houses a lavish sanctuary as well as a religious school. The congregation follows the Reform ritual.

Rodeph Shalom was the first Ashkenazic congregation in the Western Hemisphere.

INDEPENDENCE HALL—LIBERTY BELL

To mark the 50th anniversary of William Penn's Charter of Privileges of 1701, a bell was ordered from England in 1751. The bell was inscribed with a verse from the Book of Leviticus (Vayikrah), "Proclaim liberty throughout the land." The bell was transported aboard the *Myrtilla,* a ship owned by David Franks and Nathan Levy, prominent leaders of Philadelphia's Jewish community. The bell presently housed in Independence Mall is a second copy. Its crack occurred on July 8, 1835 when the bell tolled for the funeral of Chief Justice John Marshall.

DROPSIE UNIVERSITY
Broad and York Streets

This graduate institution was founded in 1907 by Moses Aaron Dropsie and is dedicated to Hebrew, Biblical, and Middle Eastern studies. It is nonsectarian and nontheological. Its students are Jews, Protestants, Catholics, Moslems, Buddhists, and non-religious—all engaged in studying the ancient languages of the Middle East. Fragments of the Cairo *Genizah* are contained in the university's library.

The building located on the northeast corner of Broad and York Streets was originally built in 1909 for Mikveh Israel, Philadelphia's oldest congregation. It was designed by the Paris-trained architect, William Tachau. He fronted the low building with a range of engaged, coupled columns of the Beaux-Arts Ionic order, which encloses the three arched doorways.

Most interesting is the novel arrangement of the women's section. Tachau replaced the second floor gallery with low tribunes which line the broad tranverse hall of worship on its short sides. He thus avoided the impression of isolation and separateness conveyed by galleries. The reading platform *(Tebah)* was placed in the usual Sephardic tradition, opposite the Ark *(Heychal)* rather close to the other end of the hall, with the space in between left free.

In the early 1960s Mikveh Israel moved into its present building located at 44 North 4th Street, near Independence Hall. It sold its former building to Dropsie University. In 1975, the building was designated a National Historic Landmark. The building was recently purchased by a local church.

RECONSTRUCTIONIST RABBINICAL COLLEGE
2304 North Broad Street

The Reconstructionist movement is a cross-fertilization of Eastern European Orthodoxy and the Reform movement's innovations. It portrays Judaism as culture, and not merely a set of religious beliefs. The Reconstructionist Rabbinical College, the first of its kind in the United States, was established in 1968. It is located near Temple University and Dropsie University. The College's 5-year curriculum requires students to engage in a Ph.D. studies program at Temple University while they study concurrently at the Rabbinical College.

FRANK MEMORIAL SYNAGOGUE
5400 Old York Road

The Harry S. Frank Memorial Synagogue, located on the grounds of the Albert Einstein Medical Center, was designed by the American-born Jewish architect Arnold Brunner in 1901. Brunner was the architect who designed New York's Shearith Israel Synagogue, North America's first congregation, in 1897.

The small stone synagogue measures 33 feet by 37 feet and 28 feet high. It has an interior portico on two Doric columns. The inscription frieze of a menorah is taken from the Kfar Bir'im synagogue (3rd century) in Galilee. There are two bold lions, cast in limestone, sitting on either side of the main entrance. The interior was recently refurbished. The building is only used for

The Frank Memorial Synagogue is a National Historic Landmark.

special occasions such as small weddings.

The Frank Memorial Synagogue was declared a National Historic Landmark in 1983. Contact Rabbi Sidney Goldstein, The Medical Center chaplain, at (215) 456-6059, for further information about the Frank Memorial Synagogue.

SOCIETY HILL SYNAGOGUE
418 Spruce Street

This official city landmark was originally built as a Baptist church in 1829. The Roumanian-American Synagogue, an Orthodox congregation, purchased the building in 1911. It is now used by a Conservative congregation.

WEST PHILADELPHIA

Other noteworthy former synagogue structures located in this once-vibrant Jewish section of Philadelphia are:

Temple Beth Israel, located at Montgomery and 32nd Street, was designed in the Moorish-Revival style in 1920 and resembles the Hagia Sophia in Constantinople.

Congregation B'nai Jeshurun, at 33rd Street, near Diamond Street, was built in 1924.

PITTSBURGH

RODEF SHALOM CONGREGATION
4905 Fifth Avenue

The Rodeph Shalom Congregation sponsored an architectural competition for its new synagogue in the Oakland section of Pittsburgh in 1906. It was won by Palmer and Hornbostel, who designed a large building seating 1500. The structure is made of brick and terra cotta and the inner dome is vaulted with Guastavino tiles. The dome itself is reminiscent of the grand mosques of Turkey, with handsome proportions. The large stained glass windows, a modern innovation, depict Biblical scenes and were designed by the Willet Studio in 1906. The architectural value of the building has been recognized; it was placed on the Registry of National Historic Buildings by the Department of the Interior in 1980, and had become a Pittsburgh Historic Landmark earlier. The Kimball organ, installed in 1907, has been designated as a historic instrument by the National Historic Organ Society. It is the only synagogue organ thus distinguished. The Rodef Shalom Congregation, founded in 1856, is the oldest congregation in the city of Pittsburgh. Its first synagogue was built in 1861 and was located on Hancock Street (now 8th Street). The congregation follows the Reform ritual.

B'NAI ISRAEL CONGREGATION
327 North Negley Avenue

The massive round rusticated fieldstone structure is capped with an aqua-colored tiled dome. B'nai Israel Congregation is a designated Pittsburgh Historic Landmark. It was erected in 1924 and was designed so that the worshippers will face east, towards

Pittsburgh's Temple Rodef Shalom is a National Historic Landmark.

Jerusalem. That presented a considerable problem to its architects, Henry Hornbostel and Alexander Sharov, since the street entrance is also the eastern side. The problem was solved through a long circular inclined gallery which carries the worshipper to the sanctuary from the lower level.

B'nai Israel Congregation is an official Pittsburgh Historic Landmark.

The windows contain abstract images—in keeping with the literal interpretation of the second commandment not to make any graven images. These windows, installed in 1966, were designed by John Jack Duval, and use a new epoxy resin technique. The congregation follows the Conservative ritual.

The interior circular ramp leads the worshipper into the main sanctuary.

BETH HAMEDRASH HAGADOL
1230 Colwell Street

The Beth Hamedrash Hagadol was the first synagogue founded by Eastern European Jews in 1873. It is the oldest Orthodox congregation in western Pennsylvania. Its first location was at 129 Washington Place. In 1960, the Federal Government bought-up all the real estate in that downtown section, including the old Beth Hamedrash Hagadol. The congregation was given enough compensation for its old building and a parcel of land just a few blocks from its original location. In 1964, a new synagogue was built across from the Civic Arena.

The original 1873 hand-carved wooden Ark was removed from the old building and transplanted into the new synagogue. The Beth Hamedrash Hagadol is the only synagogue in Pittsburgh's downtown section. There are daily morning and evening services.

CONGREGATION ETZ CHAIM

In 1864, Pittsburgh's second oldest congregation, Etz Chaim, was organized. Its first synagogue was located on Craft Avenue. That Neo-Classical building is now used as a playhouse. The congregation is still functioning and is located at Shady and Wilkins Avenues, in the Squirrel Hill section.

CONGREGATION KESSER TORAH

The original synagogue building of this congregation is located on Webster Avenue. It is a three-story brown brick structure with entrances on two sides. Atop the building is a dome which is covered with black shingles. Although the building is used as a church, the large Star of David is still visible on its front façade.

The present congregation is located in the Squirrel Hill section, at 5706 Bartlett Street.

PUNXSUTAWNEY

This town becomes a national attraction on Groundhog Day. There has been a Jewish community in the town since the turn of the century. The original synagogue was located on Indiana Avenue. It was demolished in 1948 because it was in the path of a new bridge. The present synagogue of Congregation Agudath Achim is located on Church Street and was constructed in 1949.

YORK

Temple Beth Israel's original building, located at 120 Beaver Street, was built in 1906 and is now used by a local church. The small 2-story building is an excellent example of the Moorish Revival style. The two bulbous domes are each surrounded by miniature domelets. Adjoining the former synagogue are restored Federal-style homes.

The congregation is presently housed in a modern structure at 2090 Hollywood Drive. The Eternal Light *(Ner Tamid)* consists of a cut geode, with its luxurious exposed purple quartz crystals and a fine filament of sculptured brass which serves as the light source. The congregation follows the Reform ritual.

Temple Beth Israel's first location was on Beaver Street.

THE OLD NEIGHBORHOODS

The following list contains information about synagogues which are no longer functioning as Jewish houses of worship. These addresses are located in the old sections of the city or town. It is advisable to take extra precautions while driving through these neighborhoods.

Abington Old York Road Temple *971 Noble Hill*

Aiquippa Congregation Agudath Achim *501 Church Street (ca. 1900)*
Main and 21st Streets

Allentown Congregation Agudas Achim *628 West 2nd Street*
Congregation Sons of Israel *6th & Tilghman Streets*
Congregation Kneseth Israel *31 South 13th Street*

Altoona Congregation B'nai Yaakov *19th Street (between 11th & 12th Avenues)*
Mountain City Hebrew Reform Congregation *13th Avenue & 15th Street*
Talmud Torah *13th Avenue (between 18th & 19th Streets)*

Ambridge Congregation Beth Samuel *266 Glenwood Drive*
5th and Maplewood Streets

Bangor Jewish Center *4th Street*

Barnesboro Congregation B'nai Israel *Maple & 12th Streets*

Beaver Falls Congregation Agudath Achim *6th Avenue & 5th Street*

Berwick Congregation Ohave Sholom *Freas Avenue*

Braddock Congregation Agudas Achim *1023 Talbot Avenue*
Congregation Ahavath Achim *6th Street*

Bradford Temple Beth Israel *6 East Corydon Street*
Congregation Beth Zion *South Avenue*
First Hebrew Orthodox Congregation *45 Kennedy Street*

Brownsville Congregation Ohave Israel *2nd Street*

Butler Congregation B'nai Abraham *123 5th Avenue*

California Congregation Sons of Jacob *Liberty Street*

Carnegie Congregation Ahavas Achim *Broadway & Main Street*

Chester Congregation Mispallelim *325 West 7th St*
Congregation Ohev Sholom *8th & Welsh Streets*
Congregation B'nai Abraham *208 West 3rd Street*
Congregation B'nai Israel *3rd & Floyd Streets*
Congregation of Israel *1009 West 3rd Street*

Coatesville Congregation Beth Israel *4th & Diamond Streets*
33 South 5th Avenue

Danville Congregation B'nai Zion *Front Street*

Dickson City Congregation Oheb Sholom *Main Street*

Easton Congregation B'nai Abraham *126 South 6th Street*
600 Ferry Street
Congregation Covenant of Peace *38 South 6th Street*
Jewish Community Center *660 Ferry Street*

East Liberty Congregation B'nai Israel *209 Collins Street*

East Pittsburgh Congregation Ohab Zedek *Electric Avenue*

Ellwood City Congregation Etz Chaim *Wayne Avenue & 7th Street*

Erie Congregation Brith Sholom *721 French Street*

Exeter Boro Congregation Anshe Ahavath Achim *1061 Wyoming Avenue*

Farrell Congregation Ahavath Achim *929 North Lee Avenue*
B'nai Zion Congregation *Spearman & Union Streets*

Glassport Congregation B'nai Israel *Ohio Avenue*

Greensburg Congregation B'nai Israel *Ludwick & Hamilton Streets*

Hanover Hebrew Congregation *6 Center Square*

Harrisburg Jewish Community Center *1110 North 3rd Street*
Congregation Chizuk Emunah *6th & Forster Streets*
Congregation Kesher Israel *Capitol & Briggs Avenues*
Congregation Ohev Sholom *2nd & South Streets*

Hazelton Congregation Agudath Israel *South Cedar Street*

Jenkintown Congregation B'nai Jeshurun *227 Summit Avenue*

Jesup Congregation B'nai Israel

Johnstown Congregation Rodef Sholom *Iron Street*
100 Dartmouth Avenue

Kane Congregation Beth Jacob

Kittaning Congregation Kneseth Israel *North Jefferson Street*

Lancaster Congregation Degel Israel *416 Chester Street*
Jewish Community Center *219 East King Street*
Temple Beth El *25 North Lime Street*

Lansdale Congregation Beth Israel *Green Street & Lincoln Avenue*

Latrobe Congregation Beth Israel *416 Weldon Street*

Lebanon Congregation Beth Israel *1112 Cumberland Street*

McKeesport Congregation Gemilas Chesed *Market & 3rd Streets*
Congregation Kesher Israel *Mulberry Street*
Temple B'nai Israel *812 Jenny Lind Avenue*
Congregation Etz Chaim *6th & Mulberry Streets*
111 7th Street

McKees Rocks Congregation Ahavas Achim

Mahonoy City Israel Congregation *South Street*

Meadville Hebrew Society

Monessen Congregation Kneseth Israel *Schoolmaker Avenue*

Mount Carmel Congregation Tifereth Israel *4th & Oak Streets*

Nanticoke Congregation Anshei B'nai Yehuda *184 Market Street*

New Castle Congregation Tifereth Israel *Howe Street*

Norristown Congregation Tifereth Israel *Market & Cherry Streets*

Oil City Congregation Shearith Israel *261 Elm Street*
Congregation Etz Chaim *Plumer Street*

Old Forge Congregation Bikur Cholim

Olyphant Congregation Bikur Cholim *Willow & Lincoln Streets*

Philadelphia Congregation Adath Jeshurum *21 North Broad Street*
Adath Zion Congregation *1334 Paul Street*
Montefiore Congregation *2911 North 8th Street*
Congregation Agudas Achim *5944 Katherine Street*
Congregation Ahavath Israel *2302 North Masher Street*
Congregation Ahavath Israel of Oak Lane *6735 North 16th Street*
Congregation Anshe Sholom *1920 Germantown Avenue*
Congregation Ateres Israel *84th & Harley Avenues*
Beth Aaron Temple *5300 Euclid Avenue*
Congregation Beth Am Israel *58th Street & Washington Avenue*
Congregation Beth El *135 South 58th Street*
Congregation Beth Jacob *6027 Chestnut Street*
Congregation Ezrat Israel *69th & Ogintz Avenue*
Congregation Beth Judah *5426 Sansom Street*
Congregation Beth Samuel *2212 South 5th Street*
Congregation Beth Sholom *Broad & Cortland Streets*
Beth Tefilath Israel *40th Street & Powelton Avenue*
Congregation Beth Zion *318 South 19th Street*

Congregation B'nai Israel *307 West Tabor Road*
B'nai Israel of Logan *10th & Rockland Streets*
B'nai Jeshurum *33rd & Diamond Streets*
Boulevard Temple *Tyson & Brows Street*
Congregation Brith Sholom *871 North 5th Street*
Congregation Ahavas Chesed *29 West Rittenhouse Avenue*
East Lane Temple *1100 Oak Lane Avenue*
Congregation Kneset Israel *984 North Marshall Street*
Har Zion Temple *54th Street & Wynnefield Avenue*
Congregation Linas Zedek *5944 Larchwood Avenue*
Midtown Temple *1211 Chestnut Street*
Mikvah Israel *Broad & York Streets*
Sterling Alley (north of Cherry Street)
Congregation Magen Abraham *1713 South 4th Street*
Mount Airy Jewish Center *Arleigh & Johnston Streets*
Neziner Congregation *771 South 2nd Street*
Congregation Ohav Zedek *1535 North 7th Street*
Congregation Poale Zedek Shearith Israel *1011 South 5th Street*
Congregation Raim Ahuvim *59th Street & Cedar Avenue*
Congregation Kneset Israel *1723 North Broad Street*
Congregation Shaare Shomayim *23rd & Wharton Streets*
Congregation Shaare Zedek *S.W. 52nd Street & Columbia Avenue*
Congregation Shair Israel *342 Porter Street*
Congregation Shaar Israel *2509 South 4th Street*
Congregation Sons of Halberstam *610 North 6th Street*
Temple Beth Israel *32nd Street & Montgomery Avenue*
Congregation Beth Aaron *5300 Euclid Avenue*
Congregation Rodef Zedek *10th & Ruscomb Streets*
Congregation Sinai *Washington Lane & Limekiln Pike*
Congregation Zion *Edison Avenue & Trevise Road*
Congregation Tifereth Israel *113 North Union Street*
Congregation Tifereth Israel of Parkside *3940 Girard Avenue*
Congregation Tikvas Israel *41st Street & Parkside Avenue*
West Oak Lane Jewish Center *Thonron Avenue & Sedgwick Street*

West Philadelphia Jewish Center *63rd Street & Ludlow Street*
Wynnefield Jewish Center *58th Street & Overbrook Avenue*
Congregation Zemach David *4900 North 8th Street*
Congregation Etz Chaim Zichron Jacob *3209 West Cumberland Street*

Phoenixville Congregation B'nai Jacob *124 Main Street*

Pittsburgh Congregation Adath Israel *3257 Ward Street*
Congregation Adath Jeshurun *5643 Margaretta Street*
Congregation Ahavath Sholom *Liberty Avenue & 28th Street*
Congregation Beth El *1910 Broadway*
Congregation Beth Hamedrash Hagadol *129 Washington Place*
Congregation Beth Israel *1st & East Streets*
1214 Wood Street
Congregation Beth Jacob *Franklin & Townsend Streets*
B'nai Israel Congregation *209 Collins Street*
B'nai Israel Congregation *North Highland & Hippey Streets*
B'nai Israel Congregation *6202 Penn Avenue*
Congregation Beth Yehuda *1911 Beaver Avenue*
Congregation Beth Zion *7053 Hamilton Avenue*
Congregation B'nai Emunah *886 Kennbect Street*
Congregation Chevre Tehillim *35 Townsend Street*
Congregation Chevre Torah Anshe Sinai *Fulton & Clark Streets*
Congregation Talmud Torah of South Side *1922 Carson Street*
Knesseth Israel Congregation *72 Miller Street*
Congregation Machzikei Hadas *Wylie Avenue & Granville Street*
Congregation Or Chodosh *Roberts Avenue (near Reed)*
Congregation Ohel Jacob *Roberts Avenue (near Centre)*
Congregation Shaare Tfilo *23 Miller Avenue*
Congregation Poale Zedek *129 Crawford Street*
Congregation Shaare Torah *29 Townsend Street*
Congregation Shaare Zedek *14 Townsend Street*
Congregation Tifereth Israel *Fullerton & Clark Streets*
Congregation Tree of Life *210 Craft Avenue*
Congregation Kesser Torah *Webster Avenue*

Pittston Congregation Agudas Achim *62 Broad Street*

Port Chester Congregation Kneses Tiferes Israel *258 Willet Avenue*

Pottstown Congregation Mercy & Truth *Hale Street*
High & Warren Streets

Pottsville Congregation Ohev Zedek *4th & Arch Streets*

Puxsutawney Chevre Agudath Achim *Indiana Avenue*

Rankin Congregation B'nai Israel *2nd Street*

Reading Congregation B'nai Zion *624 Penn Avenue*
Congregation Kesher Israel *8th & Court Streets*
Congregation Oheb Sholom *Chestnut & Pear Streets*
Congregation Shomre Habrith *533 North 8th Street*
Jewish Community Center *134 North 5th Street*

Scranton Congregation Ahavas Achim *South Washington Avenue*
Congregation Anshe Chesed *501 Madison Avenue*
Congregation Beth Hamedrash Hagadol *420 Penn Avenue*
Congregation B'nai Abraham & Jacob *Penn Avenue*
Congregation B'nai Israel *111 Hickory Street*
Congregation Kneseth Israel *Linden Street (between Franklin & Mifflin)*
Madison Avenue Temple *523 Madison Avenue*

Shamokin Congregation B'nai Israel *Shamokin & Commerce Avenues*

Shenandoah Congregation Kehilath Israel *315 West Oaks Street*

South Bethlehem Congregation Brith Sholom Talmud Torah *Wood & Walnut Streets*
Congregation Rodeph Sholom *26 East 3rd Street*

Steelton Congregation Tifereth Israel *South 2nd Street*

Sunbury Congregation Kneseth Israel *243 Market Street*

Titusville Congregation B'nai Gemilas Chesed *North Martin Street*

Washington Congregation Beth Israel *Franklin & Spruce Streets*

52 West Chestnut Street

West Chester Congregation Kesher Israel *New & Washington Streets*

Wilkes-Barre Congregation Anshei Sfard *340 Market Street*

Temple B'nai Brith *175 South Washington Street*

Congregation B'nai Jacob *135 South Welles Street*

Congregation Holchei Yosher *196 Lincoln Street*

Jewish Community Center *60 South River Street*

Congregation Ohev Zedek Anshe Ungarin *Pennsylvania Avenue*

Wilkinsburg Congregation Beth Israel *Wood & Hill Avenues*

Williamsport Congregation Beth Hasholom *145 Union Avenue*

Congregation Ohave Sholom *Edwin & Hepburn Avenues*

Wyncote Congregation Kneseth Israel *332 Rice's Mill Road*

York Congregation Adas Israel *South Water Street*

19 West Market Street

Hebrew Reform Congregation Beth Israel *South Beaver Street*

Congregation Ohe Sholom *Pershing & Princes Streets*

KOSHER RESTAURANTS

Allentown Groman's Bakery *19th & Allen Streets (215) 691-1131*

Kingston Goldstein's Kosher Deli *200 Pierce Street (717) 263-0653*

Levittown Best Value *1407 East Lincoln Street (215) 547-7488*

Philadelphia European Dairy *2000 Sansom Street (215) 568-1298*
Gold Cuts *245 South 17th Street 735-4762*
Pizza, Inc. *7638 Castor Avenue 725-5437*
Dragon Inn *7628 Castor Avenue 742-2575*
Michael's Bakery *6635 Castor Avenue 745-1423*

Pittsburgh Kosher Mart *2121 Murray Avenue (412) 421-4450*
Prime Kosher *1916 Murray Avenue 421-1015*
Pastries Unlimited *2119 Murray Avenue 521-6323*

Scranton Abe's Deli *325 Penn Street (717) 342-4517*
Linden Bake Shop *422 South Main Street 343-8826*

Wilkes-Barre Pennsak's Kosher Deli *41 East North Hampton Street (717) 823-0764*

York Kaplan's Deli *2300 East Market Street (717) 757-4025*

SYNAGOGUES

Abington 19001 Temple Beth Am (R) *971 Old York Road (215)886-8000*

Aliquippa Congregation Agudas Achim *21st & Main Streets*

Allentown 18104 Congregation Am Haskalah (Rec) *Ott & Walnut Streets (215)435-3775*
Temple Beth El (C) *1702 Hamilton Street 435-3521*
Congregation Knesseth Israel (R) *2227 Chew Street* 435-9075
Congregation Agudas Achim (O) *2000 Washington Street*

Altoona 16602 Congregation Agudas Achim (C) 1306 17th Street (814)944-5317
Temple Beth Israel (R) *3004 Union Avenue 942-0057*

Ambridge 15003 Beth Samuel Jewish Center (C) *810 Kennedy Drive (412)266-5238*

Ardmore Main Line Temple (R) *2233 Bryn Mawr Avenue*

Bala Cynwyd Temple Adath Israel *123 Old Lancaster Road (215)664-5626*

Beaver Falls 15010 Congregation Agudath Achim (C) *(412)846-5696*

Bensalem Congregation Tifereth Israel (C) *2909 Bristol Road (215)752-3468*

Berwick 18603 Congregation Ohav Sholom (C) *Vine & 3rd Streets*

Bethlehem 18015 Congregation Agudath Achim (O) *155 Linwood Street (215)866-8891*
Congregation Brith Sholom (C) *1190 West Macada Road* 866-8009
Brodhead & Packer Avenues)

Bloomsburg 17815 Beth Israel Congregaton (C) *144 East 4th Street (717)784-7701*

Bradford 16701 Temple Beth El (R) *111 Jackson Avenue (814)368-8204*

Bristol 19007 Jewish Center (C) *216 Pond Street (215)788-4995*

Broomall 19008 Congregation Beth El Suburban (C) *715 Paxon Hollow Road (215)246-8700*
Temple Sholom (R) *North Church Lane 356-5165*

Butler 16001 Congregation B'nai Abraham (C) *519 North Main Street (412)287-5806*

Carbondale 18407 Congregation Agudath Sholom (O) *51½ Pike Street*

Carnegie 15106 Congregation Ahavath Achim (C) *Chestnut & Lydia Streets*

Chambersburg 17201 Congregation Sons of Israel (C) *2nd & East King Streets (717) 264-2915*

Cheltenham 19012 Congregation Melrose B'nai Israel (C) *2nd Street & Cheltenham Avenue (215) 635-1505*

Coatesville 19320 Congregation Beth Israel (C) *500 Harmony Street (215) 384-1978*

Coraopolis 15108 Temple Ahavath Sholom (R) *1100 Vance Avenue*

Cornwells Heights Jewish Center *4736 Neshaminy Boulevard*

Darby Congregation Agudath Israel *641 Columbia Avenue*

Donora 15033 Congregation Ohav Sholom (O) *2nd & Thompson Avenues*

Doylestown Temple Judea (R) *300 Swamp Road 215) 348-5022*

Dresher 19025 Temple Sinai (C) *Limekiln Pike & Dillon Road (215) 643-6510*

Dubois Congregation Sons of Israel *150 West Webster Ave.*

Dunmore Temple Israel *509 East Drinker Street*

Duquense 15110 Congregation Beth Jacob (O) *431 Catherine Street (17 South 2nd Street)*

Easton 18042 B'nai Abraham Synagogue (C) *16th & Bushkill Streets (215) 258-5343*

Temple Covenant of Peace (R) *1451 Northampton Street 253-2031*
Jewish Community Center *660 Ferry Street*

Elkins Park 19117 Congregation Adath Jeshurun (C) *York & Ashbourne Roads (215) 635-6611*
Beth Sholom Congregation (C) *Old York & Foxcroft Roads 887-1342*
Congregation Knesseth Israel (R) *Old York & Township Line Roads 887-8700*
Orthodox Minyan (O) *High School Road & Montgomery Avenue 642-7870*

Elwood City 16117 Congregation Tree of Life (C) *404 Beatty Street*

Erdenheim Congregation Beth Tikvah – B'nai Jeshurun (C) *1001 Paper Mill Road (215) 242-0512*

Erie 16502 Temple Anshe Chesed (R) *930 Liberty Street (814) 454-2426*
Brith Sholom Jewish Center (C) *3207 State Street 454-2431*

Feasterville 19047 Congregation Beth Chaim (T) *350 East Street Road (215) 355-3626*

Ford City 16226 Knesseth Israel Congregation *416 Ford Street 762-2621*

Frackville 17931 Congregation B'nai Israel (C) *West Frack Street*

Greensburg 15601 Temple Emanu-El-Israel (R) *222 North Main Street (412) 834-0560*

Hanover 17331 Hebrew Congregation (C) *179 2nd Street*

Harrisburg Beth El Temple (C) *2637 North Front Street (717) 232-0556*
Congregation Chizuk Emuna (C) *Fifth & Division Streets 232-4851*
Congregation Kesher Israel (O) *2500 North 3rd Street 238-0763*
Temple Ohev Sholom (R) *2345 North Front Street 233-6459*

Havertown 19083 Temple Tel Or (C) *560 Mill Road (215) 528-5011*

Hazelton 18201 Agudas Israel Synagogue (C) *Pine & Oak Streets (717) 455-2851*
Beth Israel Temple (R) *98 North Church Street 455-3971*
Jewish Community Center *Laurel & Hemlock Streets*

Homestead 15120 Hebrew Congregation (O) *329 East 10th Avenue*

Honesdale Beth Israel Synagogue (R) *7th & Court Streets*

Huntingdon 16652 Congregation Agudath Achim *1009 Washington Street (814) 643-3591*

Huntingdon Valley Temple Zion (R) *1620 Pine Road (215) 673-7099*

Indiana 15701 Beth Israel Congregation (C) *Washington & South 5th Streets (412) 465-6721*

Harrisburg's Temple Beth El.

Jenkintown 19046 Jewish Community Center (C) *115 West Avenue (215) 885-0312*

Johnstown 15901 Beth Sholom Congregation (C) *700 Indiana Street (814) 536-0647*

King of Prussia Temple Brith Achim (R) *481 South Gulf Road (215) 337-2222*

Kingston 18704 Temple B'nai Brith (R) *408 Wyoming Avenue (717) 287-9606*

Kittaning Knesseth Israel Congregation (C) *599 North Water Street (412) 543-2701*

Lafayette 19444 Congregation Or Ami (R) *708 Ridge Pike (215) 828-9066*

Lancaster 17602 Temple Beth El (C) *25 North Lime Street (717) 392-1379*
Degel Israel Synagogue (O) *1120 Columbia Avenue 397-0183*
Congregation Shaarai Shomayim (R) *508 North Duke Street 397-5575*

Lansdale 19446 Congregation Beth Israel (C) *1080 Sumneytown Pike (215) 855-8328*

Latrobe 15650 Congregation Beth Israel (C) *707 Fairmont Street 537-4922*

Lebanon 17042 Congregation Beth Israel (C) *411 South 8th Street (717) 273-2669*

Lehighton 18235 Temple Israel (C) *Bankway Street*

Levittown 19057 Congregation Beth El (C) *21 Penn Valley Road (215) 945-9500*
Temple Sholom (R) *Millcreek Parkway & Edgely Road 945-4154*

Lewiston 17044 Ohev Sholom Synagogue (O) *20 East 3rd Street 248-8070*

Lock Haven Congregation Beth Yehdua *320 West Church Street*

Lower Merion Neshamy Valley Congregation *50 Ashland Avenue*

Luzern Congregation Ahavas Achim (O) *Academy & Walnut Streets (717) 287-2032*

McKeesport 15131 Temple B'nai Israel (R) *536 Shaw Avenue (412) 678-6181*

Congregation Gemilas Chesed (T) *1400 Summit Street 678-8859*

Congregation Tree of Life (C) *2025 Cypress Drive 673-0938*

Mechanicsburg Temple Beth Sholom *913 Allandale Road*

Media 19063 Beth Israel Congregation (Rec) *Gayley Terrace (215) 566-4645*

Merion Station 19066 Temple Adath Israel (C) *Old Lancaster Road & Highland Avenue (215) 404-5150*

Middletown B'nai Jacob Synagogue *Water & Nisley Streets*

Monessen 15062 Temple Beth Am (R) *100 Watkins Avenue*

Monroeville 15146 Temple Beth David (R) *4415 Northern Pike (412) 372-1200*

Mount Carmel 17851 Congregation Tifereth Israel (O) *135 South Maple Street*

Mount Pleasant 15666 Congregation Tree of Life (O *Church Street*

Narbeth 19072 Congregation Beth Am Israel *209 Forrest Avenue*

New Castle 16101 Temple Israel (R) *Highland Avenue & Moody Street*

Congregation Tifereth Israel (C) *403 East Moody Avenue 658-3321*

New Kensington 15068 Beth Jacob Congregation (C) *1040 Kenneth Avenue (412) 335-8524*

Newtown Shir Ami Congregation (R) *101 Richboro Road (215) 968-3400*

Norristown 19401 Tifereth Israel Congregation (C) *1541 Powell Street (215) 275-8797*

Oil City 16301 *Congregation Tree of Life (T) 316 West 1st Street (814) 677-4082*

Olyphant 18447 Congregation Bikur Cholim (O) *302 Lackawana Avenue 489-1955*

Penn Valley 19072 Congregation Beth Am Israel (C) *1301 Hagys Ford Road (215) 667-1651*

Philadelphia 19111 Congregation Adath Sholom (C) *Marshall & Ritner Streets (215) 463-2224*

Congregation Adath Tikvah-Montefiore (C) *Summerdale Avenue & Hoffnagle Street 742-9191*

Adath Zion Congregation (T) *Pennway & Friendship Streets 742-8500*

Congregation Ahavath Israel (O) *7976 Summerdale Avenue 725-2828*

Congregation Ahavath Torah (O) *7525 Loretto Avenue 725-3610*

Aitz Chaim Synagogue Center (O) *7600 Summerdale Avenue 742-4870*

Anshei Vilna Congregation (T) *509 Pine Street 592-9433*

Congregation Beth Ahavah (R) 2116 Walnut Street 569-3109

Temple Beth Ami (C) *9201 Old Bustleton Avenue 673-2511*

Beth David Congregation (R) *5220 Wynnefield Avenue 473-8438*

Beth Emeth Congregation (C) *Bustleton & Unruh Avenues 338-1533*

Beth Hamedrash Hagadol–Beth Yaakov (O) *6018 Larchwood Avenue 747-3116*

Beth Hamedrash of Overbrook Park (O) *7505 Brookhaven Road 473-9671*

Congregation Beth Judah of Logan (C) *4820-30 North 11th Street 677-6886*

Congregation Beth Medrash Horav (O) *7926 Algon Avenue 722-6161*

Congregation Beth Solomon (O) *698-1180*

Congregation Beth T'filah (C) *7630 Woodbine Avenue 477-2415*

Congregation Beth Tefilath Israel-Rodef Zedek (C) *2605 Welsh Road 464-1242*
Temple Beth Torah (R) *608 Welsh Road 677-1555*
Congregation Beth Tovim (O) *5871 Drexal Road 879-1100*
Beth Uziel Congregation (C) *500 East Wyoming Avenue 329-0250*
Congregation Beth Zion-Beth Israel (C) *18th & Spuce Streets 735-5148*
Congregation B'nai Abraham (O) *521-27 Lombard Street 627-3123*
B'nai Abraham Jewish Center (C) *9037 Eastwood Street 464-1099*
Congregation B'nai Israel-Ohev Zedek (O) *8201 Castor Avenue 742-0400*
Congregation B'nai Jacob-Bershu Tov (O) *1145-47 Gilham Street 725-5182*
Congregation B'nai Yitzchok (T) *254 East Roosevelt Boulevard 329-3712*
Congregation Brith Israel (C) *D Street & Roosevelt Boulevard 329-2230*
Congregation Emanu-El (C) *Old York Road & Stenton Avenue 548-1658*
Far Northeast Congregation (O) *1101 Bustleton Avenue 464-6206*
Fox Chase Jewish Center (C) *7816 Halstead Street 342-4722*
Germantown Jewish Center (C) *Lincoln Drive & Ellet Street 844-1507*
Congregation Kavanah T'hora (C) *7136 Horrocks Street 725-0259*
Kensington Synagogue (C) *2033 East Allegheny Avenue 634-4428*
Congregation Kesher Israel (T) *412 Lombard Street 922-7736*
Congregation Kneses Israel-Anshei Sfard (O) *6716 Bustleton Avenue 332-7655*
Congregation Lenas Hazedek (O) *2749 Cranston Road 477-4700*
Congregation Lubavitch (O) *7622 Castor Avenue 725-2030*
Temple Menorah (C) *4301 Tyson Avenue 624-9600*

Congregation Mikveh Israel (C) *44 North 4th Street 922-5446*
Congregation Ner Zedek-Ezrath Israel (C) *Bustleton Avenue & Oakmont Street 728-1155*
Oxford Circle Jewish Center (C) *1009 Unruh Avenue 342-2400*
Congregation Raim Ahuvim (O) *5854 Drexal Road 878-8477*
Congregation Rodeph Sholom (R) *615 North Broad Street 627-6747*
Congregation Rodeph Sholom Suburban Center (R) *8201 High School Road 635-2500*
Congregation Shaare Shamayim (C) *97-68 Veree Road 667-1600*
Congregation Shaare Zion (O) *520-D Lombard Street 922-2818*
Temple Sholom (C) *Large Street & Roosevelt Boulevard 288-7600*
Society Hill Synagogue (C) *418 Spruce Street 922-6590*
Congregation Tikvah Chadashah (C) *5364 West Chew Avenue 438-1508*
Young Israel of Oxford Circle (O) *6427 Large Street 743-2848*
Young Israel of Wynnefield (O) *5300 Wynnefield Avenue 473-3511*
Young Peoples Congregation Shar Eli (C) *728 West Moyamensing Avenue 339-9897*

Philipsburg Congregation Sons of Israel (O) *Spruce & 6th Streets*

Phoenixville 19460 B'nai Jacob Synagogue (C) *Starr & Manavon Streets (215) 933-5550*

Pittsburgh 15220 Congregation Adath Jeshurun (O) *5643 East Liberty Boulevard (412) 361-0176*
Bais Yoseph Congregation (O) *6225 Nicholson Street 422-7437*
Beth El Congregation (C) *1900 Cochran Road 561-1168*
Beth Hamedrash Hagadol (O) *1230 Colwell Street 471-4443*
Beth Israel Center (C) *118 Gill Hall Street 655-9253*
Congregation Beth Sholom (C) *5915 Beacon Street 421-2288*

Congregation B'nai Emunah (O) *4315 Murray Avenue 521-1477*
Congregation B'nai Israel of East End (C) *327 North Negley Avenue 661--252*
B'nai Zion Congregation (O) *6401 Forbes Avenue*
Temple David (R) *4415 Northern Pike 372-1200*
Temple Emanu-El (R) *1250 Bower Hill Road 279-7600*
Congregation Gemilas Chesed (T) *1400 Summit Street 678-8859*
Congregation Kether Torah (O) *5706 Bartlett Street 521-9992*
New Light Congregation (C) *1700 Beechwood Boulevard 421-1017*
Parkway Jewish Center (C) *300 Princeton Drive 823-4338*
Congregation Poale Zedek (O) *Phillips & Shady Avenues 421-9786*
Rodef Sholom Congregation (R) *4905 5th Avenue 621-6566*
Congregation Shaare Torah (O) *2319 Murray Avenue 421-8855*
Kneseth Israel Congregation *1112 North Negley Avenue*
Dor Chadash Congregation *Forbes & Denniston Avenues*
Chofetz Chaim Congregation (O) *5807 Beacon Street*
Temple Sinai (R) *5505 Forbes Avenue 421-9715*
Congregation Tree of Life (C)Wilkins & Shady Avenues 521-6788
Young Israel-Shaare Zedek(O) *5851 Bartlett Street 421-7224*
Lubavitch Center (O) *2100 Whightman Street*
Machzikei Hadas Congregation *814 North Negley Avenue*
Ohave Zedek Synagogue of Oakland *356 Craft Avenue*
Shaare Tefilah Congregation (O) *5741 Bartlett Street521-9911*
Torah Chaim Congregation *729 North Negley Avenue*

Pittston Congregation Anshe Ahavas Achim *231 Delaware Avenue*

Pleasant Hills Beth Israel Center (C) *Gill Hall Road (412) 655-2144*

Plymouth Congregation B'nai Israel *132 West Main Street*

Pottstown 19464 Congregation Mercy & Truth (C) *575 North Keim Street (215) 326-1717*

Pottsville 17901 Oheb Zedek Center (C) *2300 Mahantongo Street (717) 622-5890*

Punxsutawney 15767 Chevre Agudath Achim (O) *Church Street*

Radnor 19087 Har Zion Temple (C) *639 County Line Road*

Reading 19604 Congregation Beth Jacob (O) *955 North 10th Street (215) 372-8508*

Kesher Zion Synagogue (C) *1245 Perkiomen Avenue 372-3818*

Temple Oheb Sholom (R) *Perkiomen Avenue & 13th Street 373-4623*

Shomrei Habrith Congregation (O) *2320 Hampton Boulevard* 921-0881

Richboro Congregation Ohev Sholom (C) *944 2nd Street Pike (215) 322-9595*

Scranton 18510 Congregation Beth Sholom (O) *Clay Avenue & Vine Street (717) 346-0502*

Ahavath Sholom Synagogue *1733 North Main Street*

Young Israel Congregation Machzikei Hadas (O) *(501) Madison Avenue 342-6271*

Congregation Oheb Zedek (O) *1432 Mulberry Street 343-2717*

Penn Monroe Synagogue (O) *901 Olive Street 347-3704*

Temple Hesed (R) *Knox Street & Lake Scranton Road 344-7201*

Temple Israel (C) *Monroe Avenue & Gibson Street 342-0350*

Shamokin 17872 Congregation B'nai Israel (O) *7 East Sunbury Street*

Sharon 16146 Temple Beth Israel (R) *840 Highland Road (412) 346-4754*

Shenandoah 17976 Congregation Kehilath Israel (O) *35 South Jardin Street*

Spring House Beth Or Congregation (R) *Penllyn Pike & Dager Road (215) 646-5806*

Springfield 19064 Congregation Beth Tikvah *1001 Paper Mill Road*
Congregation Ner Tamid (C) *300 West Woodland Avenue (215) KI3-4241*

Stroudsburg 18360 Temple Israel (R) *660 Wallace Street (717) 421-8781*

Sunbury 17801 Congregation Beth El (C) *249 Arch Street (717) 286-1127*

Uniontown 15401 Temple Israel (R) *119 East Fayette Street (412) 437-6431*

Uniontown Congregation Tree of Life (C) *Pennsylvania Avenue 438-0801*

Upper Darby 19082 Temple Israel (C) *Bywood Avenue & Walnut Street (215) FL2-2125*

Wallingford 19086 Congregation Ohev Sholom (C) *2 Chester Road (215) 874-1466*

Warren 16365 Warren Hebrew Congregation (O) *112 Conewango Avenue*

Warrington Congregation Tiferes B'nai Israel *2478 Street Road (215) 343-0155*

Washington 15301 Congregation Beth Israel (C) *265 North Avenue (412) 225-7080*

Wayne Congregation Har Zion *County Line & Matsonford Roads*

West Chester 19380 Kesher Israel Congregation (T) *206 North Church Street (215) 696-7210*

Wilkes-Barre 18702 Congregation Anshei Emes (O) *13 South Welles Street (717) 824-1781*
Congregation Anshe Sfard (O) *53 South Welles Street*
Congregation Ohav Zedek (O) *242 South Franklin Street 825-6619*
Temple B'nai Brith (R) *408 Wyoming Avenue*
Temple Israel (C) *239 South River Street 287-9606*

Williamsport 17701 Temple Beth Hasholom (R) *425 Center Street (717) 323-7751*
Congregation Ohev Sholom (C) *1501 Cherry Street 322-4209*

Wyncote 19095 East Lane Temple (C) *501 Cedarbrook Hill TU4-4555*

Wynnewood 19096 Temple Beth Am Israel (C) *Remington Road & Lancaster Avenue (215) 649-5300*
Main Line Temple (R) *410 Montgomery Avenue 649-7800*

Yeadon 19050 Congregation Beth Tefilah (C) *Whitby Avenue & West Cobbs Creek (717) 625-2156*

York 17402 Temple Beth Israel (R) *2090 Hollywood Drive (717) 843-2676*
Congregation Ohev`Sholom (C) *2251 Eastern Boulevard 755-2714*

MIKVEHS

Allentown 1834 Whitehall Street (215) 433-2177 or 435-8097

Ardmore Wynnewood & Argyle Roads (215) 642-8679

Harrisburg 3601 North 4th Street (717) 232-2023 or 234-0097 or 238-4141

Kingston 139 3rd Street *(717) 283-1961*

Lewiston 20 East 3rd Street *(717) 283-8070*

McKeesport 1545 Ohio Avenue *(412) 678-8859 or 678-2264 or 678-2725*

Philadelphia 7525 Loretto Avenue *(215) 745-3334 or 722-7574*

Pittsburgh 2336 Shady Avenue *(412) 422-7110*

Scranton 700 Vine Street *(717) 344-5138 or 344-4427*

Wilkes-Barre 3rd Avenue & Institute Lane *(717) 287-9408 or 287-6336 or 287-2032*

Williamsport 1501 Cherry Street *(717) 322-7050 or 322-4209*

Rhode Island

The first Jews to arrive were attracted by the declaration made by Roger Williams, the founder of Rhode Island. He established Rhode Island in 1636 as a refuge for all religious nonconformists. The Jewish merchants in the British West Indies colony of Barbados shifted their base of operation to Newport in 1658. They were instrumental in making Newport one of the largest ports in North America. The Jewish ship owners and merchants were important factors in the whaling industry and in the manufacture of candles from sperm oil.

The Jewish community purchased a burial plot in 1677, making this the oldest existing Jewish cemetery in the United States. In 1759, the Jewish community decided to build a synagogue. Until that time, services were conducted in private homes. The community sought and received help from New York's Congregation Shearith Israel. In 1763, the Jeshuat Israel Congregation was dedicated. The first minister of the congregation was Isaac Touro. The synagogue has since been called the "Touro Synagogue," and is the oldest synagogue structure in the United States. In 1947, the Touro Synagogue was designated a National Historic Landmark.

At the outbreak of the Revolutionary War, when the British captured Newport, most of the Jews fled the city with the Americans. The city suffered heavy damage and commercial losses during the war, and never recovered its prewar commercial status as America's third most important port. The Touro Synagogue was closed in 1822, and did not officially reopen until 1883. The congregation has always followed the Sephardic (Spanish and Portuguese) ritual.

In the 1820s, the Sephardic Jews fled to Providence. German Jews settled in that city in the 1840s. The congregation, Sons of Israel, was organized in 1855. This congregation eventually became today's Temple Beth El of Providence. The first synagogue in Providence was built in 1890 and was located at the corner of Friendship and Foster Streets. During the 1880s, Eastern European Jews moved to Providence.

In 1877, Rhode Island had only 1,000 Jews. By 1907, there were 17 synagogues in Providence serving a Jewish population of 10,000. The Jewish population of Rhode Island is presently approximately 22,000.

NEWPORT

TOURO SYNAGOGUE
85 Touro Street

In 1658, the Jeshuat Israel Congregation was organized by Sephardic Jews who had arrived as merchants from the British West Indies colony of Barbados. They conducted religious services in private homes until they decided to build a synagogue in 1759. They asked for assistance from several other Sephardic congregations throughout the Old and New World such as New York, London, Amsterdam, Jamaica, Curaçao, and Surinam.

The congregation commissioned Peter Harrison, the architect of the Redwood Library and the Brick Market in Newport and other important buildings in Boston and Cambridge, Massachusetts. The Touro Synagogue (named after the congregation's first minister, Isaac Touro) measures about 35 feet by 40 feet, somewhat larger than New York's Shearith Israel, which was built in 1730 on Mill Street. The plan closely follows the Sephardic

The Touro Synagogue is the oldest Jewish house of worship in the United States.

ritual and resembles the Spanish and Portuguese Synagogue (Esnoga) of Amsterdam, built in 1675, and the Bevis Marks Synagogue of London, built in 1701. There are twelve columns supporting the women's gallery, the number twelve being symbolic of the twelve tribes of Israel. The annex on the side of the synagogue housed the Hebrew School.

The Ark, or *Heychal,* was designed as a built-in closet, with a delicately panelled, double tier front. The lower tier contains the compartment for the Torahs. The upper tier, an ornamental panel, displays the Tablets of the Law in a pedimented, elegantly profiled frame.

The reading platform, or *Tebah,* is situated in the center of the synagogue as required by Jewish law. There is something very unique, however, about this *Tebah*. There is a trap door in the floor of the *Tebah* which leads down to the foundations. Some say that secret stairs, rooms under cellars, and secret chambers were common in Early American houses. It is important to note that the founders of this congregation were Sephardic and descendants of the Spanish and Portuguese congregations of Amsterdam and London—descendants of the Marranos.

During the period of the Spanish Inquisition (1492), Jews were required to convert to Christianity. Many Jews chose to publicly convert to Christianity. They attended Catholic church services and actually ate pork in the public squares to prove that they were true Christians. However, at home they would still practice their Jewish faith. These secret Jews were known as Marranos, which means "pig" in Spanish. The descendants of these Marranos maintained certain elements of precaution in the design of the Touro Synagogue. The trap door in the Tebah could, if the emergency arose, be used as a means of escape. The exterior of the building does not even look like a synagogue. It has two tiers of round-arch windows separated by a belt course, which was similar to some of the more modest, early 18th century American Congregational Meeting-Houses, such as the Old South Meeting House in Boston (1729).

There is a 12-branched candelabra suspended from the ceiling brought from Europe, where it had been part of a Spanish monastery converted from a synagogue. The clock on the balcony is inscribed, "Judah Jacobs, London, Anno Mundi 5529 (1769)." The congregation's first Torah was said to have been 200 years old when it was brought from Amsterdam. The silver ornaments decorating the Torah Scrolls include two sets of *rimmonim* (finials) designed by Myer Myers, the celebrated pre-Revolutionary Jewish silversmith, who made church bells, silver plates, and buckles for the aristocracy.

There is a tale about the British army approaching Newport during the Revolutionary War. They were destroying the enemies' (American) homes and churches. As they entered the Touro Synagogue, they spotted the Crowns of the Torahs. They thought that those crowns represented the "Crown of England!" It was then, the tale goes, that the British troops "passed over" the Touro Synagogue and spared it from destruction.

The Touro Synagogue was the site of the meetings of the Rhode Island General Assembly during 1781-1784, and the first sessions of the Rhode Island Supreme Court were held there. When George Washington visited Newport in 1781, a town meeting was held in the synagogue. One of Washington's three letters to the Jews of the United States, written shortly after his election to the presidency, was addressed to the Newport congregation. This is the letter that contains his famous phrase that the government of the United States "gives to bigotry no sanction, to persecution no assistance."

The Touro Synagogue is officially owned by New York City's Congregation Shearith Israel (The Spanish and Portuguese Synagogue) and pays an annual rental fee of $1.00 for the use of its premises. The Touro Synagogue is an official National Historic Landmark. For further information about the synagogue and religious services, please call (401) 847-4794.

OLD JEWISH CEMETERY
2 Bellevue Avenue

The oldest Jewish cemetery in the United States dates back to 1677. It belongs to the Jeshuat Israel Congregation, the Touro Synagogue. Some of the distinguished Jews buried here are Jacob Rodriguez Rivera, Moses Seixas, and Abraham and Judah Touro. In the cemetery there is a monument to the Reverend Isaac Touro, the first minister of the congregation, who is buried in Kingston, Jamaica.

Continue driving up along Touro Street, which becomes Bellevue Avenue, and see the glorious historic mansions of Newport.

THE OLD NEIGHBORHOODS

The following list contains information about synagogues which are no longer functioning as Jewish houses of worship. These addresses are located in the old sections of the city or town. It is advisable to take extra precautions while driving through these neighborhoods.

Bristol Congregation Anshe Kovno *37 Goddard Street*
Central Falls Hebrew Beneficial Association *21 Central Street*
Pawtucket Congregation Beth David *Chalkstone Avenue*
Providence Congregation Sons of Israel *Friendship & Foster Streets*
Congregation Ahavath Sholom *240 Willard Avenue*
Howell & Scott Avenues
Congregation Anshe Slavite Chevre *Shonmut Avenue*
Congregation Sons of Zion *45 Orms Street*

Congregation Tifereth Israel *254 Willard Avenue*
Westerley Congregation Shaare Zedek *Canal Street*
Woonsocket Congregation B'nai Israel *Bernow & Greene Streets*
Congregation Linas Hazedek *140 Willard Avenue*

KOSHER RESTAURANTS

Providence Miller's Deli *774 Hope Street (401) 521-0368*
Spiegel's Deli *243 Reservoir Avenue 461-0425*
Kaplan's Bakery *756 Hope Street 621-8107*

SYNAGOGUES

[Note: All area codes 401]

Barrington 02806 Temple Habonim (R) *165 New Meadow Street 245-6536*
Bristol United Brotherhood Synagogue (C) *205 High Street 253-3460*
Cranston 02905 Temple Torat Yisrael (C) *330 Park Avenue 785-1800*
Cranston 02905 Temple Torat Yisrael (C) *330 Park Avenue 785-1800*
Temple Sinai (R) *30 Hagan Avenue 942-8350*
Middletown Temple Sholom (C) *220 Valley Road 846-9002*

Narragansett Congregation Beth David (O) *29 Browning Drive 789-3437*

Newport 02840 Congregation Ahavas Achim (O) *136 Kay Street*
Touro Synagogue (O) *85 Touro Street 847-4794*
Temple Sholom (C) *198 Thames Street*

Pawtucket 02862 Congregation Ohave Sholom (O) *305 High Street 722-3146*

Providence 02906 Temple Beth David Anshe Kovno (C) *145 Oakland Avenue*
Temple Beth El (R) *70 Orchard Avenue 331-6070*
Beth Israel (C) *155 Niagra Street*
Beth Sholom–Sons of Zion (O) *275 Camp Street 331-9393*
Temple Emanu El (C) *99 Taft Avenue 331-1623*
Congregation Mishkan Tefiloh (O) *203 Summit Avenue 521-1616*
Congregation Shaare Zedek–Sons of Abraham *688 Broad Street 751-4936*
Congregation Sons of Jacob (O) *24 Douglas Street 274-5260*
Congregation Tifereth Israel *Broad & Graham Streets*
Jewish Community Center *401 Elmgrove Avenue*

Warwick 02888 *Temple Am David (C) 40 Gardiner Street 463-7944*
Temple Judea *50 Lackena Avenue*

Westerly 02891 Congregation Shaare Zedek (C) *Union Street 596-4621*

Woonsocket 02895 Congregation B'nai Israel (C) *244 Prospect Street 762-3651*

MIKVEHS

Providence 688 Broad Street *(401) 751-4936*
401 Elmgrove Avenue *(401) 751-0025*

Vermont

Vermont has always had fewer Jews than any of the New England states. Its remoteness from Boston and New York, and from major ports of debarkation for Jewish immigrants, made it too difficult for many Jews to get to Vermont.

Vermont's first Jewish community sprang up at Poultney shortly after the Civil War. Jewish peddlers from nothern New York, western Massachusetts, and nearby Canada who sold their goods in the Vermont countryside grew tired of the long journey home for the Sabbath and the holidays, and decided to settle in Poultney. A congregation was founded in Poultney in the early 1870s. There was even a small synagogue. Vermont's first Jewish cemetery, established in East Poultney, contains the oldest grave, dated 1876. At the turn of the century, the economic situation in Poultney was on the decline. Most of the Jewish community moved to Burlington and Rutland.

The oldest existing Jewish community is located in Burlington. The first synagogue in the city, Congregation Ahavi Zedek, was organized in 1882. Its first synagogue was built on the corner of Cherry and Church Streets. Congregation Chai Odom, founded in 1888, built a synagogue the following year on Hyde Street.

Rutland has the second oldest Jewish community in the state. What is now the Rutland Jewish Center was founded in the early 1900s as Congregation Adath Israel in West Rutland. In 1907, a small synagogue was built in West Rutland to serve the needs of the Jewish families living there and in Rutland. The present congregation is located at 96 Grove Street and is housed in an historic landmark building, the former Baxter Memorial Library, which is clad on its exterior in Vermont marble. The construction cost of the Memorial Library in 1900 was $1 million. The congregation purchased the building for $12,000.00.

The Rutland Jewish Center was built in 1890 as the Baxter Memorial Library.

THE OLD NEIGHBORHOODS

Burlington Congregation Ohavi Zedek *Cherry & Church Streets*
Congregation Chai Adom *Hyde Street*
West Rutland Congregation Anshei Sholom Allen Street

SYNAGOGUES

[Note: All area codes 802]

Barre Congregation Tifereth Moshe *18 North Main Street*
Bennington 05201 Temple Beth El (C) *225 North Street*
Burlington 05401 Congregation Ahavath Gerim (O) *168 Archibald Street* 862-3001
Congregation Ohavi Zedek (C) *188 North Prospect Street* 864-0218
Temple Sinai *195 Summit Street* 862-5125
Montpelier Congregation Beth Jacob *10 Harrison Avenue*
Rutland 05701 Rutland Jewish Center (C) *96 Grove Street* 773-3455
St. Albans 05478 Jewish Congregation *55 High Street*
St. Johnsbury 05819 Congregation Beth El *76 Railroad Street*

MIKVEHS

Burlington 168 Archibald Street *(802) 862-3001 or 862-3293 or 863-1222*

Israeli Folk Dancing

Connecticut

Bridgeport Jewish Community Center *4200 Park Avenue (203) 372-6567*
Thursday 8:00–9:30 p.m. *Cathy Velenchik*

Hartford Jewish Community Center *335 Bloomfield Avenue (203) 236-4571*
Tuesday *7:30 - 10:00 p.m. Marla Cohen*

New Haven Jewish Home for the Aged *169 Davenport Avenue (203) 248-0291 or 387-7097*
Sunday 7:30 - 10:00 p.m.
Willa Horowitz/Dori Stern

Delaware

Wilmington Adas Kodesh Synagogue *Washington Boulevard & Torah Drive (302) 762-2705*
Sunday 8:00 - 10 p.m. *Faith Brown*

Maryland

Baltimore Baltimore Hebrew Congregation *7401 Park Heights Avenue (301) 764-1587*
Monday 8:30 - 10:30 p.m. *Bunny Gilman*

Bathesda Bradley Hills Elementary School *(301) 656-3391*
Tuesday 7:45 - 10:15 *Dorothy Solomon*

Jewish Community Center *5700 Park Heights (301) 542-4900*
Thursday 8:00 - 10:15 p.m. *Bonnie Dunn*

College Park University of Maryland Hillel *7505 Yale Avenue (301) 422-6200*
Monday 8:00 - 10:30 p.m. *Rocky Korr*

Rockville Jewish Community Center *6125 Montrose Road (301) 881-0100*
Wednesday *8:00 - 10:30 p.m.*

Massachusetts

Boston (area) Brandeis University *Usdan Student Center (Levin Ballroom)*
Thursday *8:30 - 11:00 p.m. (Sept. - May)*
Harvard Hillel House *74 Mount Auburn Street (617) 495-4695*
Monday 8:00 - 10:30 p.m. *Rebecca Diamond (Sept. - June)*
MIT Student Center (Sala de Puerto Rico) *(617) 225-9185*
Wednesday 7:00 - 11:00 p.m. *Joan Hantman*
Boston University Hillel *233 Bay Street (617) 266-3880*
Tuesday 8:00 - 10:00

New Jersey

Cherry Hill JCC of Southern Jersey *2395 West Marlton Pike (Route 70) (212) 568-4717*
Thursday 8:00 - 10:00 p.m. Lori Daren

Metuchen Temple Neve Shalom *250 Grove Street (201) 494-5660 / 321-1143*
Thursday 8:00 - 10:30 p.m. Miriam Handler

Princeton Princeton University *Corwin Hall*
(609) 771-8136
Monday 7:30 - 11:00 p.m. Ruth Markoe

Tenafly JCC on the Palisades *411 East Clinton Avenue*
(201) 569-7900 or (201) 836-2655
Sunday & Tuesday 7:30 - 10:30 p.m. Tamar Yablonski

New York

Albany Temple Israel *600 New Scotland Avenue*
(518) 438-7858
Wednesday 7:00 - 8:30 (9:30) p.m. *Lorraine Arcus/ Stanley Isser*

Ithaca Cornell University *Anabel Taylor Hall (One World Room)*
Thursday 8:00 - 11:00 p.m.

East Meadow Eisenhower Park Roller Rink - Field #4
(718) 275-0265
Tuesday 7:30 - 10:00 p.m. (July - Aug.) *Honey Goldfein-Perry*

New York City Congregation Shaare Zedek *212 West 93rd Street (718) 699-1248*
Sunday 7:00 - 11:00 p.m. *Naftaly Kadosh*
Columbia University (Earl Hall) *Broadway & West 117th Street*
Monday 7:15 - 10:15 p.m. *Ruth Goodman Burger*
(212) 280-511, 888-1770
92nd Street YMHA *1395 Lexington Avenue (2nd floor)*
(212) 888-1770
Wednesday 8:00 - 11:00 p.m. *Ruth Goodman Burger/ Danny Uziel*
Ethnic Arts Center *179 Varick Street (201) 836-2655*
Thursday 8:00 - 11:00 p.m. *Tamar Yablonski*

(Brooklyn) J.C.H. 7802 Bay Parkway (718) 331-6800
Tuesday 8:00 - 11:00 p.m. Rene Diamond

(Queens) Central Queens YMHA 67-09 108th Street
(718) 888-1770
Tuesday 8:00 - 11:00 p.m. *Honey Goldfein-Perry*
Flushing YMHA *45-35 Kissena Boulevard (718) 461-3030*
Call for schedule.

Stony Brook SUNY Union Ballroom
Monday 8:00 - 11:00 p.m.

Uniondale Hofstra University *Student Center*
(Multi-Purpose Room) (718) 275-0265
Sunday 7:30 - 10:30 p.m. (Sept. - May) *Honey Goldfein-Perry*

Rochester Hillel School *191 Fairfield Drive*
(716) 461-9015
Thursday 7:30 - 10:00 p.m. *Molly Shafer*
Jewish Community Center *1200 Edgewood Avenue*
(716) 461-2000
Sunday 7:00 - 10:00 p.m. *David Valentine*

Pennsylvania

Philadelphia YMHA *Broad & Pine Streets*
(215) 247-2965 or 834-1980
Wednesday 7:30 - 10:30 p.m. *Steve Schwrtz/Ellen Weber*

Washington, D.C.

George Washington University
Marvin Center Ballroom
800 21st Street N.W.
Monday 7:00 - 11:00 p.m. *Steven Sklarow*

Chabad Houses

CONNECTICUT

New Haven Chabad House *175 Osborne Avenue 06511 (203) 389-8335*
Trumbull Y. Stock *77 Mt. Pleasant Drive 06611 (203) 268-7700 or 268-0740*
West Hartford Chabad House *798 Farmington Avenue 06119 (203) 233-5912*

MASSACHUSETTS

Amherst Chabad House *30 North Hadley 01002 (413) 549-4094*
Boston Chabad House *491 Commonwealth Avenue 02215 (617) 424-1190*
Brookline Yeshiva *9 Prescott Street 02146 (617) 713-5330*
Framingham Chabad House *74 Joseph Road 01701 (617) 877-8888*
Lexington Chabad House *9 Burlington Street 02173 (617) 863-8656*
Longmeadow D. Edelman *1148 Converse Street 01106 (413) 567-8665*
Milton Shalom House *68 Smith Road 02186 (617) 333-0477*
Springfield Chabad House *782 Dickinson 01108 (413) 736-3936*
Worcester Chabad House *24 Creswell Street 01602 (617) 752-0904*

MARYLAND

Baltimore Chabad House *5721 Park Heights Avenue 21215 (301) 340-6858*
Columbia Lubavitch Center *9650 Santiago Road #11 21045 (301) 740-0165*
Hyattsville B. Chanowitz *6711 Wells Parkway 20782 (301) 422-6200*
Rockville Chabad House *311 West Montgomery Avenue 20850 (301) 762-2167*

NEW JERSEY

Englewood Y. Brod *409 Grand Avenue 07631 (201) 568-9423*
Elizabeth M. Kanelsky *1255 Clinton Place 07208 (201) 798-0056*
Livingston M. Kasinetz *12 Beverley Road 07039 (201) 994-0262*
Maplewood S.B. Gordon *12 Wellesley Road 07040 (201) 762-6628*
Margate Chabad House *P.O.Box 3366 08402 (609) 823-3223*
Morristown Rabbinical College *226 Sussex Avenue 07960 (201) 267-9404*
Manalapan Chabad House *89 Old Queens Road 07726 (201) 446-2701*
New Brunswick Chabad House *8 Sicard Street 08901 (201) 828-7374*
Paterson M. Greenberg *6 Manor Road 07514 (201) 271-2250*
Wanamassa M. Simon *2202 Sunset Avenue 07712 (201) 774-5921*

NEW YORK

Albany Chabad House *122 South Main Street 12208 (518) 482-5781*
Binghamton Chabad House *1004 Murray Hill Road 13903 (607) 797-0015*
Commack Chabad House *74 Hauppauge Road 11725 (516) 462-6640*
Coram Chabad House *6 Hyde Lane 11727 (516) 732-1676*
Getzville Chabad House *2501 North Forest Road 14068 (716) 688-1642*
Ithaca Chabad House *112 Schuiler Place 14850 (607) 273-8314*
Monsey Chabad House *4 Phyliss Terrace 10952 (914) 352-7642*
New City Chabad House *216 Congers Road 10956 (914) 634-0951*
New York City Chabad House *310 West 103rd Street 10025 (212) 864-5010*
Rochester Chabad House *36 Lattimore Road 14620 (716) 244-4324*
Schenectady Chabad House *1365 Van Antwerp Road 12309 (518) 377-6929*
Syracuse Chabad House *113 Berkley Drive 13210 (315) 424-0363*
Troy Chabad House *2306 15th Street 12181*
White Plains Chabad House *26 West Street 10605 (914) 681-6064*
Woodridge Chabad *P.O.Box 5 12789 (914) 434-8981*

PENNSYLVANIA

Philadelphia Lubavitch Center *7622 Castor Avenue 19152 (215) 725-2030*

Lubavitch House *4032 Spruce Street 19104 (215) 222-3130*

Pittsburgh Chabad House *5867 Marlborough Avenue 15217 (412) 681-6473*

S. Posner *2410 5th Avenue 15213 (412) 681-2446*

RHODE ISLAND

Providence Chabad House *48 Savoy Street 02906 (401) 273-7238*

VERMONT

Burlington Chabad House *158 North Willard Street 05401 (802) 658-7612*

LECTURE PROGRAMS

by Oscar Israelowitz

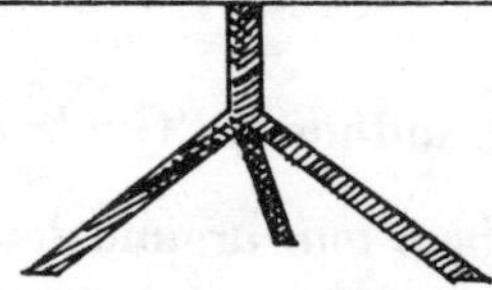

The Wandering Jews of New York City
Jewish Landmarks of New York City
The Source of the Synagogue — Ancient Synagogues of Israel
The Wandering Jews of New Jersey
The Synagogues of the United States — The Northeast
The Synagogues of Europe

The multi-media programs (lecture, slide presentation, and sound track) are available for your special organizational meetings. For further information please write to:

Lectures
c/o Mr. Oscar Israelowitz
P.O. Box 228
Brooklyn, New York 11229

Bibliography

Abelow, S.P. *History of Brooklyn Jewry*. New York: Sheba Publishing, 1937

Athearn, R.G. *The American Heritage New Illustrated History of the United States*. Vol. 10 New York: Dell Publishing, 1963

Blake P. *An American Synagogue for Today & Tomorrow*. New York: Union of American Hebrew Congregations, 1954

de Breffney, R.G. *The Synagogue*. New York: Sheba Publishing, 1978

Butler, C. *The Temple Emanu-El, New York*. Architectural Forum, Vol. 42 No. 2 (Feb., 1930) pp. 151-154

Eisendrath, M.M. *An American Synagogue for Today & Tomorrow*. Architectural Record, Vol. 114 (Dec., 1953) pp. 119-121

Feldman, S. *Guide to Jewish Boston & New England*. Cambridge: Genesis 2, 1986

Goldberger, P. *The City Observed—New York*. New York: Vintage Books, 1979

Goodman, P. *Guide for Planning the Synagogue Building*. American Institute of Architects Journal, Vol. 37 (May, 1962) pp. 70-74

Grafton, J. *New York in the Nineteenth Century*. New York: Dover Publications, 1977

Gurock, J. *When Harlem Was Jewish*. New York: Columbia University Press, 1979

Howe, I & Libo, K. *How We Lived*. New York: Plume Press, 1979

Meyers, N. *Temple B'nai Abraham, Newark, New Jersey*. American Architect Vol. 127, No. 2465

Perry, H.G. *Hora Magazine* American Zionist Youth Foundation Issue 44 Spring 1986

Pool, Rev. D. de Sola *The Mill Street Synagogue of Congregation Shearith Israel*. New York, 1930

Postal, B. & Koppman, L. *American Jewish Landmarks, Vol. I*. New York: Fleet Press, 1977

Sanders, R. & Gillon, E. *The Lower East Side*. New York: Dover Books, 1979

Tachau, W.G. *The Architecture of Synagogues*. Jewish Publication Society, 1926

White, N. & Willensky, E. A.I.A. *Guide to New York*. New York: Collier Books, 1978

Wischnitzer, R. *Synagogue Architecture in the United States, History & Interpretation*. Philadelphia: Jewish Publication Society, 1955

Encyclopedia Judaica. Jerusalem: Keter Publishing House, 1972

Brooklyn Daily Eagle Almanac. New York: Brooklyn Daily Eagle, 1889-1929

The Universal Jewish Encyclopedia, 1948

Recent American Synagogue Architecture—Catalogue. New York: The Jewish Museum of New York, 1963

Two Hundred Years of American Synagogue Architecture—Catalogue. Waltham, Massachusetts: American Jewish Historical Society, 1976

Congregation Beth Emeth of Albany, New York—A History, 1976

Beth Zion Temple, Buffalo, New York. Architectural Record Vol. 143 (March, 1968) pp. 133-136

B'nai Jeshurun Temple, Newark, New Jersey. Brickbuilder Vol. 24 (1915) pp. 305-306

Brith Kodesh, Rochester, New York. Architectural Record Vol. 133 (Nov., 1963) pp. 143-148

Charles River Park Synagogue. Architectural Record Vol. 156 (Sept., 1974) p. 140

Congregation Sons of Israel, Lakewood, New Jersey. Progressive Architecture Vol. 46 (March, 1965) pp. 138-141

Glass Towered Synagogue. Architectural Forum Vol. 100 (June, 1954) p. 145

New Synagogue Projects. The American Hebrew Vol. 126, No. 18 (March 21, 1930) pp. 673-694

New Synagogues in the United States. l'Architecture d'Aujord hui Vol. 28 (April-May, 1957) p. 70

Port Chester Synagogue. Edilizia Moderna No. 67 (August, 1959) pp. 9-14

Religious Buildings. Architectural Record Vol. 124 (Sept., 1958) pp. 137-156

Rodeph Shalom Synagogue, Pittsburgh, Pennsylvania. American Architect & Building News Vol. 93, No. 1882 (March, 18, 1908) p. 97

Synagogue at Port Chester, U.S.A. The Architect & Building News; Vol. 218 (Dec. 28, 1960) pp. 821-822

Temple Beth Zion, Buffalo, New York. Inland Architect & News Record Vol. 17, No. 1 (Feb., 1891)

Temple Ohabei Shalom, Brookline, Massachusetts. American Architect Vol. 134 (Nov. 20, 1928) pp. 707-711

American Jewish Organizations Directory. 11th Edition 1982-1983 New York: H. Frenkel, 1982

From Peddlars to Professionals—A History of Maine's Jews. Maine Times Feb. 24, 1984 & March 2, 1984

The Exodus. Newsweek Magazine March 13, 1972

History of Pioneers. Council of Jewish Organizations, Toms River, New Jersey Littman, J. & Robinson, M., 1976

Temple Beth Israel, York, Pennsylvania. 100th Anniversary Journal, 1978

Historic Brochure. Lilian & Albert Small Jewish Museum of Washington, D.C.

The Lloyd Street Synagogue. Historic Brochure

The Essex Story. Jewish Education Association of Essex County New Jersey, 1955

Photographic Credits

Adas Kodesch Shel Emeth Congregation *30, 31 165, 251*
The American Hebrew *14, 167, 289*
American Jewish Historical Society, Waltham, Mass. *44, 113, 125, 129 (bottom)*
Baltimore Hebrew Congregation *55*
Brooklyn Public Library *128*
Congregation Beth Shalom *256*
Dover Publications *192*
Drake Memorial Museum *259*
Embassy of Israel *40*
Grossinger's Hotel *170*
Jewish Historical Society of Greater Washington *37*
The Jewish Museum *164, 207*
New England Chassidic Center *79*
Newark Free Public Library *116, 119*
Temple Oheb Shalom *57*
The Ben Shahn Foundation *123*
Congregation Shearith Israel *182*
John Hopf / Union of American Hebrew Congregations *301*
The West Point Chapel *213*
Rachel Wischnitzer *265*

Guide to Jewish New York City

1983 Edition

The original 1983 edition contains 10 complete do-it-yourself tours of the largest Jewish city in the world. There are Jewish historic landmarks, Jewish museums, synagogues, kosher restaurants, Israeli folk dancing, and Yiddish theatres.

Paperback 152 pages $3.50

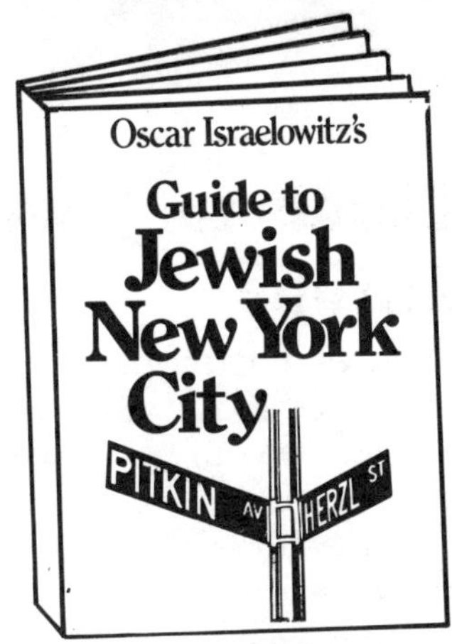

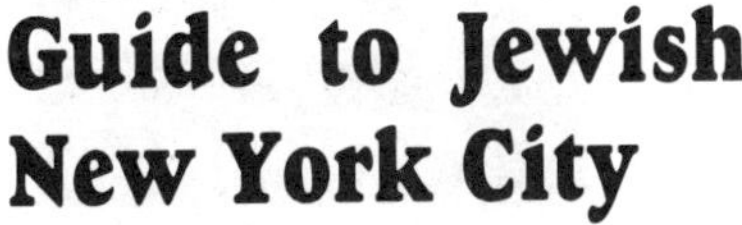

Guide to Jewish New York City

Revised Edition

The expanded and updated edition contains 12 complete do-it-yourself tours with information on Chassidic neighborhoods, the Lower East Side, historic landmark synagogues, mikvehs, and Jewish entertainment.

Paperback 200 pages $8.50

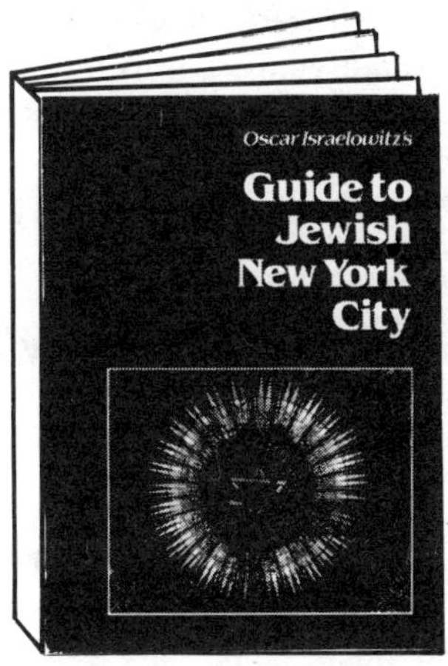

Shopper's Guide to Borough Park

A unique guide of this Chassidic section of Brooklyn, New York, known as the "Jerusalem of America." Complete with vintage photographs, a do-it-yourself walking tour, and, of course, the shopping.

Paperback 60 pages $3.00

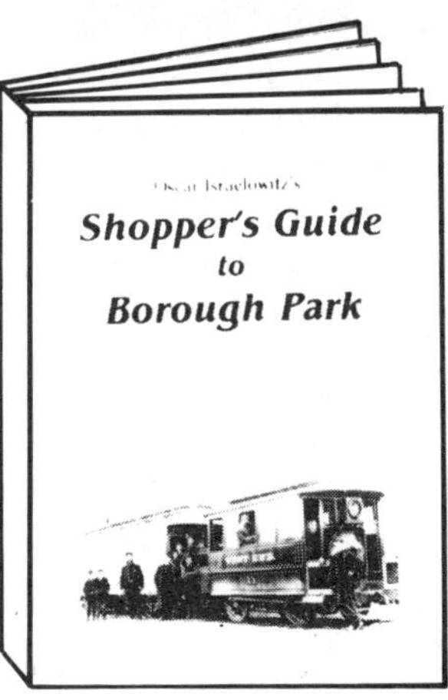

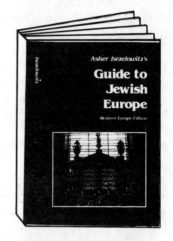

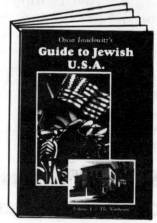

Synagogues of New York City

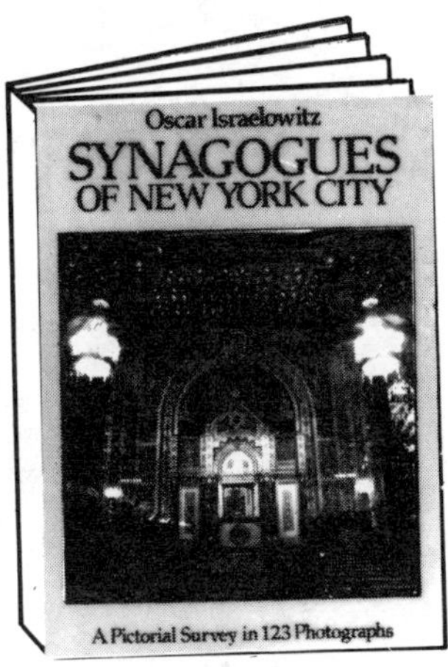

This pictorial survey of the great synagogues in all five boroughs of New York City contains 123 black and white and color photographs. These photographs outline the history of the Jewish presence in New York City and the role synagogues played in sustaining it. The high quality book makes a fine gift for the Judaica collector.

Paperback 86 pages $7.50

The Lower East Side Guide

This unique guide is designed for the tourist and contains a complete-do-it-yourself walking tour of this historic Jewish neighborhood. It is also designed for the shopper and contains a shopping directory with information on where to find the bargains!

Paperback 124 pages $6.00

Synagogues of the World Photographs

For the collector of exquisite color photographs from the private collection of Oscar Israelowitz. The 15 ready-to-frame prints (10" x 6") includes interior and exterior views of such great synagogues in Florence, Amsterdam, London, Gibraltar, Glasgow, Jerusalem, and Curaçao.

$5.00

BIOGRAPHICAL SKETCH

Born in Brussels, Belgium, Mr. Oscar Israelowitz brings a rich background to his mission of documenting Jewish New York City. Besides his rabbinical training, he is also a professional architect and photographer. Among his noted architectural projects are the Synagogue and Holocaust Center of the Bobover Chassidim in Borough Park and the Yeshiva Rabbi Chaim Berlin (elementary school) in the Flatbush section of Brooklyn. He has exhibited his photographs at museums throughout the New York area, including the Brooklyn and Whitney Museums. The photographs in this guide are his own creations. His first book, *"Synagogues of New York City,"* published in 1982, has been distributed worldwide and has received rave reviews. Mr. Israelowitz has appeared on several television and radio programs including NBC's *First Estate – Religion In Review.* In his spare time, Mr. Israelowitz gives lectures on various Jewish topics and also conducts tours of Jewish New York City.

Index